TAX
RELIEF
RESOLUTION

THE ULTIMATE GUIDE TO
PAYING LESS TO THE **IRS** STARTING NOW

STEVEN V. MELNIK
TAX ATTORNEY, CPA

 FLAMENCO PRESS, LLC

978-0-9913657-0-8 | print
978-0-9913657-2-2 | print with flaps
978-0-9913657-1-5 | ebook

To order books for special sales,
contact the publisher, Flamenco Press through:
ProtectYourAssetsCentral.com

Tax law is generally considered to be one of, if not the most complicated area of law.
This is mainly because of many exceptions to the rules, and exceptions to the exceptions.
As such, please note that while I have provided what in my opinion, are the most valuable rules
and exceptions to them, there are many more rules and many more exceptions to the rules
than what's discussed in this book.

Library of Congress Catalogue Number: 2014932398

10 9 8 7 6 5 4 3 2 1
Printed in the United States

Business & Investing | Taxation | Personal Finance | Small Business

Table of Contents

Introduction

Dealing with the Internal Revenue Service (IRS) can be a very stressful experience. It is important to understand your rights and how to deal with the IRS so that you can minimize the stress and anxiety that may result. Most cases begin when you prepare a tax return. For some, they receive a refund, some owe a tax debt, and some end up being audited, resulting in a tax balance or a reduction to their refund. *Tax Relief and Tax Resolution: The Ultimate Guide to Paying Less to the IRS Starting NOW* is designed with the intent of guiding you through:

- the maze of key elements in every tax return;
- the process of selecting a competent tax preparer;
- the IRS audit process;
- the process of selecting a competent tax professional to represent you in IRS tax matters; and
- the process of resolving your IRS tax debt.

It is always advisable to seek assistance from an experienced tax attorney. However, if you are making a decision to handle your taxes and IRS-related matters yourself, this book is a priceless tool. I know that many may not want to or don't feel they have the funds to pay for professional representation. Should you choose to deal with the IRS on your own, the purpose of this book is to help you make it through this process on your own.

Generally, the IRS strives to be professional and courteous when dealing with taxpayers. Policies and procedures have been set in place in the *Internal Revenue Manual (IRM)* used by IRS employees in conducting their duties. The IRM is accessible to taxpayers on the IRS website:

IRS.gov/irm/index.html

Although the IRM provides a uniform set of policies and procedures for IRS employees, throughout my practice, my firm has found that cases may be handled differently depending on the IRS representative that you speak to, the type of resolution you are seeking, or on the facts and circumstances of your case.

User Alert: In using this book, it is important to understand that your case may not result in the same outcomes presented in the examples found throughout. The examples provided throughout are used for illustrative purposes on the topic being discussed.

All information provided in this guide is based on *present* IRS rules and regulations. However, IRS tax laws, policies, rules, and regulations are constantly changing, and as a result, you should not rely solely on the information provided.

Although I, along with the attorneys within my practice, strive to maintain a current and up-to-date status with all IRS updates on laws, policies, rules, and regulations, I cannot guarantee that all information provided will be the most up-to-date by the time you have acquired this book.

For the links to the latest rules, regulations, and related expert advise please visit:

ProtectYourAssetsCentral.com

It's taxpayer beware!

I am very grateful
to many professionals for their assistance
in making this book possible.

Thank you very much!

PART 1

Tax Preparation

How To Select a Competent Tax Preparer and File Accurate Tax Returns, and Obtain Huge Tax Saving

Inside this chapter

CHAPTER 1

What Exactly is the Internal Revenue Service (IRS)?

The Internal Revenue Service (IRS) is an agency of the Federal Government that is responsible for the collection of tax revenue for the United States. It is responsible for processing your income tax returns, as well as interpreting and enforcing tax laws written by Congress. Its headquarters are located in Washington D.C. and are comprised primarily of four operational divisions:

- Wage and Investment Division

- Small Business/Self-Employed Division

- Large Business and International Division

- Tax Exempt and Government Entities Division

These four divisions are responsible for communicating with taxpayers, processing tax returns, collecting taxes, and conducting audits.

Contrary to the belief of many, the IRS is not out to get you, seize your property, or make your life miserable. President Abraham Lincoln enacted the first income tax in 1862 to cover war expenses.[1] He then created the position of Commissioner of the Internal Revenue Service to oversee the collection of income taxes. However, 10 years later, the income tax was repealed. Then in 1894, Congress once again tried to revive the income tax, but the Supreme Court ruled that it was unconstitutional.

> **Spoiler Alert:** Throughout the years, chat lines, the Internet, and in-person workshops surface regarding the issue of paying taxes—as in DON'T. Many encourage participants not to file under the premise that U.S. citizens are not required to pay any taxes. That extreme disillusion surfaces from what occurred in 1894 when the Supreme Court initially ruled the income tax as unconstitutional. However, do not allow these groups to influence your decision on whether to pay your taxes, because they are greatly misinformed. Disobeying the law will result in dire consequences.

In 1913, the Sixteenth Amendment was ratified giving Congress the authority to enact an income tax. That same year, Congress levied a one percent tax on personal net incomes above $3,000 and a six percent surtax on personal net incomes above $500,000. Shortly after, the first income tax return, Form 1040, was introduced. During World War

II, Congress then introduced payroll taxes and quarterly tax payments. In the 1950s, the name was changed from the *Bureau of Internal Revenue* to the *Internal Revenue Service.*

Real Life Story: Jerry disliked having income taxes deducted from his income and felt that it was unfair that the government take funds from his income that it did not provide. He then encountered an individual who was a member of an anti-income tax group. This individual convinced him that it was unconstitutional for the IRS to collect taxes from his income. This was music to Jerry's ears. He then joined the group, began advocating against the IRS and immediately submitted a new Form W-4, to his employer claiming exemption from income taxes. At that point, Jerry's employer stopped deducting income taxes from his paycheck. This went on for several years.

But Jerry did not stop there. He also stopped filing income tax returns despite receiving a W-2 from his employer that listed his income earned for each tax year. He was convinced that since he had not been contacted by the IRS, that this anti-income tax group was a legitimate organization.

Unfortunately, after several years had gone by, the IRS sent a *Lock-In Letter* to his employer. A *Lock-In Letter* is a letter sent by the IRS to an employer requiring that they change an individual's exemptions to zero "0" so that the maximum amount of taxes can be withheld. This infuriated Jerry as he was now unable to meet his monthly expenses. But the IRS did not stop there. A Revenue Officer was assigned to Jerry's case because he had several unfiled returns.

He sent several requests to Jerry and made every attempt to discuss his case with him so that he could have an opportunity to comply. Not surprisingly, Jerry refused to respond. The Revenue Officer then had Jerry's unfiled returns prepared by the Substitute for Returns Unit, an IRS unit that prepares tax returns for use by the IRS in cases when the individual fails to file. After it was determined how much taxes Jerry owed, and the appropriate notices were sent, the Revenue Officer began to levy Jerry's bank account and garnish his wages.

Jerry responded to this by quitting his job and closing his bank account, but that only made matters worse. He then received a summons to appear in Tax Court by the Department of Justice and was being charged with Tax Evasion for failure to pay his taxes.

At this point, Jerry retained our firm to represent him in Tax Court. He was completely distraught and expressed that he honestly believed that income taxes were unconstitutional and did not know that it would have gotten this bad or go this far. Jerry feared losing his home and his assets because he had already lost his job and had no income. He was now dependent upon his family to help him make ends meet. Our Attorney did not waste any time; he immediately began to negotiate with the Department of Justice.

In less than two weeks, he was able to prepare the necessary documents and negotiate a plea that prevented Jerry from serving a prison sentence, the levy was released, and he was able to enter into an affordable settlement that allowed him to pay less than the full amount owed. He was then able to return to the workforce and was counseled on the importance of paying his income taxes. He cried for joy on his Attorney's shoulders because he had been certain he would lose it all. Jerry learned a valuable lesson that day: *It is better to comply with the IRS than to ignore its existence.*

Personal Income & Business Tax Returns

Most, if not all, audits/examinations begin because of a filed or unfiled tax return. The IRS requires that individuals and businesses file all required tax returns when due. There are various guidelines provided by the IRS for determining whether you are required to file an income tax return.

Whether you are required to file an income tax return will be determined by your filing status, your age, and income.

Generally, if you are an employee, you are required to file an income tax return if your income exceeds the standard deductions (*see* Appendix E for further details and instructions).

If you are self-employed or a 1099 independent contractor, you are required to file an income tax return if you earned over $600 in income before deducting business expenses. This is because employers paying 1099 independent contractors over $600 in income in a given tax year are required to file a Form 1099 directly with the IRS, reporting all income paid for that tax year. You should file an income tax return, even if not required, if any of the following applies:

1. You paid taxes on your income and are entitled to a refund;

2. You are eligible for the *Earned Income Credit* (EIC); or

3. You take advantage of refundable credits such as the additional *Child Tax Credit*, or *American Opportunity Credit*, etc. (credits are covered in fuller detail in the section on common deductions, Chapter 5, *Tax Credits: Financial Help Many Forget*).

The IRS wants you to be in compliance. What does that mean? For individuals, the IRS considers your account to be in compliance when all tax returns were filed for the last six years. The current year is 2014, which means that an individual taxpayer must file all returns from 2007 through 2013 in order to be compliant. This is critical to note. If for some reason you enter into a tax resolution situation, *the IRS will not negotiate if you are not compliant* in most cases. Six years means six years—that means all returns for the previous years must be on file if you had a filing requirement for that tax year. And, you need to stay current with required ongoing filings as they occur.

Businesses must file all required tax returns and may go beyond the past six years to as far back as its initial date of operation.

What happens if you fail to file a return?

Simply this: the IRS may file it for you in what is called a *Substitute for Return* (SFR) ... meaning that the IRS will estimate what it believes your income and taxes paid to be based on information it has in its system. If a SFR is created, you will get a *Notice of Assessment* for taxes owed that most likely includes a penalty and fine. It will also detail how the balance owed was calculated, with a deadline to pay or file your own return and send to the IRS.

A business may *cause* the IRS to initiate an audit for not filing.

I can't stress this enough: you don't want to go down this path. It is important that you file your required tax returns on time annually. You must also ensure that your returns are accurate when filed in order to decrease the likelihood that you will be audited by the IRS.

A *Substitute for Return* is a return that the IRS prepares on your behalf without your consent based on the information provided to the IRS. After a *Substitute for Return* is prepared by the IRS, you will receive a Notice of Assessment detailing how your tax return was prepared, and the proposed balance owed on your account, with a deadline to pay or file your own return and submit it to the IRS.

Endnotes

[1]IRS.gov/uac/Brief-History-of-IRS

Inside this chapter

Form **1040**

Department of

U.S. Indiv

For the year Jar

Your first nar

Label

(See instructions on page 12.)

Use the IRS label. Otherwise, please print or type.

L A B E L

H E R E

If a joint ret

Home add

City, tow

Presidential Election Campaign ▶ Chec

1

2

3

Filing Status

Check only one box.

Exemptions

6a

b

c

If more than four dependents, see page 15.

Income

Attach Form(s) W-2 here. Also attach Forms W-2G and 1099-R if tax was withheld.

If you did not get a W-2, see page 19

Enclose, bu not attach, payment. A please use Form 104

CHAPTER 2

The Basics ... How Do you Determine Your Filing Status?

Taxpayers have to start somewhere in the filing process—identifying your filing status is the logical and critical place to begin. Although it seems simple—single or married—there are other options that taxpayers need clarity on. Different standard deductions, eligibility for various tax credits and whether you even need to file a return are all taken into consideration within each filing status. Your marital status on the last day of the year determines your marital status for the entire year.[2] Sometimes, you can actually qualify for more than one status. If that occurs, be tax smart and select the one that creates the *lowest tax obligation*.

Presently, the IRS has five types of filing statuses:

- Single
- Head of Household
- Married Filing Jointly
- Married Filing Separately
- Qualifying Widow(er) with Dependent Child

Single

You are considered *Single* if you are unmarried, divorced, or legally separated according to state law on the last day of the year (December 31).

Head of Household

You may file as Head of Household if you are: 1. unmarried, 2. paid more than half the cost of maintaining a home for you and a dependent, and 3. have a qualifying dependent that meets the six factors presented in the Earned Income Credit Section in *Chapter 5, Tax Credits: Financial Help Many Forget.*

Married Filing Jointly

You are considered to be married if at the end of the tax year (December 31), you are legally married according to state law. This requirement doesn't apply to Registered Domestic Partnerships, but applies to same-sex couples that are legally married according to the laws of the state where the marriage took place. You and your spouse must file a joint tax return in order for your filing status to be Married Filing Jointly. Filing a joint return with your spouse may have beneficial tax consequences such as:

- Higher standard deductions; • Higher tax credits;
- Lower taxes

Note: If your spouse died before the year ended, you may still file a joint return for the year in which he or she or he died.

Married Filing Separately

Although you are married, you may choose to file separately from your spouse as Married Filing Separately.

Alert: When filing separately from your spouse (Married Filing Separately), you reduce your Standard Deduction. In some cases, it may also limit tax credits for which you may be eligible. Filing *separately* from a spouse who may owe the IRS will help to prevent you from having your tax refunds seized, or prevent you from potentially owing the IRS if you were to file jointly. As an attorney, I would encourage you to get legal advice if this is your primary purpose in electing this filing status.

Qualifying Widow(er) with Dependent Child

You may be eligible to file as a Qualifying Widow(er) with a Dependent Child for two years following the year of your spouse's death. By using this filing status, you will be able to use the tax rates of the Married Filing Jointly status and the highest standard deduction amount provided you do not itemize your deductions.

Caution: You cannot file a joint return with your deceased spouse and claim this filing status unless the following conditions are met:

> Along with your Social Security Number and your name, knowing your correct filing status is an elementary step in all filings with the IRS. If your status changes, make sure future filings reflect it. It's wise to have proper documentation of any marriages, divorces, births and deaths.

- You were entitled to file a joint return with your spouse for the year your spouse died, even if you did not file jointly;

- You didn't remarry in the same year that your spouse died;

- You have a child or stepchild for whom you can claim an exemption, but foster children are not allowed;

- The child lived in your home all year, except for temporary absences;

- You paid more than half the cost of keeping up a home for the year.

Endnotes

[2] IRS.gov/uac/Eight-Facts-About-F

Inside this chapter

CHAPTER 3

How to Select a Tax Preparer to Prepare Your Tax Returns

Every tax return starts with your name and your filing status. Not difficult to determine. What is added as a return is completed, is supplied by you or a Tax Preparer.

> **Real Life Story:** Matthew was an elderly man and was receiving Social Security Benefits (SSB) and monthly annuity payments for his disability. Every year, he would have his returns prepared by the same licensed Tax Preparer but he did not research the preparer's credentials. Every year, the Tax Preparer informed Matthew that he owed taxes because he did not have sufficient withholdings from his annuity. For years, he filed his returns, but did not pay the taxes owed. Eventually, that got the IRS's attention.
>
> Several *Notices of Intent to Levy* from the IRS were sent, but Matthew ignored those notices. He also

received a *Final Notice of Intent to Levy* and he ignored that notice as well. Finally, the IRS issued a levy on Matthew's SSB and annuity income. This prompted him to finally listen to his Tax Preparer and have taxes deducted from his annuity. After adjusting the tax deductions from his annuity, Matthew did not owe taxes on subsequent returns.

However, his SSB and annuity were still being levied by the IRS. So he hired our firm to negotiate a settlement with the IRS. My associate tax attorney, who was also a licensed Tax Preparer, took immediate notice of the fact that Matthew's incomes were SSI and an annuity as a result of his disability. The Attorney determined that based on IRS law, some annuity payments were not taxable if paid as a result of disability, and SSI payments were not taxable if the SSB and other income combined for an amount below $25,000. If Matthew's annuity payments were exempt from taxation, then his combined income would be less than $25,000.

My associate tax attorney did the research and confirmed that Matthew's income was exempt from taxation. Based on this information, he determined that Matthew's original Tax Preparer had incorrectly prepared his returns. My associate tax attorney then prepared and filed amended returns for Matthew as far back as three years, reflecting that he did not owe taxes, but was actually due refunds for the full amount of taxes that were deducted from his annuity.

As a result, an immediate release of all levies on Matthew's income was obtained. After the returns were done processing, the IRS ended up issuing over $10,000 in refunds to him for both the taxes deducted from his income in the past, and for funds wrongfully levied from his SSB and annuity. Matthew vowed from that moment to always hire our firm to prepare his income tax returns. He learned a valuable lesson from all of this: *Choose your Tax Preparer Wisely!*

If you decide to seek professional assistance with preparation of your tax return, there are important things to consider. A wrong selection can send you and your return spiraling down a hole. It is important that you choose someone that is honest, professional, and provides excellent service, because you will be held legally responsible for what is reported on your tax return, even when prepared by someone else. Below are key items to consider when selecting a tax preparer:

1. Check the preparer's qualifications and credentials.
The IRS requires that all tax preparers obtain a Preparer Tax Identification Number (PTIN) in order to prepare tax returns. When you pay someone to prepare your tax return, be sure that your return includes their PTIN in the section labeled "Paid Preparer Information." You should also research the preparer's history in order to determine whether they have any derogatory remarks or disciplinary action.

Conduct independent research in order to determine whether the preparer has been sanctioned previously for preparing fraudulent returns. The most common method is to use the Internet and search for

If you are due a refund, make sure that the refund is deposited directly into your personal bank account, or that the check is sent to your mailing address.

the individual's name, or name of the company. A lot of information is available beginning with a search on Google about individuals and companies. You may use this method as a good starting point in conducting your research.

2. Inquire about the preparer's fees. Most preparers will offer their service at a flat rate per return. Avoid preparers who require a percentage of your refund for their services. Why? This is an indication that they may inflate your refund in order to receive a larger fee.

If you are due a refund, make sure that the refund is deposited directly into your personal bank account, or that the check is sent to your mailing address. Do not allow any of your refund to be deposited into the account of your preparer unless there is a valid reason and you are convinced that your preparer is trustworthy. There have been instances when a preparer recommended that the taxpayer deposit their refund into the preparer's account, and the preparer disappeared without a trace and kept the refund for themselves. It's wise to have all moneys sent directly to you.

3. Ask if the preparer offers electronic filing. The IRS requires that all paid preparers who prepare more than ten returns per year must file the returns electronically, unless the client elects to file a paper return.

Make sure that your preparer offers electronic return filing as it often ensures that your return will be prepared accurately, and processed securely and in a timely manner. If your preparer does not offer electronic filing, it is likely that they are not as experienced as they appear to be, and your return may be more susceptible to inaccuracies. Take a pass.

4. **Make sure that the tax preparer is accessible.** You should never retain the service of a preparer that you are not able to contact when needed. In some cases, you may need to contact your preparer even after the tax filing deadline. Your preparer should be available year round in the event that you have questions or concerns about your tax return. Yes, they have vacations and emergencies—but should always leave their practices, meaning clients, in the hands of a qualified preparer that can answer questions or handle an emergency in their absence.

Generally, tax preparers will try to respond to your inquiries within a stated period of time—such as within 24 hours or 48 hours. The preparer's response time may vary, but generally, tax preparers will try to respond within a reasonable time.

5. **Research the tax preparer's reputation with clients.** Conduct independent research in order to determine whether the tax preparer has other clients in your line of business or occupation. You need to ask this upfront in your initial interview. A preparer that has other clients similar to yourself is likely to understand your line of business or occupation and be more knowledgeable of how to accurately prepare your tax returns. Also, if you

know other clients who have used the tax preparer in the past or presently, ask them whether they have been audited in the past as a result of any tax preparer errors. A reputable tax preparer should receive referrals from past clients and have a great reputation with their clients.

6. **Inquire whether the tax preparer represents clients in audits.** When a tax preparer represents clients in an audit, this is an excellent indication that the preparer will stand behind his or her work. They are also more likely to have experience in auditing and be able to provide competent representation. A tax preparer that has represented clients in previous audits will likely know the type of documentation the IRS is requesting, and may also be able to detect potential audit risks that may result from items listed on your tax return. **Caution:** It is highly recommended that you hire a tax attorney in matters requiring oral advocacy or litigation.

7. **Determine how long the preparer has been in the business of preparing returns.** Experience is an important qualification for a tax preparer. You want someone who has prepared returns on a full time basis for at least a few years—not anyone who is so green that his or her expertise primarily comes from the more academic versus a more practical "in the trenches" approach that a few years of doing returns and representing taxpayers in audits creates. And not someone who does this on a part-time basis or adjunct to their regular job that is outside of tax matters.

My recommendation is that he or she should be preparing taxes for a minimum of five years, has audit experience, and works with clients who are similar in needs. Of course, you always need to have that "gut" feeling that the person you are dealing with is someone who you trust and with whom you can openly confide your financial dealings and positions.

8. **Never ignore signs of foul play.** In some cases, a preparer may ask you to do things that raise a gigantic red flag. For example:

   • **Asks you what amount of refund you would like to receive.** A tax preparer cannot inform you of your refund prior to preparing the tax return. If you are asked how much of a refund you would like, this is a clear indication that your tax preparer will prepare a fraudulent tax return.

   • **Asks you to sign a blank return.** Do not sign a blank return under any circumstances. Do not sign a return without reviewing the return. Be sure to ask questions about any items that you find may be questionable. "When in doubt, check it out!"

   • **Asks you to deposit your refund into their account.** A reputable tax preparer will not require you to deposit your refund into their account absent a valid reason that should be disclosed to you, nor will they ask for a percentage of your refund. If you are asked to do this by your tax preparer, it is likely that you will be the victim of fraud.

If it looks like—sounds like—feels like—any of the above, my best recommendation is to not work with this person or firm.

The Do-It-Yourself Filer

Every spring, your TV blasts commercials of taxpayers happily boasting about their magnificent refunds. Is that such a good thing? Maybe, maybe not. In my opinion, getting a tax refund, especially one that exceeds several hundred dollars is a sign of mediocre or no tax planning. Tax preparers should be looking forward with you and asking questions. Questions that would include income projections, anticipated tax deductions, increases or decreases in charitable contributions, changes in mortgage interest, job related and education expenses, potential gains or losses on investments, and other areas that could affect the bottom line to your taxable income.

And every spring, a variety of cornerstone tax preparer ads pop up as well as those for software to just fill in the blanks and Do-It-Yourself. The question becomes: Do you or don't you? From my experience as a tax attorney, I have discovered that most of the Do-It-Yourself filers have cheated themselves out of several hundred, if not thousands, of dollars of refunds. The fact is that you will not know if your refund is accurate unless you are experienced in calculating taxes, exemptions, and credits. When you prepare your return yourself, you rely heavily on your software to guide you through the process, and it may not ask all of the pertinent questions, or discover all of the errors relating to your return. Having a competent tax preparer will help to ensure that you receive the maximum refund possible.

You may have noticed that during tax season, several software companies advertise a "free second look" at your tax return by one of their paid tax preparers in order to ensure that you receive the maximum refund possible. This is because reliance on your tax software alone does not ensure that you will receive all of the exemptions and credits to which you are entitled. So be tax smart, and hire a competent tax preparer to prepare your tax returns. This will also help to ensure that you receive the maximum refund possible, while also reducing the likelihood that your tax return will be audited by the IRS.

Having a highly competent and qualified tax preparer on your team will not only ensure that you file your return on time, but they will also ensure that you include all relevant pieces to your financial and tax puzzle, are adequately represented against the IRS if the need arises, and will also bring peace of mind and sanity to your everyday life.

Steven's Tip: The savvy taxpayer looks before he or she leaps. Ask for references, and follow up with all of them. You want to work with a tax professional who "gets you"—who also works with other taxpayers who work within your profession, your industry, your expertise. Not all tax-payers can be treated with a "cookie cutter" approach.

Inside this chapter

CHAPTER 4

Deductions: Don't Leave Them Off Your Return

W hen preparing your income tax return, it is important that you claim all of the deductions to which you are entitled. Deductions can make the difference between owing the IRS, or obtaining a sizeable refund.

Real Life Story: Emily decided to prepare her tax return on her own. She relied on a "home-based software" and simply filled in the blanks as required by her software. By the time she was finished entering all of her information, the software determined that she owed the IRS approximately $15,000. Emily was devastated because she was sure that she had entered her information correctly, and now she owed the IRS $15,000! Before submitting the return, she hired our firm to review her return and to provide her with options for resolving the taxes owed.

My associate tax attorney reviewed Emily's tax return and determined that she did not receive several deductions and credits to which she was entitled. So the attorney revised the tax return, and after all of the revisions, she was entitled to a refund, rather than owing the IRS. Emily learned a valuable lesson: *It is better to have a professional prepare your tax return than to do it yourself.*

Although I recommend that you have a professional prepare your tax return, if you decide to prepare your tax return on your own, double check the return to ensure that you have claimed all of the deductions to which you are entitled.

What Are Personal Exemptions?

Think of you and those that you support and are dependent on you, for starters—you and yours. *Personal exemptions* are pre-set amounts established by the IRS that a taxpayer may deduct for themselves and any dependents claimed on their income tax return. The personal exemption is similar to a tax deduction; it reduces your taxable income, and reduces your taxes due. The IRS adjusts the personal exemption annually to account for inflation.

In 2013, the personal exemption was $3,900. This amount is expected to increase to $3,950 in 2014. You may only claim the personal exemption if someone cannot claim you as a dependent. When spouses file a joint tax return, they may claim a personal exemption for each spouse even if one spouse did not earn any income during the year. However, if they file as Married Filing Separately, they may each claim only one personal exemption for themselves. Also, spouses are prohibited from claiming the same dependent when filing as Married Filing Separately.

What Are the Differences Between the Deductions?

A *Tax Deduction* is an item that you can claim that will reduce the amount of your income that can be taxed by the IRS. Generally, tax deductions are allowable if related to the production of income. You want to deduct what is allowable and deductible. There are three types of tax deductions allowed by the IRS:

1. Standard Deductions

2. Itemized Deductions

3. Above-the-Line Deductions

This area is one where many taxpayers encounter some confusion. Taxpayers are not allowed to claim both standard and itemized deductions. As a result, you must choose one of the two methods when preparing your income tax return. Generally, you should choose the method that will result in the lowest tax owed, or the largest refund if one is due to you. However, if you choose to itemize your deductions, you are more likely to be audited by the IRS if your deductions are found to be unreasonable in comparison to your income.

What Are Standard Deductions?

The *Standard Deduction* is fairly easy to explain. It is a predetermined amount that a taxpayer may subtract from his or her income based on the filing status. Taking the standard deduction will automatically reduce your income level upon which taxes owed are calculated. Every year, the IRS increases the standard deduction for each filing status. The Standard Deduction may be claimed only by citizens of the United States, and resident aliens. Spouses filing as Married Filing Separately are prohibited from claiming the standard deduction where one spouse itemized their deductions. Also, nonresident aliens residing in the United States may not claim the standard deduction on a return that is filed. Taxpayers who claim it are not likely to be audited by the IRS as no proof will be required for this deduction.

The chart below provides the standard deduction allowed by the IRS from 2007 through 2014. As always, future years can change and it's recommended to always check rates for the current year.

Filing Status					
Year	Single	Married Filing Jointly	Married Filing Separately	Head of House-hold	Qualifying Widow(er)
2014	$6,200	$12,400	$6,200	$9,100	$12,400
2013	$6,100	$12,200	$6,100	$8,950	$12,200
2012	$5,950	$11,900	$5,950	$8,700	$11,900
2011	$5,800	$11,600	$5,800	$8,500	$11,600
2010	$5,700	$11,400	$5,700	$8,400	$11,400
2009	$5,700	$11,400	$5,700	$8,350	$11,400
2008	$5,450	$10,900	$5,450	$8,000	$10,900
2007	$5,350	$10,700	$5,350	$7,850	$10,700

In special cases such as:

1. taxpayers 65 years of age or older;
2. taxpayer's spouse is 65 years of age or older;
3. if a taxpayer or spouse is blind; taxpayers are allowed to add an additional $1,550; if 65 or older and blind, the standard deduction is $3,100 to their standard deduction if married, or a maximum of $1,500 for unmarried individuals in 2014.

For individuals who may be claimed as a dependent, the standard deduction is generally limited to $1,000, or the dependent's earned income for the year plus $350 if it does not exceed $6,200 (or standard deduction for the single filing status), whichever is larger in 2014. If the dependent is 65 or older, or blind, his or her standard deduction will likely be higher. [3]

What Are Itemized Deductions?

Any eligible expenses that taxpayers may claim in order to reduce their taxable income are called *Itemized Deductions.* Generally, taxpayers choose to itemize their deductions when it will result in a larger tax refund, or lower taxes. A taxpayer whose spouse filed as Married Filing Separately and itemized his or her deductions will be required to also itemize deductions, and will be prohibited from choosing the standard deduction on the tax payer's return. The smart taxpayer will maintain records in order to substantiate any itemized deductions in the event of an IRS audit. You should also ensure that your itemized deductions are reasonable in comparison to your income.

Where taxpayers who take the standard deductions are less likely to be audited by the IRS, taxpayers who choose to itemize on their tax return are more likely to have their tax returns audited by the IRS. Taxpayers choosing to itemize their deductions must file a Schedule A with their Form 1040.

Itemized deductions are also reduced by one-third of the lesser of one: three percent of the excess of Adjusted Gross Income (AGI) over the limitation set by the IRS for that tax year; or two: 80 percent of the total itemized deductions. This is known as the "Pease Limitations." The Pease Limitations were repealed for the years 2010, 2011, and 2012. The Pease Limitation has taken effect once again in 2013. Taxpayers filing as Married Filing Jointly with a combined AGI of $300,000 or higher, or $250,000 for single taxpayers, will have their itemized deductions reduced by 3% of the amount by which their AGI exceeds these thresholds. The reduction caused by the Pease Limitation is capped at 80% of the total itemized deductions. Since the last time this limitation was used was 2013, we will use the figures provided for that year.

Example: A taxpayer with an AGI of $300,000 in 2013 and itemized deductions of $30,000 is limited to a total itemized deduction of $19,004. Follow these steps in figuring your maximum itemized deductions:

- **Step 1**—3 percent of AGI: **.03 x $300,000 – $250,000** (Pease Limitation for Single taxpayer) = **$1,500**

- **Step 2**—80 percent of itemized deductions: **.80 x $30,000 = $24,000**

- **Step 3**—Determine the lesser of Steps 1 and 2: **$1,500** (value from Step 1)

- **Step 4**—Reduce itemized deduction by figure in Step 3: **$30,000 – $1,500 = $28,500**

Itemized deductions are limited to those expenses listed on the Schedule A. Allowable itemized deductions include the following:

Medical Expenses

Medical expenses are deductible to the extent that the total medical expenses exceed 10 percent of the taxpayers AGI. For example, a taxpayer with an AGI of $30,000 with medical expenses of $5,000 would be eligible to deduct $2,000 (**$30,000 x .10 = $3,000; $5,000 - $3,000 = $2,000**) and insert on Schedule A under medical expenses. Taxpayers over the age of 65 however, may deduct medical expenses if it exceeds 7.5 percent of their AGI. Medical expenses include capital expenditures advised by a physician that is reasonable under the circumstances (i.e. swimming pool for someone with degenerative spinal disorder); payments to medical practitioners (i.e. dentist, doctors, surgeons, etc.); premiums for medical insurance (not if paid by someone else or pre-tax money); payments for prescriptions; payments for medical devices (i.e. eyeglasses, hearing aids, crutches, etc.); mileage for travel to and from medical visits; and other necessary travel expenses.

Medical expenses do not include: over-the-counter drugs; health club memberships; or cosmetic surgery (except for corrective cosmetic surgery to restore normal appearance after an injury, or genetic deformity).

State and Local Taxes

You may deduct state or local income taxes, vehicle registration and license fees, and property taxes. Any payments on Use Taxes, Excise Taxes, Fines, or Penalties are not allowed.

Mortgage Interest Expense

Mortgage interest may be deducted for up to two homes not to exceed $1,000,000 in financing debt, and $100,000 in home equity loans. You may also claim mortgage points.

Investment Interest

Investment interest (interest paid or accrued on indebtiness for property held for investment that produces interest, dividends, royalties, or annuities) may be deducted but *cannot exceed* the taxpayer's net investment income for the year. If your investment interest expense is greater than your investment income, you can defer the excess balance until more investment income is declared.

Charitable Contributions

Charitable contributions may be deducted, although such deductions are limited to an amount equal to 30 to 50 percent of your AGI, depending on the type of property contributed. Charitable contributions include money or goods donated to a charitable organization recognized by the IRS. Donations made to individuals, political campaigns, or political action committees are not deductible. The value of donated services cannot be deducted, while reasonable and necessary expenses incurred in providing a charitable service may be deducted (i.e. mileage, meals, special uniforms, etc.). Non-cash items valued at more than $500 will require special substantiation and are deductible at the lesser of the fair market value or the donor's cost.

Casualty and Theft Losses

Casualty and theft losses are deductible up to 10 percent

of the taxpayer's AGI, or to a greater extent if the taxpayer resides in an area that has been declared a disaster area.

Gambling Losses

Gambling losses are also deductible but cannot exceed the gambling winnings. For example, a taxpayer who won $1,500 during the tax year, but lost $2,000 during the same year can only deduct a maximum of $1,500 in gambling losses. If you win money via a lottery, it's taxable. You can deduct all those losing tickets that you purchased the year of your winning as long as you kept them. If you win $500, you can deduct up to $500 in losing tickets to offset your winnings. Of course, if you win one of those multi-million dollar grand prizes, a few hundred dollars in loss ticket slips will be insignificant!

Miscellaneous Itemized Deductions

Miscellaneous deductions are allowed, provided they are job related (i.e. uniform, union dues, unreimbursed travel, education, or other work related education, fees paid to tax preparers or tax software, subscriptions to periodicals, or newspapers directly relating to your job, etc.). Taxpayers are allowed to deduct miscellaneous itemized deductions that exceed two percent of their AGI. For example, a taxpayer with an AGI of $25,000 and miscellaneous work-related expenses of $2,500 can claim a maximum of $2,000. (**$2,500 x 0.02 = $500; $2500 – $500=$2000**).

What Are Above-the-Line Deductions?

Another common area that taxpayers encounter is the difference between the below- and above-the-line deductions.

Above-the-line deductions have great value for taxpayers. They are deductions taken from your income *prior* to arriving at your AGI in order to determine your taxable income. These deductions are outlined in the Internal Revenue Code (IRC) Section 62. Any deductions allowed after computing your AGI are called below-the-line deductions and are found in IRC Section 63.

What adds to the value of the above-the-line deductions is how they are treated by the IRS. *They are not subject to the limitations that may apply to below-the-line deductions.*

Above-the-line deductions are allowed for most ordinary and necessary business expenses that are related to a trade or business conducted by the taxpayer, so long as the taxpayer does not perform services as an employee. These deductions include the following:

- *Trade and/or business deductions*—includes allowance for salaries or other compensation for personal services, reasonable travel expenses, and rental or other payments.
- *Deductions of employees*—incurred in conducting the trade or business.
- *Reimbursed expenses of employees*—in connection with performing their job.
- *Expenses of performing artists*—incurred as an employee in connection to performances.
- *Expenses of officials employed by a state or political subdivision*—that is compensated on a fee basis.
- *Expenses of elementary or secondary school teachers*— not in excess of $250 paid for books, supplies, computer and other equipment, and other supplementary materials used in the classroom.
- *Losses from sale or exchange of property*—so long as the property generated rental income or royalties.

- *Life tenants and income beneficiaries of property*—may deduct depreciation of the property.
- *Expenses for members of reserved sections of the Armed Forces of the United States*—for any period in which the taxpayer was more than 100 miles away from home in connection with performing their service (i.e. travel expenses, meals, etc.).
- *Pension, profit-sharing, and annuity plans*—for self-employed individuals.
- Retirement savings.
- Alimony or Maintenance.
- Jury Duty pay remitted to employer.
- Clean-fuel vehicles and certain refueling property.
- Moving expenses.
- Interest on education loans.
- Higher education expenses.
- Health savings accounts.

Too many times, taxpayers don't claim deductions they are entitled to. Make sure that you have receipts for those you do claim, and keep them with a copy of your return.

Steven's Tip: Deductions are deductions—some are considered "sacred cows" like the mortgage deduction for a primary residence; others have had changes to them over the years. Because of that simple fact, determining what is allowable and not allowable can vary year to year. If there is any question, professional advice is recommended.

Endnotes

3 IRS.gov/pub/irs-pdf/p17.pdf

Inside this chapter

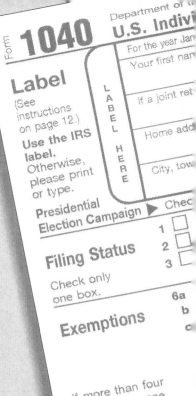

CHAPTER 5

Tax Credits: Financial Help Many Forget

When taxpayers receive tax credits, they think of them as a bonus when it comes to their income tax return. Tax deductions are used to reduce taxable income; tax credits reduce taxes owed.

If you have a tax obligation of $3,200 and a deduction of $2,000 is discovered to have not been deducted before the final tax amount was determined, your taxable income will be adjusted downward. It will be reduced by the $2,000 and the amount of tax you owe will be recalculated with the new amount based on your tax rate. A $2,000 tax credit is treated differently. It would reduce the $3,200 obligation to $1,200.

> A *Tax Deduction* reduces taxable income. A *Tax Credit* reduces tax owed.

Earned Income Tax Credit

The *Earned Income Tax Credit* (EIC or EITC) is a refundable tax credit available to workers earning low or moderate incomes.

The value of the EIC decreases or increases based on your filing status, whether you claim a qualifying child (QC), and your adjusted gross income (AGI). The EIC will reduce the amount of tax you owe, and in some situations, you may even receive a refund.

A *Qualifying Child* must be:

1. A relative either by birth or adoption;

2. Under the age of 19, or a full time student under the age of 24, or permanently disabled regardless of age;

3. A child for whom you have provided more than half of their individual's support;

4. Resided with you for more than half of the year;

5. Cannot file a joint return if he or she is married; and

6. Claimed by only one person who is entitled to claim them, either by law or mutual agreement.

If you are the claimer, you may also be able to claim the child of a girlfriend or boyfriend as a *Qualifying Relative* so long as factors two through six above are met.

In order to be eligible for the EIC for 2014, both your earned income and AGI must be less than[4]:

- $46,997 ($52,427 Married Filing Jointly) with three or more qualifying children;

- $43,756 ($49,186 Married Filing Jointly) with two qualifying children;

- $38,511 ($43,941 Married Filing Jointly) with one qualifying child; or

- $14,590 ($20,020 Married Filing Jointly) with no qualifying children.

Those who qualify for the EIC for tax year 2014 can a get a credit of:

- $6,143 with three or more qualifying children;

- $5,460 with two qualifying children;

- $3,305 with one qualifying child; or

- $496 with no qualifying children.

If your only income is *Investment Income*, it must be $3,350 or less for the year in order to be eligible for the EIC.

Child Tax Credit and Additional Child Tax Credit

The *Child Tax Credit* provides a tax credit of up to $1,000 for each child under the age of 17, depending on your income. In order to qualify, the child must also meet factors two through six provided in the previous discussion on the Earned Income Credit. The credit is limited to the amount of income tax owed. For example, if you are entitled to a Child Tax Credit of $1,000 but owe $500 in taxes, your Child Tax Credit will be reduced to $500.

However, if the amount of your credit is greater than the amount of income tax you owe, you may be able to claim the *Additional Child Tax Credit* for the remaining balance of your Child Tax Credit if your earned income was less than the following:

- $110,000 for Married Filing Jointly;
- $75,000 for Single, Head of Household, or Qualifying Widow(er);
- $55,000 for Married Filing Separately.

American Opportunity Tax Credit

The *American Opportunity Tax Credit* modifies the existing Hope Credit (discussed below) and is available to a broader range of taxpayers, including those earning higher incomes and those who do not owe any taxes. It adds course materials, supplies, and equipment as a qualifying expense in conjunction to college tuition and course fees. This credit may be claimed for up to the first four years of college at an undergraduate institution for a maximum credit of $2,500 per student.

The full credit can be awarded if your AGI is $90,000 for single taxpayers and $180,000 for married taxpayers who file a joint return. Forty-percent of this credit (up to $1,000) is refundable, which means that you may obtain a refund of $1,000 *even if you do not owe taxes.*

This credit does not apply to:

- room and board,
- transportation,
- insurance,
- medical expenses,
- student fees not related to enrollment or attendance,
- same expense paid with tax-free educational assistance, or
- same expense used for any other tax deduction.

Note: The American Opportunity Credit will only be available for the years 2009 through 2017 unless Congress decides to extend it beyond those years.

Hope Credit

The *Hope Credit* applies to tax years prior to 2008. It is a nonrefundable credit that may be claimed for the first two years of your post-secondary education for a maximum of $1,800 or $3,600 if you reside in an approved Midwestern disaster area (also includes spouse and dependents). This credit may only be claimed on qualified tuition and enrollment fees. Also, because it is nonrefundable, it cannot exceed your tax debt. This means that if you owe $1,000 in taxes, you may only claim a maximum of $1,000 of the Hope Credit. If your credit is greater than your tax debt, the excess will not be refunded to you. Also, the IRS will not allow you to claim an education credit and the Hope Credit at the same time.

In some instances, it may be more beneficial to claim the tuition and fees expenses rather than the Hope Credit. Remember to choose the deduction that results in the least amount of taxes owed, or a larger refund.

In general, you can claim the Hope Credit if all three of the following requirements are met:

- You pay qualified education expenses of higher education such as tuition and enrollment fees.

- You pay the education expenses for an eligible student which is either a full-time student or part-time student.

- The eligible student is either you, your spouse, or a dependent claimed on your tax return.

Lifetime Learning Credits

Lifetime Learning Credit is a tax credit available to college students. The credit provides a credit of 20 percent of tuition expenses for a maximum of $2,000 to $4,000 depending on your income. This credit may be claimed even if you only take one class in college. Qualifying expenses for the Hope/Lifetime Learning Credits are tuition and any required fees such as registration and student body fees. *Expenses such as books, supplies, equipment, room and board, insurance, student health fees, transportation or living expenses are not qualifying expenses for this tax credit.*

When figuring your tax credit, you will need to reduce your qualifying expenses by the amount received in grants, scholarships, or reimbursements from your employer.

Note: You do not need to reduce your expenses if you paid for your qualifying expenses using student loans or with gifts from family members.

In order to claim this credit, you or your dependent must be going to college, and if it is a dependent or spouse, you must claim them as a dependent or file a joint tax return. You may claim the maximum of $4,000 if your income is less than $65,000 for single taxpayers, or less than $130,000 for married taxpayers filing jointly.

If your income exceeds $65,000 for single taxpayers, or $130,000 for married taxpayers filing jointly, the tax credit is limited to $2,000 maximum.

Note: Unlike the American Opportunity Credit and Hope Credit, the Lifetime Learning Credit has no limit to the amount of years it can be claimed. You may claim this every year so long as you meet the eligibility rules.

Child and Dependent Care Credit

You may be able to claim the *Child and Dependent Care Credit* if you paid someone to care for your child, spouse, or dependent providing the following conditions are met:

- The child must be your dependent and 12 years old or younger. If it is a spouse or adult dependent, they must be physically or mentally incapable of caring for themselves. They must also be claimed as a dependent on your tax return.

- The care must have been provided so that you and your spouse (if married) can work or seek employment.

- You and or spouse (if applicable) must have earned income from wages, salaries, tips, net earnings from self-employment or other taxable income.

- The payments you made for child or dependent care cannot be paid to your spouse, parent of the child or dependent, someone you claim as a dependent or to one of your other children who will not be age 19 or older by the end of that year. The care provider's information must also be provided on your tax return.

- Your filing status must be Single, Married Filing Jointly, Head of Household or Qualifying Widow(er) with a Dependent Child.

- The child or dependent must have lived with you for more than half of the year with the exception of the birth or death of your qualifying child or dependent.

- The credit can be up to 35 percent of your qualifying expenses, depending on your AGI.

- In 2010 the IRS allowed up to $3,000 of expenses paid in one year for one child or dependent, or up to $6,000 for two or more children or dependents in order to figure the credit.

- The qualifying expenses must be reduced by the amount of dependent care benefits provided by your employer, if applicable, if you deduct or exclude it from your income.

- You may be subject to pay Social Security, Medicare Tax, and Federal Unemployment Tax if you pay someone to come to your home to care for your child or dependent.[5]

Obamacare Tax Credit

This is a government subsidy paid directly to your health insurance company after your taxes have been filed and processed based on your household size and income.

However, individuals who have coverage through an employer or spouse's employer may not be eligible unless one of these exceptions applies:

Houshold Size	400%
1	$45,960
2	$62,040
3	$78,120
4	$94,200
5	$110,280
6	$126.360
7	$142,440
8	$158,520

For each additional person, add $16,080.

1. Employer's plan covers less than 60% of covered health benefits, or

2. You pay over 9.5% of income for your share of the health insurance premium.

If either of these exceptions applies, you may enroll through your state health insurance coverage exchange.

Penalty

Taxpayers who do not have health insurance in 2014 or meet an exemption under the Affordable Care Act will have to pay a penalty of one percent of their taxable income or a fee of $95 for each uninsured adult and $47.50 for each uninsured child for a maximum of $285 per family, whichever is higher. This fee is expected to increase to $325 in 2015 and $695 in 2016.

Health Coverage Tax Credit

Health Coverage Tax Credit (HCTC) is allowed for up to 80 percent of the amount paid for qualified health coverage as specified in Section 53 of the Internal Revenue Code. A Health Plan is qualified if monthly payments were made directly to a health plan administrator on your behalf. This tax credit may be claimed yearly or on a monthly basis by enrolling in the monthly HCTC program. In order to claim this tax credit you must also meet the following requirements:

- You must be:
    1. A Pension Benefit Guaranty Corporation (PBGC) payee and age 55 and older; or
    2. An eligible Trade Adjustment Assistance (TAA) or Reemployment TAA (RTAA) recipient; or

    3. A qualified family member of an individual who fell under item one or two.

- You or your family members must meet the following requirements:

    1. Be covered by a qualified health plan;

    2. Not be enrolled in Medicare Part A, B, or C;

    3. Not be enrolled in Medicaid or the Children's Health Insurance Program;

    4. Not be enrolled in the Federal Employees Health Benefits Program;

    5. Not be enrolled in the U.S. Military Health System (TRICARE);

    6. Not be imprisoned under federal, state, or local authorities; and

    7. Not be claimed as a dependent on someone else's return and your qualified family members must be your spouse or dependent claimed on your return.

- You must be enrolled in a qualified health plan such as:

    1. COBRA;

    2. A state-qualified health plan;

    3. A spousal coverage plan;

    4. A voluntary employee's beneficiary plan;

    5. A non-group, individual health plan; etc.

Note: The Health Coverage Tax Credit will not be available for tax years after 2013.

Premium Tax Credit

If you obtained your health insurance coverage from the Health Insurance Marketplace, you may be eligible to claim the Premium Tax Credit (PTC). You may be eligible to claim the PTC if you meet all of the following criteria:

1. Buy health insurance from the Health Insurance Marketplace (established under the Affordable Care Act),
2. Are ineligible for coverage through your employer or government plan,
3. Are within certain income limits,
4. File a joint return if married, and
5. Cannot be claimed as a dependent by another person.

You have the option to receive the credit immediately, or receive it when you file your income tax return for 2014. If you choose to get it now, you may have all or some of your estimated credit paid in advance directly to your insurance company so that your monthly out-of-pocket premiums will be lowered. However, the estimated amount may not be accurate, and receiving too much or too little in advance can affect your refund or tax owed when you file your 2014 income tax return.

If you choose to to claim the credit when you file your 2014 income tax return, you would claim the out of pocket expenses on the return.

You must file an income tax return in order to claim this credit regardless of whether you chose to receive this credit now or later.

The open enrollment period to purchase health insurance from the Health Insurance Marketplace was October 1, 2013 through March 31, 2014 in order to claim this credit on your 2014 income tax return.

Adoption Tax Credit

The *Adoption Tax Credit* (ATC) is the largest tax credit available to individual taxpayers: up to $13,190 per child. About 70 percent of taxpayers claiming the Adoption Tax Credit had their returns audited by the IRS. If you are claiming this credit, you must file a paper return and include the following:

- Adoption order decree;
- Subsidy Agreement; and
- Proof of adoption expenses.

For a more exhaustive list of acceptable documents, see the Instructions for Form 8839.[6] It may take the IRS six to eight weeks to issue a refund when all documents have been attached.

Endnotes

[4] IRS.gov/Individuals/Preview-of-2012-EITC-Income-Limits,-Maximum-Credit--Amounts-and-Tax-Law- Updates

[5] IRS.gov/uac/Ten-Things-to-Know-About-the-Child-and-Dependent-Care-Credit

[6] IRS.gov/pub/irs-pdf/i8839.pdf

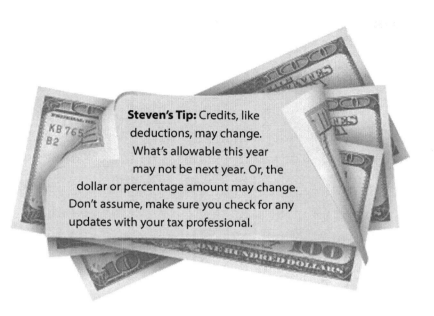

Steven's Tip: Credits, like deductions, may change. What's allowable this year may not be next year. Or, the dollar or percentage amount may change. Don't assume, make sure you check for any updates with your tax professional.

Inside this chapter

Form **1040**

Department of
U.S. Indi

For the year J
Your first n

Label

(See instructions on page 12.)

Use the IRS label. Otherwise, please print or type.

L A B E L   H E R E

If a joint r

Home ac

City, to

Presidential Election Campaign ► Che

Filing Status

Check only one box.

1
2
3

6a

Exemptions

If more than four dependents, see page 15.

Income

Attach Form(s) W-2 here. Also attach Forms W-2G and 1099-R if tax was withheld.

If you did no get a W-2, see page 1

Enclose, b not attach payment. please us Form 10

CHAPTER 6

Commonly Overlooked Deductions and Credits

Let's face it—taxes are overwhelming for most. Where a root canal maybe be preferable to doing ones own taxes, it doesn't need to be. Routinely, tax preparers find common oversights that many taxpayers make when preparing their own income tax return.

There are so many deductions and credits allotted within the IRS Tax Code that some are often forgotten. Below is a list of commonly overlooked deductions and credits that may help to reduce your tax obligation:

Charitable Non-cash Contributions: Many taxpayers donate non-cash items to charities such as Goodwill, Salvation Army, church, etc. It is important that you obtain a written receipt listing your non-cash charitable contributions.

> Take photos of items that you are donating prior to your transfer. Keep them as a backup with the copy of your income tax return.

Refinancing Points Credit: Many homeowners have taken advantage of the low interest rates in the housing market by refinancing their homes. If you have refinanced your home and have paid points on your mortgage (a point is a percentage of your mortgage loan), you may claim up to $10 per month for a maximum credit of $120 per year.

Health Insurance Premium: If you paid health insurance premiums, including long-term care premiums that exceed 10 percent of your Adjusted Gross Income (AGI), you may claim the health insurance premiums as a deduction under the current Affordable Healthcare Act.

If you are self-employed, and are not covered by an employer-paid plan, you can deduct 100 percent of your health insurance premiums based on your net income. The Small Business Job Act of 2010 also allows self-employed individuals to deduct their health insurance premiums when computing their Social Security taxes.

1. Small Employer Health Insurance Credit

To be eligible for this credit, a small employer/small business owner must purchase insurance through the SHOP (Small Business Health Options Program) Marketplace and cover at least 50 percent for the cost of single health care coverage for each employee of average wages below $50,000 annually. The employer must also have less than 25 full-time employees. You must file Form 8941 "Credit for Small Employer Health Insurance Premiums," in order to claim this credit.

Educator Expenses: If you are a qualified educator, you may deduct a maximum of $250 for materials purchased to be used in the classroom such as books, supplies, computer equipment, etc. Don't forget art supplies, copying of handouts, even movies you purchase or rent for classroom lessons.

Higher Education Expenses and Credits: If you paid for higher-education expenses and have an AGI of $90,000 or less, for single tax filers, or $180,000 for joint returns, you may be eligible for the American Opportunity Tax Credit for a maximum of $2,500 per student or the Lifetime Learning Credit for a maximum of $2,000 per return.

If you do not qualify for either credit, you may be able to *deduct* a maximum of $4,000 for your higher-education expenses.

Energy Savings Home Improvement Expenses and Credit: You may claim 10 percent or a maximum of $500 for home improvements made to make your home more energy efficient.

Investment and Tax Expenses: If you paid for tax preparation, legal, accounting, or tax planning fees, you may deduct these expenses if the total spent exceeds two percent of your AGI.

Casualty Deductions: If you live in an area that the president declared as a "Disaster Area," you may be eligible to claim your losses experienced from a natural disaster in addition to what may be claimed in a "non-disaster area."

Retirement Tax Credit: If you have made contributions to a retirement account and have low to moderate income, you may be eligible for a credit of as much as $1,000 or $2,000 if filing jointly and is determined by the qualifying contribution amount.

- AGI for Single, Married Filing Separately, or Qualifying Widow(er) can be $27,750 or less,
- AGI for Head of Household can be $41,625 or less, and AGI for Married Filing Jointly should be $55,500 or less

Interest on Student Loans: Contrary to what many believe, student loan interest is also deductible even if co-signed by someone else. The co-signer may only claim this deduction if they are actually making the payments on the loan or if you are claimed as a dependent on their income tax return.

Business Use of Home: One of the most abused deductions, as well as one of the most over-looked deductions is the use of a portion of your home for business. It is also one that can trigger an audit. That doesn't mean that you shouldn't take the deduction—it means that you must have it documented. If an audit occurs, you must have proof that the space is used for business.

This deduction applies to both self-employed individuals and W-2 employees. You may be able to deduct certain expenses incurred for business use of your home if one of the following applies:

- Your home was used exclusively and regularly as your principal place of business or used as a place to do managerial/record keeping-type tasks and there is no other fixed place where such tasks are performed.
- Your home was used exclusively and regularly as a place where you meet and deal with your clients or customers.
- You have a separate structure that is used for your place of business that is not attached to your home.
- You use your home on a regular basis for storage use.

- You use your home as a rental.

- You operate your home as a daycare facility.

You cannot deduct business expenses for any part of your home that you use for both business and personal purposes. Generally, your home must be the place where most of your time is spent in order to operate your business. **Red flag:** Refer to the next chapter, *What is an Audit?*

A W-2 employee may only deduct this expense when a part of the home was used exclusively and regularly to complete tasks related to their employment and for the employer's convenience.

Deductible expenses for business use of your home includes: mortgage interest, real estate taxes, rent, casualty losses, insurance, utilities, maintenance and repairs, and depreciation. The amount you determine should be based on what percentage of the home is used for business purposes. You cannot claim the full expenses if the entire home was not used for business purposes.

Be smart. Measure what portion is used. Take a picture of it. If there are utilities—gas, electricity, cable, etc.—then have those bills, along with the percentage calculation in reference to total square footage of your residence. Working out of the home is something that millions of Americans do on a daily basis—document what is used for tax purposes. In 2014, taxpayers may claim a standard deduction of $5 per square foot up to a maximum of 300 feet for the area used as a home office for a maximum deduction of $1,500.

Steven's Tip: Credits reduce the dollar amount of actual tax that is owed. Deductions reduce the amount of income that your tax is based upon. Claim what is appropriate for you.

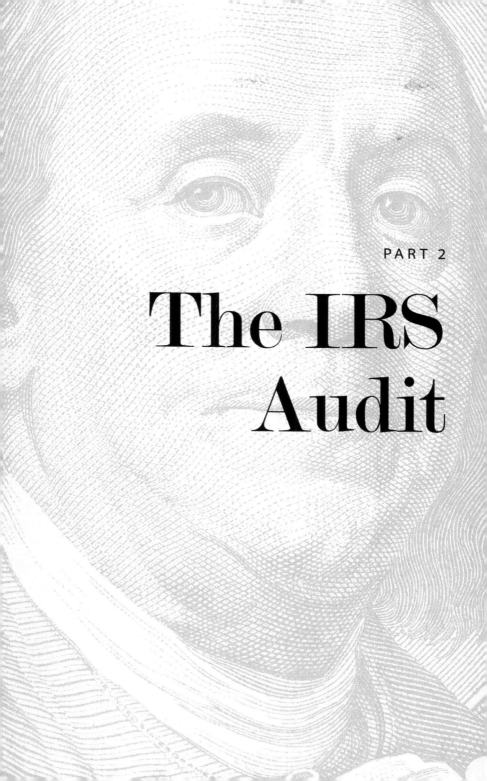

PART 2

The IRS Audit

Inside this chapter

CHAPTER 7

What Is an Audit?

Simply put, an *Audit* is the examination of a taxpayer's income tax return to make sure it accurately calculates the taxpayer's tax liability in accordance with the Internal Revenue laws of the United States.

There are five different types of audits. The basis of each type is that the IRS is examining the tax return filed by the taxpayer to make sure he or she has provided the IRS with all necessary information and that taxpayer has correctly calculated their tax liability based on that information. I'll share the process and steps of each type throughout this section.

Each taxpayer is initially charged with providing such information by filing a tax return on the forms created by the IRS, and with determining their own tax liability in accordance with such form(s). It is often said, based on this "self-assessment," that the United States has a *voluntary tax system*.

> The United States currently employs a taxation system based on self-assessment,[7] which means that each taxpayer is responsible to provide the IRS with the information necessary to determine the taxpayer's tax liability.[8]

However, this is not accurate.[9] The IRS is responsible for making sure that each taxpayer correctly calculates his or her tax liability and has been granted the power to examine any books, papers, records, or other data which may be relevant in making such calculations.[10]

Real Life Story: Phillip hired a tax preparation company to prepare his tax returns. He provided his tax preparer with all of his tax documents in hopes of receiving the maximum refund possible. Phillip was informed by his tax preparer that if he were able to claim his three-year old daughter, he would be eligible for the Earned Income Credit (EIC). He thought about it and determined that since his daughter's mother did not work for the year, that he should be able to claim his daughter without any problems. First mistake—he did not ask his daughter's mother for permission despite her being the custodial parent. His tax preparer included his daughter on his return and Phillip filed it electronically.

Two days later, Phillip was surprised to receive a call from his tax preparer that his return was rejected because someone had already claimed his daughter on their income tax return. Second mistake—he refused to contact the mother to find out whether she had claimed their daughter. Third mistake—the tax preparer informed him that if he was sure that the mother could not claim his daughter, he could sign the return and mail it.

He did and submitted it by mail to the IRS. Eight weeks later, Phillip received a refund check in the mail and cashed it—mistake four. He assumed that this meant that he was allowed to claim his daughter—mistake five.

About six months later, Phillip received a *Notice of Audit and Assessment* in the mail informing him that his return was selected for an Audit and it was determined that he was not allowed to claim his daughter nor was he eligible for the EIC. The IRS proposed to assess taxes that would have been owed had he not claimed his daughter, and the amount of the refund he received, plus interest and penalties for a total of approximately $8,000. Phillip was given 30 days to respond to the notice. He was so distraught and angry, he immediately hired my firm to represent him in the Audit.

My associate tax attorney immediately began to work with him in finding out who claimed his daughter. After investigation, it was determined that the child's mother did not claim her; she had no income and did not work that year. What she had done was to allow a friend to claim their daughter, without Phillip's knowledge or permission, who did not reside in the same home as the child. The Attorney presented evidence that Phillip met the requirements for the EIC while the other individual did not.

As a result, the mother's friend's return was also audited. After 30 days, the IRS determined that Phillip was eligible to claim his daughter and that the other person was ineligible. He was able to keep his refund, and did not owe the IRS a dime. A positive outcome for Phillip ... yet it didn't have to have happened. The five mistakes Phillip made started with him not communicating with the mother of his child which would have clarified quickly that the wrong person claimed his daughter. The financial burden of un-scrambling the mess wouldn't have had to happen.

When can a return be Audited?

Upon being audited, a taxpayer should always determine whether the tax year or years are barred from being examined. The IRS is restricted from auditing some returns after a certain amount of time has passed and from auditing the same tax year multiple times, although exceptions may apply.

Top 10 reasons your return may be Audited

No one wants to be audited by the IRS. While some returns may be randomly selected for an audit, there are some instances in which the IRS will be more likely to select your return for an audit. The top ten reasons why most returns are selected for an audit are:

1. **Errors.** Having errors on your tax return can trigger an IRS audit. Errors in the spelling of your name, social security number, or in calculations may trigger an audit. It is important that you double check all of your information to ensure that all of the information is reported accurately.

2. **Underreporting your income.** Inaccurately reporting your income is likely to trigger an IRS audit, so be honest about your earnings. When you are a wage earner (W-2 employee), or 1099 independent contractor, the IRS will receive a copy of your W-2 or 1099 that was

provided to you by your employer. If the information you provide is different from that provided to the IRS, you are likely to be audited.

Make sure that you are relying on all of the tax documents provided to you, and do not leave anything out. If you are self-employed, be honest about all of your earnings, as the IRS is sure to compare your income to that of others in your same line of business or profession.

3. **Making over $200,000 annually.** There is such a thing as making "too" much money. While only one percent of the population is audited annually, about 3.7 percent earns over $200,000 per year, and one in every eight earning over $1 million are audited every year. If you fall into this category, be sure to report your information accurately, and maintain accurate records of all information provided on your tax return.

4. **Claiming excessive business expenses.** Businesses and self-employed individuals may incur an audit when the expenses claimed appear to be excessive or unreasonable based on the income of the business or industry. Do not claim excessive travel, meals, and entertainment deductions as this will also trigger an audit. The IRS requires that your expenses be *ordinary* and *necessary,* so only claim business expenses that are ordinarily incurred in your line of business, and necessary in order for you to operate and earn a profit.

5. **Claiming false dependents or exemptions.** Each dependent claimed on your tax return provides you

with an additional exemption, which decreases your tax obligation, and increases your eligibility for various tax credits. This leads some individuals to falsely report dependents that they are not authorized or not eligible to claim on their return. This will trigger an IRS audit when you add dependents that you did not claim in the past, or have a pattern of adding and removing dependents.

In some cases where spouses have divorced, both parents often claim the same dependent on their separate returns. This will also trigger an IRS audit. So, ensure that you are authorized and eligible to claim someone as a dependent prior to including them on your return (see previous section on who can be claimed as a dependent).

6. Claiming rental losses. Generally, renting an asset is considered a *passive activity* because you are not actively performing a service, instead you are merely in possession of an asset that may or may not generate income. For this reason, the IRS typically will not allow rental losses as a deduction against ordinary income.

If you actively participate in the management of the asset, or hire a manager, then you may be eligible to claim up to $25,000 in rental losses, but your adjusted gross income (AGI) cannot be over $150,000.

When claiming rental losses, be sure to keep accurate records, you will need them if there is an audit.

7. Claiming home office expenses. If you operate a business out of your home, you may deduct business related expenses such as mortgage/rent of your home, insurance, utilities, etc. To validate your claim, you must have an area in the home that is used exclusively for your home office such as a guest bedroom. If the area is used for other purposes such as a living room, you may not claim home office expenses as the living room is used for more than just operating your business.

Claiming home office expenses is a common trigger. Be sure to keep accurate records of your expenses and have an area in your home that is used exclusively for the operation of your business.

8. Operating a cash business. One of the most difficult tasks for the IRS is to verify the income reported by cash businesses such as taxi cabs, salons, car washes, wait staff, etc. If you work in a business where customers pay with cash, be sure to keep receipts and accurate records of all of your cash transactions.

Be completely honest when reporting your income to the IRS and ensure that your expenses claimed are reasonable. Do not try to underreport your income in the mistaken belief that the IRS may never find out. The IRS has broad authority to obtain information, and they may even contact third parties. You have expenses as well; make sure you keep adequate records of all transactions, including transactions you pay for in cash.

9. Claiming excessive charitable contributions. While it is good to give back to society through charity, giving too much may raise a red flag. The IRS will generally allow you to donate about three percent of your total income without becoming suspicious. However, when giving to charities, you must ensure that the organization is registered with the IRS as a non-profit/charitable organization, and obtain a receipt for all of your transactions.

If you donate items valued at over $500, you must also keep an itemized appraisal of those items. If the organization cannot provide you with a receipt or refuses to provide you with a receipt of the transaction, chances are they are not registered legally as a charitable organization. Do not claim donations to organizations if you do not have proof of the transactions.

10. Using too many round numbers. The IRS requires that you provide accurate information on your tax return. The use of round numbers (100, 500, 700, etc.) is an indication that you may be guessing or falsifying the information provided. The probability of an audit is high.

When reporting your income and expenses, be sure to provide the most accurate information, and have documentation to support the information you provide on your return. While it is permissible to round your figures to the nearest dollar (i.e. rounding $76.99 to $77), it is impermissible to make up the numbers and report false information. Be sure to report exact figures, and keep accurate records of the information that you provide on your return.

How Long Does the IRS have to Audit My Tax Return? The Statute of Limitations

A *Statute of Limitation* (SOL) is the length of time the IRS has to perform a specific act before it becomes time barred. Specifically, the IRS has three years from the date a tax return is filed, or three years from the due date of the tax return, whichever is later, to assess (impose a tax deficiency) on a taxpayer's tax return.

Contrary to some of the media hype, my experience is that the IRS does not make it a practice to target individuals or groups. That doesn't mean that your anxiety meter might not jump if you get a letter notifying you that your tax return is being audited.

Example: Alicia filed her tax return for 2012 income on April 15, 2013. Therefore, in this case, the IRS is time barred under the statute of limitations from assessing the return after April 15, 2016.[11]

Can the 3-Year Statute of Limitations be extended?

There are many instances in which the three-year statute may be extended. For example, the statute of limitations for a partnership, with fewer than ten partners, does not begin to run until the individual partner reporting the pass-through income, files the partner's return. Cases involving foreign accounts may also have the SOL extended.

Example: Brendon lived outside of the United States but failed to disclose his foreign accounts on his 2009 income tax return filed on April 15, 2010. In May of 2013, he assumed that the IRS audit window was closed because it was beyond the three-year SOL. On June 6, 2013, Brendon received a notice from the IRS that he was being audited for non-disclosure of his foreign accounts. The window for foreign account related audits is six years. For Brendon's return, the IRS had until April 25, 2016 to audit the return.

Substantial Understatement of Income

One common extension applies to an understatement of Income. If the taxpayer omits income representing more than 25 percent of the gross income reported on a tax return, the three-year SOL period is extended to six years.[12] Is that a hard and fast rule? No. If the taxpayer discloses the taxpayer's position on a tax return, the limitation is three years even if there is an omission of more than 25 percent.

For example, let's say that you take a position that a particular item (which is in excess of 25 percent of gross income) is not income and do not include it on your return, the SOL will be six years. To handle, or clarify this, you attach a statement to your tax return stating your position and apprise the IRS of the fact that you did not include such income. When you do this, the SOL will be three years.

Example: Dianne filed her return 2008 tax return on March 10, 2009. She received an IRS underreporting notice for her 2008 tax return on April 15, 2013 for failure to include all income reported to the IRS. Dianne thought that she had included all of her income on the 2008 return and explained she never received the income statement that the IRS provided.

The IRS determined Dianne had demonstrated she honestly did not receive the income statement, it reduced the SOL back to three years instead of six years and closed the audit. Dianne owed no additional taxes and was not assessed any penalties.

False or Fraudulent Return

If the taxpayer files a return with the intent of evading his or her tax obligations, the IRS may audit the return and assess additional taxes at any time.[13] Some taxpayers hold bank accounts off-shore and intentionally fail to report the income from such accounts for tax purposes.

Some taxpayers don't disclose income from a variety of sources—whether it's income from work done or received from an investment. Unreported income means that a false or fraudulent tax return has been filed and the IRS may audit and assess additional taxes on their income at any time. Likewise, if no return is filed for a tax year, or if a return that is filed is deemed to be insufficient, the SOL will not begin to run. Filing an amended return does not begin the SOL if the original return was false. The SOL on a fraudulent return will *never* begin to run even if an amended return which is not fraudulent is filed.[14]

Example: Edward filed his 2005 tax return on February 7, 2006. He failed to report his off-shore accounts on his tax return intentionally. On April 10, 2012, the IRS determined that Edward had filed a fraudulent return and was informed of his off-shore account. He thought that since six years had passed, his 2005 return was barred from an audit due to the statute of limitations. Wrong thinking. Because his return was false or fraudulent, the IRS could audit Edward's return at any time.

Can the IRS Audit a Tax Return More Than Once?

Rarely is going through an audit an experience a typical taxpayer looks forward to. The thought of a repeat can send chills down most taxpayers' spines. Unless an extreme situation arises, the Internal Revenue Code prevents a tax return for a particular tax year from being audited more than once.[15] In theory, once an audit is closed, the taxpayer can rest assured that they will not re-visit the tax year. In practice, this is not the case. The IRS has developed a list of reasons that will allow them to re-open a closed audit. One of the reasons listed is substantial error by the IRS in the previous audit.[16]

Example: Fred and Susan filed their 2010 income tax return on April 15, 2011. The IRS audited the return on March 7, 2012, and the audit was closed on June 7, 2012. The IRS cannot audit the return again in the future because the audit was previously closed.

However, and it's an important "however," there is a bit of a Catch-22 here. If the IRS finds that there were substantial errors made by the previous IRS auditor, Fred and Susan's return may be audited again, so long as it is within the three year SOL from the original filing. The IRS could re-open their 2010 return before April 15, 2014.

Types of Audits the IRS Performs

Contrary to some of the media hype, my experience is that the IRS does not make it a practice to target individuals or groups. That doesn't mean that your anxiety meter might not jump if you get a letter notifying you that your tax return is being audited.

In general, the IRS will notify a taxpayer that the IRS is auditing taxpayer's tax return for a particular year or year(s) via a letter. There are five different types of audits, each with a varying level of scrutiny and complexity, and the letter from the IRS will be the first indication of which type of audit is being conducted. The five different types are audits are:

- Automated Underreporter Program[17]

- Correspondence Examinations

- Office Examination

- Field Examination[18]

- Research Audit

The first two types of audits are generally the least complex and are usually conducted by the IRS at an IRS "campus" formerly known as an IRS Service Center. The other three types of audits generally deal with more complex tax issues and will require the taxpayer, or taxpayer's representative, to meet with an IRS examiner face-to-face.

Face-to-face is not what you would normally wake up one morning and think this would be a good way to spend your afternoon. No, when a face-to-face meeting is called for, you will quickly understand that this is going to take some of your time and there is the "unknown" out there. You don't know where it's going, how long it will take, and are uncertain of the outcome possibilities. Let me take you through the process of the key components of what happens within each.

Automated Underreporter Program[19]

The *Automated Underreporter Program* is the least complex of the various types of audits.[20] Under this type of audit the IRS compares the information that you, the taxpayer, have provided on your tax return with information about you, provided by third parties.

> The audit connected with underreporting is designed for issues which can be settled by submission of records (via facsimile or mail) and for which no substantial disagreement is anticipated.

Income reported by any taxpayer may be cross-referenced against 1099s or W-2s filed by the payer of such amounts. That would be you.

If the IRS finds a discrepancy, a computer-generated letter will be sent requesting that you provide documentation of a particular item (only send copies of documents provided, as opposed to originals) or notifying you of a proposed change in your tax return—and the resulting amount of additional tax due as a consequence of the change.

This type of audit is designed for issues which can be settled by submission of records (via facsimile or mail) and for which no substantial disagreement is anticipated. No agreement is reached, or additional issues arise, you, or the IRS, may request to have the audit transferred to an *Office Examination* (discussed below) in which you can have a personal meeting with the IRS examiner.[21] The Automated Underreporter type of audit is not considered to be an "examination" and therefore, the IRS reserves the right to re-examine your return at any time.[22]

> **Example:** George filed his 2010 income tax return on April 15, 2011. He failed to include all of his income, as the income reported on his tax return did not match the IRS records—meaning that 1099s received from banks, mutual funds, brokerage firms, etc., for 2010 did not match what he disclosed on his original filing. Because of this, George's return was selected for auditing by the IRS Automated Underreporting Program.

The Correspondence Examination

The second type of audit, the *Correspondence Examination*[23] is also designed to be handled over the phone or by mail and therefore should not encompass complicated issues. In this examination, the IRS will send a letter to you requesting information or substantiation of a limited number of issues or items identified on your tax return.

Common issues that arise in a Correspondence Examination include: Contributions to an IRA or Keogh plan, small casualty or theft loss, disability income exclusion, Alternative

Minimum Tax, Math Clerical Abatement, Self-Employment Tax, Unallowable Items, Erroneous Refund, Taxable Gain on Sale of Residence, Social Security Form SSA-7000, Alimony, Charitable Contributions and Medical Expenses among others.[24]

The letter received from the IRS should indicate exactly which item on your tax return is being examined and should ask for specific documentation or substantiation for the item. For example, the IRS letter could ask the taxpayer to provide receipts for medical expenses or a charitable contribution. Again, you should provide only copies, as opposed to originals, to the IRS.

Under this examination, the letter received will generally not list any proposed changes to the return. Instead, the IRS will review the documents you provide before making a proposed adjustment.[25]

Like the Automated Underreporter Program, this type of audit is designed for issues for which no substantial disagreement is anticipated. If no agreement is reached, or additional issues arise, you should request to have the audit transferred to an Office Examination. As the taxpayer, you can have a personal meeting with the IRS examiner and discuss problem items in person.[26]

Example: Helen filed her 2011 tax return on April 10, 2012. On November 15, 2012, the IRS detected some erroneous calculations and questionable items on her tax return. In order to verify the information provided on Helen's return, the IRS issued a Correspondence Examination in order to request verification of the questionable items.

The Office Examination

An *Office Examination* usually takes place in the IRS examiner's office and involves a face-to-face meeting. You may appoint a representative to attend the meeting to act on your behalf or attend in person. An Office Examination usually includes issues that require a degree of interpretation of the tax law as well as verification of items reported on your return.[27]

When conducting an Office Examination, the IRS will usually send a letter directly to the address you provided when you last filed your income tax return with a copy of your return which states the date, time, and location of the examination, as well as a detailed list of the documents and information that you should provide at the examination, and the items on your tax return that are under examination.

> **Example:** Irv's 2011 tax return was selected for an IRS audit/examination. However, because he owned a business, the IRS sent a letter to Irv requesting that he bring certain information to a specified local IRS location. This is called an Office Examination because the audit will be conducted at a local IRS office.

Where Is the Office Examination Located?

The IRS does not intend to make it inconvenient for any meeting. Typically, the location of the examination will be the IRS area office closest to the address listed on taxpayer's tax return that is capable of handling the audit.[28] If you can demonstrate a *need* to have the location of the audit changed, you should notify the agent listed on the letter via writing (and telephone) of why you need to change the meeting location. The IRS will accommodate you. A *need* does not include the convenience of a taxpayer or taxpayer's representative.[29] An example of a *need* would be you are physically incapable of traveling a great distance, or if your records are too voluminous to transport to the location listed by the IRS.

Will the Letter List the Information and Tax Issues the Examiner is Looking For?

Always a good question, and the answer is that you will not know exactly what the examiner is looking for until you get there. Although the letter sent by the IRS will provide some details on the items to be discussed at the examination, it will usually not reveal the exact nature of the examiner's thought process, nor will it list all of the tax issues that are likely to be involved. For example, the letter may request that you provide documentation for all expenses and/or deductions listed on the tax return.

Note: The purpose for this request, in addition to verifying that expenses were actually made, may be to determine whether your expenses relate to a *passive activity* which could have tax implications for the taxpayer. A passive activity is one in which an individual is not directly involved, or fails to take action that would demonstrate a desire to make a profit from the activity. An example of a passive activity loss is owning a rental property, but you do not advertise that the property is for rent, or make any efforts to obtain a tenant. However, you try to claim rental losses on your tax return for the mortgage and property taxes that you have paid for the property. This type of loss is not allowed by the IRS because you did not take action to rent the property to a tenant or obtain a property manager to assist you in obtaining a tenant.

Another item often requested by the IRS for an Office Examination is the *Statement of Annual Estimated Personal and Family Expenses* (Form 4822). As evidenced by the title, this form requests that you provide estimated living expenses as well as personal assets. The information contained in this form may be used by the IRS examiner to determine whether the net income reported on the taxpayer's income tax return is reasonable in light of their living expenses and assets. Under the tax code, the IRS examiner needs a "reasonable indication that there is a likelihood of unreported income" [30] in order to employ indirect methods (such as reviewing taxpayer's bank accounts) of probing whether the taxpayer has underreported income.

Form 4822 becomes the examining agent's road map. For example, if a taxpayer reports $10,000 of income and the completed Form 4822 reflects $32,500 in living expenses and no reference to interest, dividends, gains or draw down in assets, it catches the agent's eye.

Thus, the IRS examiner would have a reason to employ additional *indirect* methods of determining the taxpayer's income. This may include, obtaining copies of your bank accounts or interviewing third parties who may have information concerning your income, assets, and living arrangements from the information you provided on the Form 4822 or through independent investigation.

Example: Jonathon and Anne owned a family dog grooming business. When they filed their tax return, they reported that they had earned a profit of $25,000. The IRS determined that this was almost 60 percent less than what they had reported in previous years, and about 50 percent less than the amount reported by other businesses in the same industry. So the IRS decided to conduct an Office Examination in order to verify whether they were under-reporting their income.

When Jonathon and Anne completed the Form 4822, they reported living expenses of $55,000 annually, but their total income and assets reported were insufficient in comparison to their living expenses. This prompted the IRS examiner to investigate further. The examiner requested bank statements, and corresponding statements for each of their investments that were reported on the Form 4822. At the end of the investigation, the IRS examiner found that Jonathon and Anne had underreported their income, and issued a report containing their findings and proposed an increase in their taxes, which included penalties for underreporting their income and interest. They ended up owing the IRS almost $65,000. Jonathon and Anne learned that it is important to be truthful in your reporting of information to the IRS, as it will be much more costly in the end for attempting to conceal information.

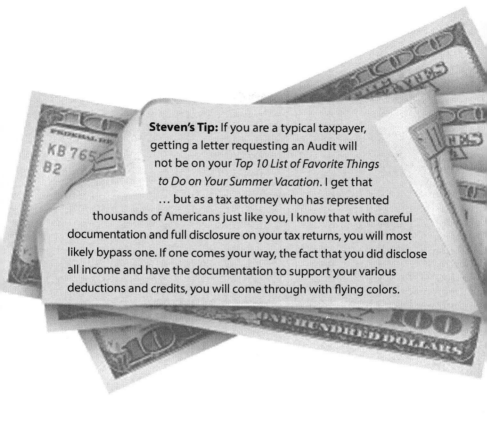

Steven's Tip: If you are a typical taxpayer, getting a letter requesting an Audit will not be on your *Top 10 List of Favorite Things to Do on Your Summer Vacation.* I get that … but as a tax attorney who has represented thousands of Americans just like you, I know that with careful documentation and full disclosure on your tax returns, you will most likely bypass one. If one comes your way, the fact that you did disclose all income and have the documentation to support your various deductions and credits, you will come through with flying colors.

Endnotes

[7] BNA 623 2nd I-A

[8] §6011(a)

[9] BNA 623-2nd I-A

[10] 7602(a)(1) and (2)

[11] 6501(a)

[12] 6501(e)(1)

[13] 6501(c)

[14] CCH PP 1007 and 1008

[15] 7605(b)

[16] Rev. Proc. 2005-32

[17] CCH Federal Tax and Procedure PP403 (page 86)

[18] CCH 406, BNA

[19] CCH Federal Tax and Procedure PP403 (page 86)

[20] CCH PP 403

[21] BNA II-B. citing IRM 4.22.5.4.3 (10-1-10)

[22] CCH 403

[23] CCH 404

[24] CCH 404 and BNA 623 2nd II b-1. See IRM 4.19.11

[25] CCH 404

[26] BNA II-B. citing IRM 4.22.5.4.3 (10-1-10)

[27] BNA 623 2nd II C. 3

[28] CCH 405

[29] 301.7605-1(c)(2) and CCH 405

[30] 7602(e)

Inside this chapter

CHAPTER 8

Common Issues Covered Within an Audit

If an audit is in your midst, you will have plenty of questions. I'll start with the most common and then dig into a variety of issues that can occur throughout the process.

An *Office Examination* may cover a myriad of issues, but some common issues include: Verification of travel

> An Audit may negatively affect a taxpayer's ability to participate in certain IRS programs.

and entertainment expenses under IRC Section 274, which will include not only documentation that the expense was made, but also documentation of the purpose for the expenses, large itemized deductions, home office expenses, dependency exemptions, income from rents or royalties, and bad debts.

Sales reps and truck drivers often file tax returns with many of the items that are of the type to be examined in an Office Examination. They (and all other taxpayers) should keep careful records of not only receipts, credit card statements, and cancelled checks, but also of other facts and circumstances which may influence the deductibility of an expense.

For example, a truck driver should keep a log of where he travels, and document the business purpose for the travel with daily mileage and destination points. Merely showing that an expense was made through a credit card bill or other payment verification is often not enough to document to the IRS that the expense was actually for a business, as opposed to a personal purpose.

In a similar vein, loans to relatives or friends may be easy to document, but hard to prove that they were not a gift and thus qualify as a bad debt. A savvy taxpayer should make sure that a loan looks like and acts like a loan. That means that there is a written (and signed) loan agreement between the parties, a due date, payment schedule, and what happens if there is a default. The only reason why there would be a loss claim on a tax return is via a default. Included would be:

> Keep careful records of not only receipts, credit card statements, and cancelled checks, but also of other facts and circumstances which may influence the deductibility of an expense.

- What proof exists that it was a valid loan?

- What proof exists that the taxpayer/lender attempted to collect on it?

- What proof exists that the recipient of the loan funds refused payment?

Consequences of an Audit

Audits may negatively affect a taxpayer's ability to participate in certain IRS programs. For example, the IRS currently offers a voluntary disclosure program for taxpayers who have failed to report foreign bank accounts. With an Audit, the taxpayer may first realize that such a requirement exists. Unfortunately, the mere presence of the audit simultaneously prohibits the taxpayer from taking part in the program.[31]

An Open Audit will also prohibit a taxpayer from pursuing an *Offer in Compromise* for that tax year until the audit has been closed. In some cases, the Offer in Compromise unit may delay a case if there is a current audit, or may return your Offer in Compromise, requiring that you refile your offer after the audit is resolved. In some cases, once an audit has been closed, you may be indicted on criminal charges such as fraud, tax evasion, etc., and face being fined and/or imprisoned.

Real Life Story: Rosemary attended a seminar in which a group opposing taxation taught individuals how to falsify their income in order to obtain tax refunds of $100,000 or more. The organization required that individuals give a percentage of their refunds to others in need, of their own choosing, but the funds must be used to help others, not just you. They convinced Rosemary that it is legal to do this as the income documents that they create would be provided to the IRS, and the individual would not be audited.

Everything the individuals needed to prepare their return, from the income documents to the tax preparer, was provided by this organization. She enthusiastically joined the organization and had her return prepared by one of the organization's accountants. She received a tax refund of over $200,000 and immediately began to disburse the refund to various relatives and friends in need. She even donated to charitable organizations. Rosemary felt good about her decision to join the organization as she was able to do a lot of good with the money she obtained.

Approximately four months later, her return was audited by the IRS, and it was determined that it was false and based on falsified documents. The IRS demanded that Rosemary return the refund she obtained, and assessed interest and penalties for filing a fraudulent return. The $200,000 no longer existed ... Rosemary had no money left. It didn't take her long to realize that she had been bamboozled by this organization. When she tried to contact the leaders and other members of it, she was not able to get in contact with anyone.

At the close of the audit, a Revenue Officer was immediately assigned from the Department of Justice. Rosemary was notified that if she could not return the refund received, she would be indicted on criminal charges for filing a fraudulent return. If found guilty, a prison sentence as well as being obligated to pay back the refund and additional penalties and interest was now facing her.

This sounds grim. Rosemary discovered my firm and hired it to represent her in this matter. We immediately did three things:

1. Began to investigate the organization and was able to obtain names of the individuals involved;

2. Assisted her in contacting everyone that she had given some of the refund in order to obtain as much of the funds back;

3. Contacted the IRS and started negotiating;

4. Provided sufficient evidence to the IRS that Rosemary was taken advantage of;

5. Succeeded in getting over half of the moneys back and directed them to the IRS.

Because of our efforts along with the remorse demonstrated by Rosemary, she was not given a prison sentence. She was, though, on the hook for the balance and required to pay it back. After negotiating a reasonable payment plan based on her present financial situation, she learned a valuable lesson: "If it is too good to be true, it probably is."

Don't falsify documents or provide inaccurate information on your tax return; it is not worth it.

What Occcurs at a Face-to-Face Meeting?

Most taxpayers want to know what happens during a meeting with an examiner. It's a good question. At your examination, the IRS examiner will start by reviewing the documents you provide and discuss the relevant tax issues being examined. Don't be surprised if the examiner asks for additional information. If additional information is requested, he or she will give you adequate time to produce the documents or respond to particular issues. The scope of the examination may be increased at this point, based on the information received by the examiner pursuant to the initial request.

A second meeting is not uncommon. What if you want to record the meeting? You can, provided you give the IRS a 10 days' notice and you consent to the IRS also recording the meeting.[32]

Once all documents have been produced, or at a time when the examiner determines you have had ample opportunity to present your documents and/or position, the examiner will explain his or her finding to you (or your representative). If the examiner makes changes to the tax return, the examiner will detail the calculation of any additional tax proposed and provides Form 4549 Income Tax Examination Changes.[33]

At this point, you and the IRS agent will either be in agreement or disagreement as to your tax liability. What you do is obviously the next step: you either agree or disagree.

When you agree with the audit

If it is determined that the tax liability shown on the return is correct, the examination is terminated, and the tax liability shown on your return becomes the final IRS determination. If the IRS examiner makes an initial determination that you have not correctly determined your liability and that additional tax is due, the examiner will provide you with Form 4549

Income Tax Examination Changes (except in cases where criminal prosecution is recommended[34]) and if you agree with the examiner's determination (or choose not to contest), it becomes a final determination of tax liability.

It is important to understand that Form 4549 contains a statement to the effect that the report is subject to acceptance by the area director, which means you could receive notification that agreed upon examination changes has been rejected and that the examiner must make additional changes. Once the examination changes are agreed upon (and agreed to by the area director), the case could still be subject to internal review.

What's an *internal review?* Audits can generate questions, and certain issues are looked at closely, such as the claim of "innocent spouse." Internal reviews are done by the IRS technical staff and subject to being returned for further work if a substantial error was made.

In the normal course of an audit, after you and the examiner agree upon the examiner's adjustments, you will be issued a Form 870 (Waiver of Restrictions on Assessment), which waives your right to petition the examiner's findings in Tax Court. At the same time, you will pay any additional amounts due in accordance with the examination. If you cannot pay the amount due, a payment arrangement such as an installment agreement may be negotiated.

When will the audit be closed?

An agreed case is generally considered closed when you receive notification in writing of adjustments to your liability or of acceptance of your tax return without change.[35] Certain types of cases, such as large refund cases, are not "closed" for IRS purposes until the case has been reviewed.[36] In general, the IRS should only audit any one tax year at one time. Once a tax audit is closed, you should not have to worry about being audited for that year again.[37] In practice, the IRS may re-open a closed audit for a tax year if the IRS made a substantial error or if fraud is discovered.

What happens if you disagree with the audit?

When you and the examiner cannot come to agreement on the correct amount of tax liability, the examiner will issue a "Notice of Proposed Deficiency" also known as a *30-Day Letter*. In an effort to avoid the 30-Day Letter, you may request to have a conference with the IRS examiner's group manager. Such a conference is intended to resolve only factual issues and will not address actual settlements or liabilities. If no agreement is reached after the conference, the 30-Day Letter will be sent to you along with a copy of the examiner's report.[38]

What is the 30-Day Letter?

The 30-Day Letter provides you the opportunity to request that an Appeals Officer review the IRS examiner's determination before going to court. The Appeals Officer review is called an Appeal and is discussed below. Depending on the case, the 30-Day Letter may also give the taxpayer the opportunity to provide additional information to the examiner during the thirty day period. This opportunity to provide additional information may be helpful in examinations where you have not produced all the information requested by the examiner prior to the issuance of the 30-Day Letter.

In some cases, the examiner may not grant extensions, or further extensions of time for you to produce the documents requested and will issue the 30-Day Letter when he feels the case should move forward. If you have produced all the information requested, or have indicated that no further information will be provided, the 30-Day Letter may not afford you the opportunity to provide additional information. Instead, it may include Form 870 and a demand for payment. In either case, you will have thirty days to request that an Appeals Officer review the case before going to court.

Will the IRS grant more time?

It's a rare taxpayer who doesn't want more time to gather information … or to not deal with the IRS. With that said, the IRS will generally grant the taxpayer, or his or her representative, an extension of time to respond to the 30-Day Letter. It is not automatically given, and justification should be provided with the extension request.

Can you appeal the audit?

Any taxpayer may respond to the 30-Day Letter by sending a written request for review by an Appeals Officer to the IRS. Although it is the taxpayer's right to request an appeal, understand that not all requests are accepted. Appeals will generally not accept the case if additional information needs to be gathered.[39] If you do not provide the information requested by the IRS examiner, you may not be able to go to Appeals.

What happens if you do not appeal or respond?

If you do not appeal, receive satisfaction on appeal, or do not respond to the 30-Day Letter, the IRS examiner will issue a "Notice of Deficiency," also known as a *90-day Letter*. The 90-Day Letter allows you to file a petition for redetermination with the Tax Court (go to Tax Court), within 90 days, before the IRS examiner's determination may become final.[40]

What happens if you partially agree with the audit?

If you and the IRS examiner agree to some of his proposed changes, but not all, you can sign Form 870 with respect to the agreed changes and pay the additional tax liability (if there are any) with respect to just those changes. If there are issues not covered on Form 870, an appeal and/or a petition to the tax court is still an open option to you.[41]

What is the 90-Day Letter?

The 90-Day Letter allows you to file a petition to have your case heard in front of the Tax Court without prepaying the tax liability. You may, though, want to prepay the tax liability to prevent interest from accruing. If the eventual hearing is in your favor, you will be reimbursed any excess moneys paid. The IRS is required to include in each 90-Day Letter the date determined by the IRS as the last day on which you may file a petition with the Tax Court.[42]

Can the IRS cancel the 90-Day Letter?

The IRS may, under certain circumstances, rescind a 90-Day Letter with your consent.[43] Most likely, this is done if new material information has surfaced that could either change the examiner's determination or could make the case acceptable for Appeal.

What can I do during the 90-Day time frame?

You may request a conference during the 90-Day period available to petition the Tax Court. Even if the conference is granted, the 90-Day time frame will not be extended unless after the conference, the taxpayer and the IRS *mutually agree* to rescind the 90-Day Letter. This is generally only useful when you have not corresponded with the IRS and delivered information/documents that could change the IRS examiner's determination in a beneficial manner that was not previously available to the IRS.

Be forewarned: if a 90-Day Letter is rescinded, the IRS retains the right to re-issue a new 90-Day Letter.

When will your case be closed?

In general, an income, estate, or gift tax case is closed after examination when the period for filing a petition with the Tax Court (90-Day Letter) expires and no petition is filed.[44] There are other rules for determining a closed case for other types of tax not discussed here. Cases referred to Appeals are not considered closed.[45] The IRS should only audit any single tax year of your taxes once. Typically, once a tax audit is closed, you should not have to worry about being audited for that year again with a few exceptions.[46]

In practice, the IRS may re-open a closed audit for a tax year if the IRS made a substantial error or certain other conditions are met. Here are the conditions upon which the IRS may reopen a case:

1. The taxpayer has provided information that was not previously considered.

2. The IRS made an error that prevented the case from being resolved.

3. The taxpayer provided a late response on a case that was closed due to their failure to respond.

4. The taxpayer was not satisfied with the resolution, and corrective actions are available.

5. After internal review by the IRS, it was determined that the case was not completely, or was incorrectly, resolved.

The IRS office that closed the prior case must also decide whether or not to reopen a case. The IRS also categorizes cases based on nine criteria. Those criteria would then determine how soon a decision must be made to reopen your case. For example, cases assigned a criteria of 1 through 4 should receive a decision within one workday, and cases assigned a criteria of 5 through 9 should receive a decision within three workdays. If the decision to reopen the case is made, it must then be assigned to Taxpayer Advocate Management Information System (TAMIS).

Does an audit affect the IRS collecting against you?

Any audit of a particular tax year or years will prevent the IRS from taking collection action for that tax year or years. The IRS must wait until the audit is closed and a determination has been made concerning the amount of taxes owed if any prior to taking collection action.

You will first receive the proposed assessment or audit determination and be given 90 days to file an appeal request. If no appeal is filed, or once a final decision has been made, the IRS will then begin to issue notices starting from the first notice of intent to levy before taking collection action against you.

If you are involved in an Offer in Compromise while an audit is pending for a tax year in which you wish to have included in your offer, it will result in a delay of your case, and in some cases, your offer may also be returned. Make sure you read closely Chapter 21, *Resolutions, Offers, and Agreements.*

Should you fight an audit?

The question for most is: do you embrace the outcome of the audit or do you choose to fight it? That decision to accept or reject is always going to be by a case-by-case basis if a professional is advising you. First, review the IRS audit examination and determine whether you agree or dispute the findings made. If you believe that you have substantial evidence to make a valid and persuasive counter argument, then fighting the audit may be beneficial. When in doubt, have a Tax Attorney or CPA review the audit and your documentation and provide their recommendation on what your next course of action should be.

If you are looking at a difference of a few hundred dollars—the cost of professional advice will most likely exceed the IRS settlement. If you are looking at a more significant amount, get advice.

How long should your fight an audit?

There is no cookie-cutter approach to an audit or how long they will last. Your decision on whether to continue fighting the audit should be based on how confident you are in your position. If it's high and your documentation supports your position, including being more credible than the IRS audit report, it may make sense to hang in there until you have exhausted all of your options. But, it's also important to consider the financial burdens that fighting an audit may cause. Make an informed decision by weighing the pros and cons.

When should you involve a Taxpayer Advocate?

Another player who can help you in the audit is the Taxpayer Advocate (TPA). Part of the IRS, the TPA's duty is to ensure that you are treated fairly, and that you know and understand your rights. They offer free guidance to assist you through confusing processes—audits are just one of the many areas that a TPA is available to a taxpayer. If you are unable to represent yourself in an audit or cannot afford to hire a Tax

Attorney or CPA to represent you, then you should consider contacting the TPA for assistance at 877-777-4778. More information on TPAs can be found in Chapter 10, *Representation during an Audit.*

Steven's Tip: When a notice of audit arrives in your mailbox, there are always questions. Ideally, you would like to know exactly why you are being audited—that may not happen until the actual audit occurs. Items may be uncovered that open a door to the Revenue Officer to probe in a different direction. If you are audited, take only the documents that are requested in the notice letter. If you are reprresented by an accountant, enrolled agent, or tax attorney, let her or him do the talking—it's what you pay them to do. And, it may prevent you from divulging something that could open a can of worms.

Endnotes

[41] 7602(e)

[42] CCH pp 405

[43] CCH 405

[44] BNA 623-2nd II E 4. Citing IRM 4.10.8.3 (8-11-06)

[45] BNA 623-2nd II E 6 a 1

[46] BNAII E 6 a 1

[47] BNA II E 6 1. Citing 7605(b) and rev proc. 85-13

[48] §601.105(d)(1). BNA 623 2nd IV C 1 a

[49] IRM 8.2.1.6 (10-18-07). BNA IV G 2

[50] 6213(a), BNA 623 – 2nd II E. 1 c

[51] BNA II- E 1. d

[52] §3463 of the 1998 IRS Restructuring Act requires BNA II E d 1

[53] 6212(d)

[54] II E 6 a 2

[55] Rev proc 2005-32 and BNA II E 6 a 2

[56] BNA II E 6 1. Citing 7605(b) and rev proc. 85-13

Inside this chapter

Form **1040**

Department of

U.S. Indi

For the year J

Your first n

Label

(See instructions on page 12.)

Use the IRS label. Otherwise, please print or type.

L A B E L

H E R E

If a joint r

Home a

City, to

Presidential Election Campaign ▶ Che

1

Filing Status

Check only one box.

2

3

6a

Exemptions

If more than four dependents, see page 15.

Income

Attach Form(s) W-2 here. Also attach Forms W-2G and 1099-R if tax was withheld.

If you did no get a W-2, see page 1

Enclose, b not attach payment. please us Form 10

CHAPTER 9

What is a
Field Examination?

Not all audits are conducted within the confines of an IRS office, especially when it comes to businesses. Taxpayers who claim deductions for home offices or have separate physical sites may get the request for an onsite audit or a Field Examination. **It is generally applicable to businesses or more complex individual returns.**

A Field Examination is conducted at your place of business or wherever the taxpayer keeps its book and records.

If you receive notice of one, you may request in writing to schedule the examination at a time that would be least disruptive to your business. This type of examination may include the same issues as an Office Examination mentioned earlier, and often deals with valuation and depreciation issues where a business is concerned. The same procedural rules generally apply to a Field Examination as to the Office Examination.

Example: Jerald owned an automotive manufacturing company. His 2011 tax return was selected for an IRS field examination/field audit. Because of this, the IRS auditor scheduled a date and time to visit his business location where the records were kept in order to conduct the audit.

If the records had been at his accountant's office or another site at another location, Jerald would notify the examiner for a site change as well as a date change if needed.

For most businesses, the IRS is sensitive to the fact that there are "busy" times that may involve customers as well as business related travel. Time and locations will be reset.

What is the Research Audit?

The Research Audit is the most annoying type of audit. In short, every item on your tax return is examined regardless of dollar amount and even when there is no apparent error on the return.[47] Many taxpayers and professionals view it as a fishing expedition—you bring everything and the IRS will find something, somewhere in all your papers.

Appealing an Audit

With mail audits, you may have the results of an IRS examination report reviewed by an Appeals Officer. The time for this to be done is after the taxpayer receives a 30-Day Letter. The taxpayer must specifically request that their examination be reviewed by an Appeals Officer should the taxpayer's wish that this be done. As discussed below, an appeal should be based on a specific item of disagreement with the examiner's report or based on a legitimate litigation risk. Otherwise the appeal will be rejected.

What is the purpose of an Appeal?

The purpose of an Appeal is to resolve a tax controversy without litigation.[48] Most appeals are handled by one Appeals Officer. The Appeals Officer is specifically authorized to enter into settlement with a taxpayer based on the perceived hazards of litigation.[49] However, an appeal should be based on an actual dispute of a finding in the examiner's report. It should not be viewed as a chance to have a different person to perform the audit in hopes that they will reach a different conclusion.

How do I Prepare a Request for Appeal?

Some Audits, including those in which the proposed tax liability is in excess of $25,000, require the taxpayer to submit a "formal protest" which should include the following information:

- A statement that says you want to appeal the examiner's findings to the Appeals office. Include your name and address and daytime telephone number;

- A copy of the letter showing the proposed changes and findings being protested, or the date and symbols from the letter;

- The tax periods or years involved;

- An itemized schedule of the adjustments with which the taxpayer does not agree;

- A statement of facts supporting the taxpayer's position on any contested factual issue;

- A statement outlining the law or other authority, if any, upon which you are relying;

- A declaration under penalties of perjury attesting that the statement of facts is true and accurate.[50]

Other audits for tax assessments below $25,000 require only that you submit in writing, during the 30-day time frame, the changes on the examiner's report with which you do not agree and any reasons for disagreement.[51]

What happens if the 30-Day time period expired?

In general, a protest letter sent to appeals must be filed within 30 days of receiving the 30-Day Letter. As described above, once 30 days has passed, the IRS will send a 90-Day Letter. If for any reason, you have not received a 90-Day Letter and believe it would be worthwhile to go to Appeals, you should file a protest letter with Appeals. The Appeals Officer may, if a good reason is given, decide to review the examiner's report. The 90-day time frame to file a petition to go to Tax Court is not delayed even if Appeals agrees to accept your protest letter.[52]

What Should the Protest Letter Include?

The protest letter should provide a good reason for an Appeals Officer to agree to review the examiner's report. The protest should deal with any defects and deficiencies in the examiner's report, such as improperly framed issues, misstatements or omissions of fact, or incorrect conclusions of law. A protest letter is not automatically accepted for review, and, even if accepted, is not a worthwhile effort unless specific reasons for changing the examiner's report are provided and substantiated. The following is a list of circumstances that could cause an appeal to be returned:

- the protest fails to set forth your position or is otherwise seriously deficient;

- substantial additional information is required to resolve an important issue;

- there has been a failure to secure timely consents extending the statute of limitations for assessment;

- significant unresolved factual variances exist between the examination report and the protest;

- there is a clear misapplication of the law that renders an important issue indefensible;

- the case is a reopening of a previously closed case contrary to IRS practice;

- new issues are discovered which would otherwise be raised because the ground for such action is a substantial one and the potential effect upon the tax liability is material;

- some further action must be taken or some further event must occur before Appeals can adequately consider the case, such as Headquarters must complete consideration of valuation of works of art, or coordination is needed with the appropriate offices within Division Counsel or Associate Chief Counsel;

- the claims are for abatement of excise tax, employment tax, or trust fund recovery penalty which the IRS does not deem meritorious.

What are Your Rights During an Audit?

It is important that you know your rights during an audit so that you do not become intimidated by the IRS representative, or divulge more information than necessary. The IRS is required to apprise the taxpayer of the taxpayer's rights when dealing with the IRS. In order to comply with this requirement, the IRS has created updated versions of Publication 1, *Your Rights as a Taxpayer;* Publication 5, *Appeal Rights and Preparation of Protests for Unagreed Cases*; Publication 556, *Examination of Returns, Appeal Rights and Claims for Refund*; Publication 594, *The IRS Collection Process;* and Publication 1660, *Collection Appeal Rights.* Publication 1 should be included with the initial correspondence sent to the taxpayer. Publication 5 should be included with the 30-Day Letter.

If you are selected for an audit, you have the right to know why the IRS is asking for information. You also have the right to know how the IRS will use the information you have provided, and what will occur if you refuse to provide the requested information. During an audit, you should try to be as cooperative as possible. The IRS is likely to have access to information that you may feel is privileged, and your failure to provide that information will not deter the IRS from using other means to obtain the information by obtaining a summons or subpoena from a court of law.

- You have the right to have representation by an authorized representative.

- You have the right to have your information kept private and confidential.

- You also have the right to appeal any disagreements concerning the audit either within the various departments of the IRS, or in a court of law.

- You are entitled to receive professional and courteous treatment from IRS employees.

> It is important that you know your rights during an audit so that you do not become intimidated by the IRS representative, or divulge more information than necessary.

If you believe that you were not provided with professional and courteous service, you should request to speak to the manager of the IRS representative, or seek the assistance of the Taxpayer Advocate (TPA) explained in the next chapter.

Endnotes

47 CCHPP 407

48 IRM 8.1.1.1(1) (2-10-12), BNA IV A

49 BNA IV A

50 §601.105(d)(2)(v). BNA IV C 1 a

51 Ban IV C 1 a

52 BNA IV C 1 b

Inside this chapter

Representation During an Audit

In selecting a tax professional for representation in an IRS audit, you should choose someone who is knowledgeable of the tax issues presented in the audit. It is also important to determine whether the individual's license allows them to represent you in the audit. The four most common types of individuals that may represent you in an Audit are:

1. Licensed Tax Preparer (LTP)

2. Enrolled Agent (EA)

3. Certified Public Accountant (CPA)

4. Attorney (A)

You may also retain the services of the TPA if you are experiencing difficulties in resolving your tax matter with the IRS, or require guidance throughout the process.

The Licensed Tax Preparer

Also called a Registered Tax Return Preparer (RTRP), the Licensed Tax Preparer (LTP) is an individual that has obtained a Preparer Tax Identification Number (PTIN) from the IRS by registering as a tax preparer, and has successfully passed the RTRP Competency Test administered by the IRS, and also passed a tax compliance check (they do not owe any back taxes to the IRS), and have filed all required tax returns.

An LTP/RTRP must also renew their PTIN every year, and complete 15 hours of continuing education administered by the IRS annually. LTPs/RTRPs are allowed to prepare and sign tax returns on behalf of taxpayers.

They can:

Represent taxpayers in an audit if they prepared the tax return that is being audited.

They cannot:

Represent taxpayers on other matters not related to the tax return they prepared. In an audit, the LTP/RTRP *can only* focus on your tax return and whether the items were correctly reported by them.

Represent you in Tax Court or in litigation before the IRS. They are limited to representing taxpayers in an audit for the tax returns that they have prepared.

Give tax advice not relating to preparing a tax return.

It is important to understand that LTPs/RTRPs are not likely to be skilled in argumentation or oral advocacy, so it is recommended that you hire an Attorney when items on your return are in dispute that you are confident should be allowed by the IRS, or when you believe that you are being treated unfairly by the IRS.

The Enrolled Agent

Similar to an LTP or RTRP, the Enrolled Agent (EA) receives his authorization by taking an examination with the IRS, or because he was a former IRS employee. EAs must complete 72 hours of continuing education courses every three years in order to maintain eligibility to practice before the IRS. Similar to attorneys and CPAs, EAs have unlimited practice before the IRS. This means that they may represent taxpayers in all 50 United States and Territories, and can handle all tax matters, including the preparation of tax returns.

Note: Unlike CPAs who have obtained their education in Accounting, EAs may lack the same education and skill in preparing tax returns. Also, unlike attorneys, EAs are not trained in advocacy, and are not likely to be as effective in representing taxpayers in matters requiring litigation or oral advocacy.

The Certified Public Accountant

An accountant who has successfully passed the uniform Certified Public Accountant Examination in the United

States earns the title of Certified Public Accountant (CPA). They have also met the required education and experience required to obtain certification as a CPA. CPAs are skilled in preparing tax returns, and some may also assist in financial audits. This makes having a CPA valuable in an IRS audit because they have the skill along with the education required to accurately prepare and defend matters involving tax returns.

CPAs, like EAs and Attorneys, may represent taxpayers from all 50 United States and Territories, and can handle all tax matters. **Note:** Unlike Attorneys, CPAs are not trained or skilled in oral advocacy. As a result, for matters requiring litigation or oral advocacy, you should consider retaining an attorney.

The Attorney

Attorneys (A) are individuals who have passed the bar in a state or country, and are charged with applying the law to solve individual problems. There are many variations of Attorneys but for purposes of the IRS, anyone who has a valid bar license may represent taxpayers from all 50 States within the United States and Territories on all tax matters, including representing taxpayers in matters involving litigation in US Tax Court or other courts of law. Attorneys may also prepare tax returns.

It is common for an Attorney specializing in tax law to obtain a CPA certification by passing the CPA examination, as well as obtaining a Masters of Laws (LLM) Degree in Taxation. This makes such representatives highly desirable as they have both the education of a CPA, and the oral advocacy skills in order to represent taxpayers before the IRS.

Note: Where CPAs, EAs, and TRPs work with numbers and accounting related matters on a daily basis, not all attorneys do. If you engage one to assist you in tax matters with the IRS, make sure that he or she has the necessary tax background to assist you.

The Taxpayer Advocate

Taxpayers want help if they feel they are getting the run around or not being assisted by the IRS. Within the IRS is an independent organization that offers free services to taxpayers and was designed to assist taxpayers experiencing problems with IRS agents or representatives, or confused about various IRS procedures, including audits. Meet the Taxpayer Advocate Service (TAS) and the Taxpayer Advocate (TPA).

This individual can guide you through the audit process and help you respond to the auditor/examiner's request. He or she also will remain on your case until the matter is resolved with the IRS. TPA offices are located in all 50 United States, District of Columbia, and Puerto Rico. In order to be eligible for TPA assistance, you must demonstrate that you cannot resolve your tax problem with the IRS, and one of the following:

- Your problem is causing financial difficulties for you, your family, or your business.

- You or your business are facing an immediate threat of adverse action.

- You have tried repeatedly to contact the IRS but received no response, or the IRS has not responded by the date promised.[53]

How do I decide who should represent me before the IRS?
In deciding whether to choose an LTP/RTRP, EA, CPA, or Attorney, determine whether the information requested by the IRS will require you to verify items listed on your tax return, or whether it requires argumentation on various deductions and applicable tax laws. For matters requiring you to verify items listed on your tax return, an LTP may be able to assist you, but for matters that may result in a dispute of items, it is best that you hire an Attorney, CPA or EA.

It is important that you research the tax professional in order to determine whether they have adequate experience in providing audit representation (5 years or more), and whether they have any disciplinary actions on their record. Select one that is a reputable representative in order to ensure that your case will be handled professionally and competently from beginning to end.

Real Life Story: Theresa owned a real estate business and was being audited by the IRS for misclassifying employees as independent contractors in order to avoid paying payroll taxes. She faced a possible tax assessment of $500,000 or more. Theresa had all of her returns and bookkeeping handled by a Licensed Tax Preparer (LTP) rather than an accountant or CPA because they charged minimal fees. The IRS agent requested to conduct a Field Examination by visiting her place of business. Since the LTP handled all of her accounting and bookkeeping, she felt that the LTP would be adequate to represent her in the audit.

Theresa wasn't aware that her LTP had no prior experience representing businesses in audits despite being experienced in bookkeeping and preparing tax returns, and he disclosed this to her when she requested that he handle the audit. She insisted that the LTP handle the matter because she viewed it was his fault that she was being audited. Fearing that he would jeopardize his license and Theresa's business, the LTP convinced her to hire a Tax Attorney, offering to pay the legal fees. Theresa accepted the offer.

She then hired our firm to represent her in the audit. My associate tax attorney immediately contacted the IRS agent and requested to be present during the Field Examination. The IRS agent agreed to a time and date. Prior to the appointment, our firm's attorney visited Theresa's business to inspect all of the records and found several discrepancies and inaccurate data. The attorney then presented her with possible outcomes if the discrepancies and inaccuracies were not resolved prior to the audit examination. Somewhat shaken with what was uncovered, she agreed to implement the solutions that we suggested.

On the day of the audit, the IRS agent was able to rectify who was an employee, and who were 1099 independent contractors. Initially, Theresa faced a possible tax bill of $500,000 but ended up paying under $100,000. She learned that it does matter who represents you in an audit. Paying minimal fees for an LTP could have cost her more than the legal fees paid to retain an attorney who is skilled in tax relief and resolution.

Who has the burden of proof in an Audit?

When your return is selected for an audit, the burden of proof is upon you to show that the items you reported on the return were correct. Failure to provide sufficient evidence to support the items being disputed will result in the IRS assessing the proposed changes. If your case involves a criminal matter such as tax evasion, or fraud, then the burden of proof is upon the IRS to prove beyond a reasonable doubt that you are guilty of the allegations presented. It is important that you keep adequate records in the event of an audit so that you will be able to overcome your burden of proof.

Where real estate professionals chant "location, location, location"—when dealing with the IRS, it's, "documentation, documentation, documentation."

Will the IRS involve third parties in the Audit?

In some cases, the IRS may be required to involve third parties or obtain information from third parties. In Related

Examinations where the return selected involves other parties such as business partners or shareholders, the IRS may audit the return of all related parties if they involve the same transaction or issues.

You do have the right to request a list of all persons contacted by the IRS in your case.

In these types of audits, it will be necessary for the IRS to include and disclose information to the other parties involved. If further information is needed that you were not able to provide, the IRS may seek to verify that information by contacting third-parties such as your employer, neighbor, bank, employees, friends, etc.

Note: The IRS is prohibited by law from disclosing any more information than necessary in order to obtain and verify the information it is seeking. The IRS may continue to contact third parties so long as there is continued activity on your case. You do have the right to request a list of all persons contacted by the IRS in your case.[54]

Real Life Story: Donald owned and operated a law firm, but failed to make his payroll deposits and pay the taxes owed by the law firm. This continued for several years. After several attempts requesting that he pay the outstanding balance totaling $400,000, the IRS took the next step. It decided to conduct an audit of his entire business and its operations.

The IRS requested several different documents from Donald, including a record of his payroll and bank statements for the past three years. Fearing that the IRS would shut down his business if he disclosed the information, he decided to ignore the notice and act like he never received it. Donald had already made several mistakes; this one ignited the spark. The audit notice was certified, which meant that the IRS would be able to confirm that he signed for the notice.

The notice that Donald chose to ignore required that he respond within 30 days, which he allowed to expire. After the deadline had lapsed, the IRS sent a notice to him that if he failed to provide the information within the next 30 days, the IRS would summons the individuals and entities provided on the list for the requested information. That got his attention.

Fearing that his employees and financial institutions would find out about his IRS tax problems, Donald hired our firm to represent him in the audit. Immediately, my associate tax attorney began to obtain the information requested by the IRS. After analyzing the documents, he advised him of the areas that needed improvement, and counseled him on how to make his payroll deposits so that he can avoid owing the IRS in the future.

The attorney then negotiated with the IRS to allow Donald to continue operating so that he will be able to rectify the problem, and negotiated a reasonable payment plan so that he could pay off the payroll taxes owed. The hard lesson he learned that day is there is no avoiding the IRS, and if he won't provide the information, the IRS will summons third-parties who are able to provide the information he tried to withhold.

Audit Prevention

An audit can be a frightening and stressful event. There are seven critical steps that you can take in order to avoid being audited by the IRS. It is important to understand that the proposed steps do not guarantee that you will never be audited, but may reduce the odds of you being audited.

Seven ways to prevent an Audit

1. **Report all of your income and complete your return accurately.** It is important that the income you report on your income tax return match the income reported to the IRS. When the information you report does not match the information received by the IRS, you are likely to be audited.

2. **Maintain adequate records and documentation.** If you are a W-2 or 1099 employee, your employers will report your information to the IRS on either a form W-2 or 1099. As a general rule, you should keep your tax records for at least three to five years. This will ensure that in the event of an audit, you will have sufficient records to support the items reported on your tax return.

3. **Double check your return for errors.** Errors of any kind reported on your tax return may trigger an audit. The most common error is mathematical errors. Be sure to calculate all items accurately. Also ensure that your personal information is entered correctly such as

the spelling of your name, social security number, and address is correct. Don't ever sign a return that you did not review.

4. **Keep track of and limit transactions involving large sums of money.** Transactions involving large sums of money often require a reporting by financial institutions of the transaction. It is important that you keep detailed records of such transactions when they occur. In most cases, an individual may switch from an employer held retirement account to an IRA which may appear to be double income when reported by both institutions. Keeping adequate records of your transactions will ensure that you are able to explain any discrepancies presented in the audit report.

5. **Choose your deductions wisely and responsibly.** If you choose to itemize your deductions, be sure that your deductions are not too high when compared to your income. The IRS has guidelines set in place in order to determine the reasonableness of your deductions claimed in relation to your income. Exceeding the average for your income level is likely to trigger an IRS audit.

6. **Avoid Tax Scams.** If it sounds too good to be true, it usually is. Do not be fooled by a tax preparer that promises you a refund prior to preparing your tax return, or one that exaggerates your deductions and exemptions. Be prudent and wise when selecting any tax preparer (see section on how should you select a tax

preparer for further details). Also avoid organizations that protest against paying taxes alleging that it is unconstitutional. The Constitution allows the government to tax your income, so do not be bamboozled because you don't want to pay your tax obligations. Ensure that you do not file fraudulent returns. Rely only on records provided to you by your employer and/or reputable entities. If you are not used to receiving a large refund and nothing has changed from prior years, there is a strong likelihood that your return is fraudulent, and you should contact the IRS immediately.

7. **File All Required Returns on Time.** The IRS may issue an audit because you have demonstrated a pattern of non-compliance by failing to file your returns on time. This is especially true for business owners as the IRS is more likely to audit a business if it demonstrates a consistent pattern of non-compliance. For individuals, your returns are due by April 15. Most Corporate returns are due by March 15.

If you are unable to file your tax returns by the applicable deadlines, be sure to file an extension. The IRS imposes penalties and interests for failure to file your return on time if you should have the misfortune of having a balance due on your return.

Some corporations filing a late return may also have penalties and interest imposed even when no taxes are owed on the return. So file all required returns when due, and file on time.

Having the right representation when you create the various tax forms and returns is critical. Learn to ask key questions involving skill level when you first engage someone to assist you in your tax matters.

Ask what types of clients has the professional represented? What experiences do they have in audits? Are they new or have they been practicing for several years? What are their rates and how do they charge? Don't be shy, ask if there has been any complaints filed against them and then you do your homework.

Do an Internet search with a name of the person or firm and the words following the name: complaint, problems, ripoff, lawsuits, con, and scam.

Read everything. What you are looking for is a pattern of incompetency or misrepresentation. This is a consumer beware world and you want someone working with you who is skilled and knowledgeable in the areas you need assistance in.

Steven's Tip: Ideally, we should all be adept and savvy about tax law, the nuances of what to expect with an Audit, and how to negotiate the financial issues that back taxes create. But ideal isn't reality. It's a skill and a specialty that takes years of being in the field fine tunes.

Make sure you use the suggestions within this book to identify a tax professional who you can work with and has had years of practice of dealing not only over the phone with the IRS, but face-to-face. With Audits, Offers in Compromise, and Installment and Streamline Agreements—anything that involves Tax Resolution—I would recommend that your representative have at least five years of experience along with all the necessary credentials.

Endnotes

[53] TaxpayerAdvocate.irs.gov/About-TAS/Who-We-Are

[54] IRS.gov/pub/irs-pdf/p1.pd

Inside this chapter

CHAPTER 11

Common Mistakes
You Can Avoid

Individuals often make costly mistakes when they receive an IRS letter notifying them of an audit. In most cases, the notice of audit/examination will outline the reasons for the audit, the items being disputed, and the next step in the process.

> When you receive a notification from the IRS that you will be audited, i.e. a Notice of Audit and Assessment, get help.

Real Life Story: Alana owned a taxi cab service and was being audited by the IRS. She received a *Notice of Assessment* from the IRS proposing to increase the taxes owed on her return. The notice allowed her 30 days to respond by either providing additional evidence or accepting the proposed assessment. Alana ignored the notice and decided that she would not respond because she did not have any evidence to dispute the IRS findings. About two months later, she received another notice from the IRS requesting payment of over

$20,000 as proposed in the initial notice which included penalties and interest. Once again, she decided not to respond to the notice.

The IRS then proceeded to send her two consecutive *Intent to Levy* notices, and one *Final Notice of Intent to Levy*. The final notice allowed 30 days to respond to the notice, but once again, she did not respond.

After all of the time had elapsed for Alana to respond, the IRS issued levies on all of her bank accounts. When she received the Notice of Levy from her banks, she became furious and distressed. The IRS had taken all of her money—about $10,000. Fearing that her assets would be next, Alana hired our firm to represent her against the IRS. Luckily for her, a Bank Levy lasts for 21 days before the bank remits the money to the IRS. The $10,000 was being held by her banks but had not been sent to the IRS. As with most businesses, she needed this money to pay her cab drivers and business expenses, and had about 15 days left before the funds would be sent to the IRS.

My associate tax attorney immediately obtained proof of Alana's payroll and verification of the purpose of the funds. He then negotiated with the IRS to obtain a release of the full $10,000 so that she could pay her cab drivers and business expenses—if he hadn't, the business would have been immediately shut down. To the attorney's credit, he did not stop there. He reviewed the audit report and determined that Alana might be able to have her taxes lowered. Amended tax returns were completed that reduced her obligation to $5,000, a significant reduction from the original $20,000 the IRS had billed her for.

If Alana had not ignored the notices and contacted my firm sooner, she would have saved herself from the stress and anxiety that can occur when the IRS is in your path. She was fortunate to not have all of her funds seized by the IRS by responding in time. Alana learned a valuable lesson: *Responding to the IRS in time, saves your peace of mind.*

We all make mistakes. In dealing with the IRS, there are several common ones that can be avoided to remove the stress that tax time brings and especially a dreaded letter that notifies you that you have been selected. When you receive a notification from the IRS that you will be audited, or you receive a Notice of Audit and Assessment, get help. Below are 11 mistakes made by taxpayers that consistently resurface year after year.

1. **Ignore the Audit/Examination letter.** The number one mistake made by taxpayers when selected for an audit is to ignore the letter. It is important that you review the letter in its entirety, and respond within the time frame given by the letter. Failure to do so will result in an assessment of the proposed changes against you, and you may also miss your deadline to appeal. Do not ignore any notices received by the IRS. It is important that you cooperate with the IRS during the audit so

that you may have an opportunity to refute any items or changes made by the IRS.

Failure to respond may cause the IRS to disallow all questionable items. Also, if you do not respond by the IRS deadline, the IRS may then assess any tax balances due, penalties and interest will continue to increase, and the IRS may start collection action against you to collect the balance due.

2. **Thinking that you can blame your Accountant/Tax Preparer for the Errors.** It is a mistaken belief that you may be allowed to point the finger at your tax preparer and blame them for the errors in order to escape the audit. Reliance upon a professional is not a defense in an audit because you made the decision to hire that tax preparer. It is important that you hire a competent tax preparer so that your returns may be created accurately and without error. Always review the return prior to submitting it to the IRS so that you can ensure that it was accurately prepared.

Once you sign the return or submit the return electronically, you will be held liable for any inaccuracies or tax liability that may be determined from an audit of that return. When you sign your return, you approve all entries.

3. **Do not have all required support or documentation.** It is important that you keep your tax records for at least three to five years. Generally, the IRS has three years in which to audit your tax return. Also,

because the length of an audit may vary, your audit may last for two years depending on the complexity.

Failure to keep adequate records may prevent you from successfully refuting any of the changes proposed by the IRS, or prevent you from supporting the items being questioned by the IRS. Having all of the required documentation may also help to shorten the time it takes to complete the audit.

4. Lie, conceal, or falsify records. During an audit, it is important that you retain your integrity. Do not lie, conceal, or falsify records. This will likely hinder progress and cause serious ramifications if your falsity is discovered. Remain honest when communicating with the IRS and provide accurate records and documentation. Providing true and accurate records will help you to have a more successful audit and may also shorten the length of time it takes to complete the audit. This may also result in an audit of other tax years and criminal charges may be filed against you for fraud or tax evasion.

You may be fined or imprisoned for such actions, so do not attempt to lie, conceal, or falsify records when dealing with the IRS. This is not a position you want to expose yourself to.

5. Talk too much and offer too much information. During an audit, never offer more information than necessary, or more information than what is being requested by the IRS. Do not talk too much or disclose more information than what has been requested by the IRS. Providing more information than necessary may lead to other discrepancies, or may also provide information that makes other returns or other information you have submitted questionable.

Remember:

- When asked for information, provide only the information requested.

- When you are asked a question, answer only that question asked and be brief and direct in your responses.

6. Delay the Audit. Some taxpayers make the mistake of thinking that asking for an extension of time and taking a long time to respond will help their case. You cannot exceed the patience of the IRS, so it is not a good idea to keep requesting more time than necessary. Typically, the IRS will set deadlines specifying the length of time you will have to respond to the IRS request or audit report. Failure to respond within the allotted time will likely result in the examiner closing the audit and your only recourse at that time would be to file an appeal.

Do not try to delay an audit. Try to meet all IRS deadlines in order to preserve other forms of resolution that you may have prior to the close of an audit, such as speaking to a manager or involving the TPA.

7. Failure to request more time to respond. When warranted, the IRS may grant an extension of time for you to respond to the audit. You should contact the IRS agent specifically handling your case or the number provided on your notice in order to request an extension. The sooner, the better.

If you can demonstrate "good cause," the IRS is likely to grant your request for an extension. Good cause is generally found where an individual demonstrates that the time requested is reasonable and necessary in order to provide the requested information or to effectively respond to the IRS notice.

8. Failed to hire a competent tax professional. Some audits may be so complex in nature that you are better off hiring a competent tax professional to assist you rather than handling the case yourself. If unsure about the audit and audit process, it is always better to hire a tax professional. He or she will also be able to advise you about what information to provide, and help guide you as well as represent you throughout the entire audit process.

Having a tax professional can also help to ease some of the stress and tension that you may experience when going through an audit. Make sure you follow the previous suggestions when selecting a competent tax professional.

9. **Mistaken belief that hiring an Attorney will solve all of your problems.** While hiring an attorney can help to ease the stress and anxiety that an audit may cause, do not assume that hiring one will somehow stop the IRS from auditing you or that you no longer need to cooperate. Having an attorney represent you allows you to deal indirectly with the IRS through your attorney. You will still need to cooperate and participate in the process. Your attorney will request information in order to competently represent you, so your cooperation and participation will be essential in the success of the case.

10. **Mistaken belief that hiring an Attorney will make you appear guilty.** The belief that hiring an attorney will somehow make you appear guilty is a huge misconception and far from the truth. It is important that you determine whether you are able to handle the IRS on your own or whether hiring an attorney to represent you would be more beneficial. In all of my years of practice, I know that you should not handle complex matters on your own.

Many audits may be highly complex and you may become more confused and stressed if you attempt to handle such matters on your own. If you are in doubt, it is better to hire a Tax Attorney from the beginning than to hire one later on to fix a mess that you have created after attempting to handle the case on your own. When in doubt, get help.

11. Failing to choose your battles wisely. If the IRS is disputing an item that is small compared to other potential errors that you have detected but are not noticed by the IRS, accept the proposal so that you can avoid any further disputes. In some cases, agreeing with the IRS can help to prevent them from investigating your return even further.

> **Example:** Paul and Audrey were audited by the IRS. On the examination report, the IRS disputed medical expenses of $1,000. In representing them, it was discovered that they may have also miscalculated their income because of some cancelled debt from a credit card in the amount of $5,000. Paul and Audrey were advised to accept the proposed change in order to have the audit closed.
>
> Why? Because the rule is the IRS can only audit the return once per tax year. As a result, they paid the slight increase in tax owed for the $1,000 disputed medical expenses in order to avoid an additional declaration of $5,000 in income that the cancelled debt would create. Paul and Audrey came out ahead in their audit.

Mistakes happen, we all know that. To avoid getting embroiled in an IRS spiral, follow the above suggestions. Declare it a personal victory.

Inside this chapter

CHAPTER 12

What Happens if the IRS Audits Your Business?

With the Internet, a recession or two, and the changing work and lifestyles of the average American, businesses have changed. A far greater number of small businesses and the self-employed are spread across the landscape of our broad country. Many are headquartered within a home. Because there is plenty of "gray" out there in what's deductible and what's not; what is legitimate and what isn't, small businesses often find themselves more vulnerable to IRS audits.

Innocently, or purposefully mislabeling employees, expensing incorrectly—from items that should be depreciated and depreciating items that should be expensed, to declaring items as marketing when they were for entertainment—all get the attention of the IRS.

The IRS may select your business tax return for an audit through Random Selection. If selected through random selection, it does not mean that you have made any errors on your return, only that the IRS has selected your return and would like to review it to ensure that it is accurate.

The IRS audits a business for several different reasons:

1. You may be a part of random selection where your return was selected completely at random;

2. You may be selected through computerized under-reporting because the information you reported on your return does not match the information obtained by the IRS;

3. You are an employer and failed to file your payroll tax returns or make your payroll tax payments on time; or

4. You have misclassified employees as 1099 when they should be W-2 employees.

The Random Selection

The luck of the draw, the spin of the wheel or it's just "your time," a random selection has identified you as the company being audited. Anyone who gets a notice immediately wants to know: what are they (the IRS) looking for? Businesses are no different—what are they looking for? You will soon find out.

During this audit, the auditor may analyze both you and your business in order to verify that your lifestyle matches up with the information reported on your return. If your lifestyle and your income do not match, the IRS auditor may be inclined to dig deeper into your business operations and request further information in order to verify the accuracy of your tax return.

What do I mean by "match up"? Let's say you report $50,000 a year in income. Your personal tax return states you pay out $6,515 in various memberships, dues and subscriptions; $5,000 in charitable deductions; $3,258 in business expenses; $8,121 in medical expenses; $2,842 in real estate taxes; $19, 288 in mortgage interest; and $2,215 in state withholding taxes.

On the income side, outside of your W-2 reported wages of $50,000 (or it could be the "flow through" amount stated on Schedule C) and just a few dollars from interest and dividends. Nothing else.

The auditor's warning alarm sounds—where does the money come from to pay for memberships, charitable contributions, and business expenses in addition to everyday living expenses? You get to explain it. Such as:

> If you are claiming deductions on your personal return that are disproportionate to the income claimed from your business, the IRS wants to know how you are able to pay out more than what you declare comes in.

- If you are claiming deductions on your personal return that are disproportionate to the income claimed from your business, the IRS wants to know how you are able to pay out more than what you declare comes in.

- If you are claiming thousands in travel related expenses, yet your business is a location-based service business, the IRS will be interested in how you justify such an expense.

- If you are claiming a portion of your home as office space, the IRS is going to want to know what the percentage of that space is in relation to your overall home; how you calculate any percentage allocated to your utilities; and if your office is used for anything other than your office. If it doubles as the kitchen table, don't deduct it. You may be using your garage as an office, a garage that no longer is welcome to cars, tools, etc.,—it's a building (attached or not) to your home that is exclusively used for your business—you shouldn't have a problem.

> During the audit, the IRS auditor may find an intentional under-statement of your income.

Smart taxpayers frequently have photos of their actual office space with them during an audit. You don't need your space spruced up—what you want is to demonstrate that it's a living/breathing workspace that supports your claim for deductibility.

What is Computerized Underreporting?

When you conduct business with others, your company may be issued a 1099, K-1, or other income document that provides your gross receipts or transactions. This information is provided to both you and the IRS. So when you prepare your tax return, it is important that the information you provide match the IRS records. If you provide less income than what is reported to the IRS, your business tax return is likely to be selected for an audit through what is known as *Computerized Underreporting* by the IRS automated system.

The IRS computer automated system is used by the IRS to verify the information you provide on your tax return by cross-referencing it with the data provided to the IRS by other sources. During the audit, the IRS auditor may find an intentional understatement of your income. If that happens, the IRS Criminal Investigation team may be called to investigate your business, and you may be charged with tax evasion and be fined or imprisoned.

Needless to say, this would not be a pleasant experience. If the auditor determines that it was a plausible mistake, he will proceed to assess the additional taxes owed and include any additional interest and penalties. Not a pleasant experience either, but better than the alternative.

It is important that you report all of your business income. Do not make the mistake of thinking that you can hide certain transactions or income from the IRS. This will cause you more trouble than it is worth.

Failure to File Payroll Tax Returns or To Make Payroll Tax Payments on Time

Every business that has W-2 employees is required to file its *Payroll Tax Returns* quarterly, and make all required payroll tax payments on time. Payroll taxes are the tax deductions that you withhold from the income of your W-2 employees in addition to any taxes required to be paid by the employer. Failure to comply with this rule will result in the IRS auditing your business operations in order to verify compliance.

If you have employees, be sure to file your Payroll Tax Returns on time and make the required tax deposits. Companies that demonstrate inconsistent behavior or unwillingness to comply with this requirement may have their business shut down by the IRS. Do not take that chance. File your returns and make your required payments on time.

Misclassification of Employees as 1099 Instead of W-2 Employees?

In some cases, businesses have *Misclassified Employees as 1099 independent contractors instead of W-2 employees* in order to avoid filing payroll tax returns or paying payroll taxes. Employers are responsible for correctly classifying workers. Failure to correctly classify anyone who works for you may result in you owing employment taxes, penalties, and interest to the IRS. In determining whether an employee is a W-2 or 1099 employee, the IRS analyzes three key factors:

1. Behavioral control

2. Financial control

3. Relationship of the parties

What is behavioral control?

The IRS will analyze whether you have behavioral control by

reviewing whether you provide extensive instruction on how the work is to be performed or carried out.

Do you provide extensive instruction to your workers or are they on their own?

If you also control how and where the work takes place, provide the equipment being used, and if you provide training to the worker, the IRS is likely to find that the worker is a W-2 employee and not a 1099 independent contractor.

The less behavioral control you have over the worker, the more likely it is that the worker is a 1099 independent contractor. If the worker is found to be a W-2 employee, you will be held responsible for payroll taxes and payroll tax return filings. You have no obligation to pay Payroll Taxes or file Payroll Tax returns if the worker is found to be a 1099 independent contractor,

> If the worker is found to be a W-2 employee, you will be held responsible for payroll taxes and payroll tax return filings.

What is financial control?

The IRS will also analyze whether you have *Financial Control* over the worker by evaluating three factors:

1. Significant investment

2. Expenses

3. Opportunity for profit or loss

A significant investment isn't on your side, it's the worker's. He or she is required to *purchase the items* in order to conduct the work you are requiring. If you provide the items or the money to purchase them, the worker is likely to be classified as a W-2 rather than a 1099 independent contractor.

When the worker is *responsible for their own expenses* such as office expenses, utilities, supplies, etc., the IRS is likely to classify the worker as a 1099 independent contractor rather than a W-2 employee. However, if you reimburse the worker for their business related expenses, the worker is likely to be classified as a W-2 employee.

Lastly, if the worker is provided with an *opportunity to incur a loss or make a profit*, then the IRS is likely to classify the worker as a 1099 independent contractor. This means that the worker may have had to invest personal funds for items like a computer, car, specific software, tools, etc., to do the work you are engaging them to do. The return is the money they make. It could actually be less than what is received when the job is done.

When no opportunity to earn a profit or incur a loss exists, then they are likely to be classified as a W-2 employee and you will be responsible for payroll taxes and also required to file Payroll Tax returns.

What is the relationship of the parties?

In evaluating the Relationship of the Parties, the IRS will analyze whether there is a **written** contract between the employer and employee, and whether employee benefits are provided. When a business contract is involved, the IRS will analyze the contract in order to determine whether it adequately clarifies the relationship between the employer and the worker.

If you provide the worker with insurance, pension, and paid time off, the IRS is likely to find that the worker is a W-2 employee despite the existence of a contract classifying the relationship as an Independent Contractor relationship. If you are unsure about how to classify workers, you may seek the assistance of a Human Resource Professional or an Employment Law Attorney.

The IRS will evaluate each of these factors independently, and then combine the results in order to determine whether the information obtained demonstrates more of one classification than the other. Having a clear and concise contract and established procedures within your company will help to alleviate the possibility that you have *misclassified workers*. If you hire *1099 independent contractors*, be sure to exercise minimal behavioral control and financial control, and ensure that your actions demonstrate a business relationship rather than the relationship of an employer and W-2 employee. Be sure to take the time to review each worker individually and insure that they are classified correctly.

Preparing for the Audit of Your Business

If you decide to handle the audit on your own, here are some tips for preparing and being ready for your business audit:

1. **Find the records that support the items listed on your tax return or that are being disputed by the IRS.** You should organize your records in a neat and organized fashion. This will help the audit to run smoothly and may also reduce the time it takes to resolve it.

2. **Make a list of problems or obstacles that you would incur during the audit.** If you are unable to support various items on your return or find other possible issues that were not addressed by the IRS audit report, make a list of those items, then determine whether it is better to approve the IRS audit before these issues are detected, or whether it would be best to dispute the items proposed by the IRS. The savvy taxpayer chooses which battles to engage in.

3. **Remain honest and professional.** Do not falsify information or act unprofessionally. Remember that the IRS simply wants to verify the information you have provided, or investigate whether your business operations complies with the US Tax Code. Do not take it personally and disrespect the representative.

   By being honest and professional, you will be able to detect whether the IRS representative is professional or abuses his or her authority. When you detect abuse or unprofessionalism, you should immediately contact the representative's direct manager, or TPA.

4. **Do not seek to delay the audit.** Respond to all IRS notices and requests on time, and never request an

extension unless you honestly cannot meet the required deadline set by the IRS. Delaying an audit will only frustrate both you and the IRS representative and may provide the representative with more time to investigate further into your business or tax return.

5. **Learn from previous mistakes or from the mistakes of others.** Do what you can to correct any errors or mistakes detected by the auditor, or through your own examination. Showing that you have taken steps to rectify your past mistakes is a good indication that your current error was unintentional and you are likely to receive a more sympathetic response from the auditor. Failing to correct your errors or past mistakes may cause the IRS to take stricter measures to ensure your compliance, and in some cases may result in your businesses being shut down by the IRS. Take corrective measures when and where necessary.

Real Life Story: Judith received a notice for an audit of her business. Within it, there was an indication of two areas that the IRS was looking at. One of them was the payment for actual rent of office space used within her home that was recommended by her CPA. The amount was paid to her and was consistent with what she would have paid if she rented space outside the home where she lived.

At the audit, she represented herself and took all the records the initial notice had requested. They reflected the percentage of the office space in relation to the total square footage of the house (an entire floor of the home); utility bills she deducted a percentage of; photos of the working space for the auditor to view if necessary; plus her files that contained the backup for all business expenses claimed.

What she didn't know was that her CPA had incorrectly advised her to pay herself the rent. It's not an allowable expense for home office usage—if she had written the check to someone else for renting space, it would have been.

Because she had all her files, the auditor created a new tax return. The item for rent paid of $12,000 was deleted. But, as Judith went through the business expense files, she discovered several items that were not expensed at all and were now added in as new expenses. In the end, her new return was close to "washing" out the old return. The rental deduction was lost … and new expenses were discovered that left her owing the IRS approximately $150.

Judith declared it a win, quickly realized that she had the wrong CPA and terminated him, hiring one who was knowledgeable about home-based businesses and her type of work. She felt that the IRS was working with her in resolving the incorrect advice and return.

As a business owner, it's critical to have on your team tax professionals who not only understand your business but are fully versed in accounting practices that relate to your type of business.

Steven's Tip: If you get audited, it does not necessarily mean you did something wrong. It could merely be the "unluck" of the random draw. Just remember if you are audited, only bring the documents that support the item(s) being scrutinized. If you are unsure of yourself, consider having an IRS accepted tax professional represent you at the audit in your place. Why? Many times, taxpayers let their mouths runneth over. Meaning, you talk too much and may reveal information that the IRS might not know it would like to take a closer look. Better to be safe than sorry.

Inside this chapter

CHAPTER 13

Foreign Financial Assets: When and How to Report

There are many types of taxes that require taxpayers to file tax returns such as: income, employment, estate and gift, and excise taxes. Each type of tax has its own set of rules and filing requirements with which the taxpayer must comply. Although each set of rules and requirements are challenging and complex, two sets of rules and requirements seem to cause problems on a consistent basis and they involve foreign assets.

The *Foreign Bank and Financial Accounts Report* (FBAR) and more recently, the *Specified Foreign Financial Asset* reporting requirements introduced under the *Foreign Account Tax Compliance Act* (FATCA) are probably some of the least "known" and least intuitive reporting systems imposed by the United States. The result is they have become problematic for any taxpayer who falls subject to their reach. Why? Because these systems are not intuitive. They are not based on income earned, or even on the receipt of money or assets. They are simply reporting requirements that mandate that taxpayers disclose certain information about their financial accounts to the U.S. Government. This is a time when ignorance is not bliss. The failure to comply can lead to very hefty penalties. Feeling confused? You are not alone.

If you generate all of your income in the U.S., have all of your assets: cash, investments (and NONE of your investments have investments outside of the U.S.), businesses, trusts, etc., in the U.S., you get to skip this next section. But, if you receive/earn moneys (even if you don't take actual receipt of them) or have anything outside of the U.S., read on and read closely.

Foreign Bank Account Reporting (FBAR)

Any United States person that has a financial interest in, or signature authority over foreign financial accounts, must file Form TDF 90-22.1 if the aggregate value of the foreign financial accounts exceeds *$10,000* at any time during the calendar year.[55] Even if no income is earned by a U.S. person's financial account, or if no distributions are made to a U.S. person from his or her financial account, or in the case of signatory authority, even if a U.S. person has no actual financial interest in a foreign account (meaning they will never receive a distribution from such account), the U.S. person is still required to file a FBAR with the IRS. If married, spouses need to file separate FBARs, the exception is that if all accounts are jointly owned, only one spouse needs to file, provided the FBAR is signed by both spouses. If you have a combo—meaning both single and joint accounts, separate FBARs need to be filed.

> **Example:** Katherine had an off-shore account at Swiss Bank valued at $20,000 US Dollars. As a result, she was required by the IRS to file an FBAR even though she received no interest or distribution from the account.

> **Example:** Tryon and Amanda had offshore accounts in the Cayman Islands. They each had separate accounts and a joint one. Three FBAR forms had to be filed, one for the joint account signed by the both of them, and then two separate forms for their separate accounts.

Who is a U.S. Person?

The term *U.S. Person* includes U.S. citizens and resident alien individuals as well as all entities created or organized in the United States or under the laws of the United States.[56] This includes an entity that is disregarded for tax purposes, such as, but not limited to, a single member limited liability company (LLC).[57]

Trusts and Estates are also included in the definition of a U.S. person, even if the trust is a grantor trust (a trust in which the income, deductions, and credits are taken into account by another person and not the trust). However, the beneficiary of an IRA account does not have to report a foreign financial account held in the IRA.

> **Example:** Lloyd was born in the United States in the state of Florida. Currently, he lives in Paris, France. Because he

was born in the United States, Lloyd will be considered a U.S. person even though he does not currently reside in the United States.

The Foreign Account Tax Compliance Act (FATCA)

Any U.S. citizen, resident alien, or non-resident alien who makes an election to be treated as a resident for the purposes of filing a joint tax return, as well as a non-resident alien who is a bona fide resident of American Samoa or Puerto Rico who, during any taxable year, holds any interest in certain financial assets (referred to as *Specified Foreign Financial Asset*) must attach a Form 8983 to their tax return.

Form 8983 requires the individual taxpayer to report information about specified foreign financial assets if the aggregate value of all such specified foreign financial assets exceeds a specified amount based on the taxpayer's filing status and location of residence ($50,000 for unmarried individuals living in the United States).[58] In addition, the Treasury Department has issued proposed regulations which require certain domestic entities that are created for the purpose of holding specified foreign financial assets in the same manner as an individual would hold such assets, to file Form 8983.[59] Such entities include certain domestic, closely held corporations, domestic partnerships, and certain trusts.[60] These regulations will not take effect until tax years beginning on January 1, 2013, at the earliest, and possibly later, pending further guidance by the IRS.[61]

Example: Millie is single, and is a U.S. citizen residing in the State of California but has financial assets in Madrid, Spain of $100,000 US Dollars. As a result, the IRS required that she file a Form 8983 with her income tax return.

What are Specified Foreign Financial Assets?

In general, *specified foreign financial assets* include only assets which would be commonly referred to as a financial asset, such as a foreign mutual fund or an interest in a foreign partnership, as opposed to a non-financial object that might also have substantial value, such as a house or piece of art. More specifically, the Internal Revenue Code defines a "specified foreign financial asset" to include:

1. a depository, custodial, or other financial account maintained by a foreign financial institution;

2. a stock or security issued by a person other than a U.S. person;

3. a financial instrument or contract held for investment that has an issuer or counterparty other than a U.S. person; and

4. an interest in an entity that is not a U.S. person.[62]

This definition is somewhat cumbersome and a chart created by the IRS further delineates what assets are subject to FATCA.

Types of Foreign Assets and Whether They are Reportable on Form 8938	
Financial (deposit and custodial) accounts held at foreign financial institutions	yes
Financial account held at a foreign branch of a U.S. financial institution	no
Financial account held at a U.S. branch of a foreign financial institution	no
Foreign financial account or asset for which you have signature authority	No, unless any income, gains, losses, deductions, credits, gross proceeds, or distributions from holding or disposing of the account or asset are or would be required to be reported, included, or otherwise reflected on your income tax return
Foreign stock or securities held in a financial account at a foreign financial institution	The account itself is subject to reporting, but the contents of the account do not have to be separately reported
Foreign stock or securities not held in a financial account	yes
Foreign partnership interests	yes
Indirect interests in foreign financial assets through an entity	no
Foreign mutual funds	yes
Domestic mutual fund investing in foreign stocks and securities	no
Foreign accounts and foreign non-account investment assets held by foreign or domestic grantor trust for which you are the grantor	Yes, as to both foreign accounts and foreign non-account investment assets
Foreign-issued life insurance or annuity contract with a cash-value	yes
Foreign hedge funds and foreign private equity funds	yes
Foreign real estate held directly	no

Types of Foreign Assets and Whether They are Reportable on Form 8938	
Foreign real estate, held through a foreign entity	No, but the foreign entity itself is a specified foreign financial asset and its maximum value includes the value of the real estate
Foreign currency, held directly	no
Precious Metals, held directly	no
Personal property, held directly, such as art, antiques, jewelry, cars and other collectibles	no
'Social Security'- type program benefits provided by a foreign government	no

Source: IRS

Reporting Requirements for FBAR and FATCA

As mentioned above, each of the FBAR and FATCA regimes require that the taxpayers file an information return with the IRS.

FBAR cases require Form TDF 90-22.1 to be filed and *must be received by June 30* of the year immediately following the calendar year being reported. *Warning*: The IRS does not provide extensions for this form.

In FATCA cases, Form 8983 must be attached to the taxpayer's federal income tax return when filed with the IRS.

Each of these forms require the taxpayer to disclose fairly detailed information about the relevant account or asset such as: account or asset values, the name and address of the financial institution

> Each of these forms requires taxpayers to disclose fairly detailed information about the relevant account or asset. Failure to file them on time will lead to extensive penalties.

where the account is maintained, and any information needed to identify the asset, along with the names and addresses of all issuers and counterparties. Although no tax is imposed by either the FBAR or FATCA, failure to comply subjects the taxpayer with extensive penalties discussed below.

Penalties Assessed for Non-Compliance with FBAR or FATCA

Think big, really big. The penalties for failure to file can be high. The penalty for failure to file an FBAR is $10,000 if the failure is non-willful or the greater of:

- 50 percent of the account value, *or*
- $100,000 if the failure is willful.

That should get your attention—yet there is more—criminal penalties may apply.

The penalty for failure to file form 8983 is $10,000 plus an additional $10,000 for each 30-day period of failure to file after an IRS notice of failure to disclose, up to a maximum of $60,000. Criminal penalties may also apply. These penalties are not imposed if the taxpayer can show a reasonable cause for failure to report. This can be a difficult hurdle. The fact that a foreign jurisdiction imposes a fine or penalty for disclosing such information is not considered reasonable cause. Additionally, a 40 percent accuracy-related penalty is imposed for underpayment of tax, on taxpayer's income tax return, that is attributable to an undisclosed foreign financial asset understatement.[63]

Example: Nicholas had unreported foreign assets of $200,000 U.S. Dollars. The IRS determined that his failure to report the foreign assets was intentional. As a result, it fined him $100,000 which was half of the value of his assets, and also imposed a penalty of $100,000 for his *willful* failure to file the return, as well as additional interest for each 30-day period in which Nicholas failed to file. As a result, he ended up paying the IRS more than the actual value of his assets.

How Long Can the IRS have to Review a Return?

It can get worse. The *Statue of Limitations*, the time allowed for the IRS to assess additional tax to a taxpayer's return, is extended from three (3) to six (6) years for an omission of income related to an undisclosed foreign financial account, if the omission of gross income is in excess of $5,000. Again, the statute of limitations does not begin to run on any return that has not been filed or is incomplete.

Example: Olivia failed to report her foreign account in London, England, valued at $20,000 when she filed her 2006 return on March 5, 2007. On April 15, 2011, she received an audit report from the IRS assessing additional taxes for the unreported account. Olivia thought that the statute of limitations prevented the IRS from reviewing her account because three years had passed. Not so. Because the audit involved a foreign account, the IRS actually had six years to review the return, until March 5,

2013. As a result, the statute of limitations did not prevent the IRS from auditing her return.

Requirements to Comply with Both FBAR and FATCA

The information reporting requirements, and the penalties imposed, by the FBAR and FATCA are not mutually exclusive. One taxpayer may need to report identical information under FBAR and FATCA. Supplying the information under one requirement does not relieve the requirement to supply the same information under another requirement. The penalties are also not exclusive. Remember, they are significant. Penalties imposed by each requirement may apply even if the penalties relate to the same account or asset. Additionally, these penalties are in addition to any other penalty or tax imposed by any other code section, even if it relates to the same asset or account.

Example: Under separate revenue laws, taxpayers are required to:

1. Pay a separate tax for ownership in any Passive Foreign Investment Companies (a PFIC is basically a foreign mutual fund); and

2. Report/disclose certain interests in foreign trust on Form 3520-A.

Failure to comply with either of these requirements results in the imposition of penalties on the taxpayer. Therefore, if a taxpayer "has" a foreign trust which owns a foreign account which holds PFICs, the taxpayer will be required to file Form TDF 90-22.1, Form 8983, Form 3520-A, and calculate the PFIC tax/penalty. Failure to do so would impose all four penalties upon the taxpayer, even though all penalties stem from one account or one asset.

The Voluntary Disclosure Program

The best way to avoid the penalties imposed by one or more of the above-mentioned disclosure programs is to fully comply with its reporting requirements in a timely manner. Given that it may be easy for a taxpayer to fail to recognize such reporting requirements prior to the reporting deadline, the question becomes what a taxpayer who has undisclosed foreign accounts and/or undisclosed foreign entities, can do to be brought into compliance with United States tax laws?

Before a taxpayer gets hung out to dry, the answer may depend on whether the taxpayer has failed to report taxable income or has merely failed to file the FBAR return.

What happens if There is No Unreported Income?

For a taxpayer who has reported all income, but has failed to file an FBAR, the taxpayer may file a delinquent FBAR report along with an attachment explaining the circumstances of the failure to file. Provided there is no unreported income and the taxpayer has not been contacted by the IRS in regards to such failure to disclose, the IRS will not impose a penalty for failure to file. Other reporting requirements may have similar delinquent procedures.

Example: Phillip filed his 2010 tax return and reported all of his income. Unbeknowst to him, he was required to file an FBAR but failed to do so because he was unaware of his requirement to file. Phillip then immediately filed his FBAR and explained that he honestly did not know of the requirement. The IRS accepted his explanation and did not impose penalties because he had reported all of his income on his 2010 tax return.

What Happens if There is Unreported Income?

Not reporting foreign income also isn't a pretty picture—although, it isn't fatal either. Many taxpayers who fail to disclose a foreign account have also failed to pay tax on income earned in that account. In response to taxpayers who find themselves in this situation, the IRS has implemented a voluntary disclosure program. Prior to 2012, IRS had voluntary disclosure programs which imposed lower penalties than the current 2012 program. Beginning in 2012, a taxpayer who voluntarily discloses their non-compliance with regard to foreign disclosure requirements may avoid criminal prosecution and be subject to a 27.5 percent penalty on the highest year's aggregate value of the taxpayer's foreign accounts and foreign assets.

This is *in addition* to the tax, penalty, and interest on the income omitted from taxpayer's return.

I need to say this: this is current and can be changed in subsequent years. The benefits of the voluntary disclosure program are that taxpayers can generally avoid criminal prosecution. In many cases and depending on the facts, taxpayers can reduce the amount of the penalty calculated as opposed to the penalty calculated when he or she is not part of the voluntary disclosure program.

> **Example:** Claris had a foreign account valued at $100,000 U.S. dollars. She failed to disclose these assets on her income tax return and as a result underreported her income. When she realized that FATCA required her to file the Form 8983 with her return, she immediately filed an amended return to include the Form 8983. As a result, the IRS then imposed lower penalties on Claris' return and did not file criminal charges against her.

Voluntary Disclosures

Voluntary Disclosure generally means that the taxpayer does not know and has no reason to know of any investigation into his taxes prior to the disclosure. Therefore, any taxpayer who learns of their failure to disclose under audit will not be eligible for the Voluntary Disclosure Program. Additionally, taxpayers who have filed amended returns which report additional previously unreported foreign income, without specifically notifying the IRS, are subject to criminal investigation and cannot avail themselves of the 27.5 percent preferential penalty rate should such amended return be audited, or the existence of additional reporting requirements come to the IRS' attention for any reason.

Example: Ruth had foreign assets valued at $500,000 U.S. dollars but failed to disclose this on her 2011 tax return. Her tax return was then audited by the IRS. Ruth did not know that she was required to disclose her foreign assets. However, because she learned of her error during the audit, the IRS found that she did not meet the requirements of Voluntary Disclosure and was assessed the maximum penalty for failure to disclose her assets.

Requirements of the Voluntary Disclosure Program

As part of the *Voluntary Disclosure Program,* a taxpayer must, among other requirements, file accurate amended returns and copies of the originally filed income and informational returns for the years covered by the Voluntary Disclosure Program. He must provide all additional information regarding the foreign accounts as requested by the U.S. government, and pay all "accuracy" and "failure to file" penalties, along with a voluntary disclosure letter and statement.

Real Life Story: Rodney was born in the United States. As an adult, he relocated to a Caribbean island and became a prominent business man. He owned several businesses in several different countries across the globe. He owned no businesses in the U.S. because he wanted to avoid the high tax obligations. As his empire grew, Rodney had several bank accounts in various foreign locations, and investments all generating substantial interests. He was so successful that he spent most of his time on vacation and had others managing his business and financial affairs.

Unfortunately, none of the individuals managing his financial affairs informed him of the requirements of FATCA or FBAR. Rodney had been in business for decades without realizing that as a U.S. citizen living abroad, he had reporting requirements in the U.S.

Eventually, the IRS obtained information from a whistleblower about Rodney's activities, and he was immediately audited by the IRS. During the audit, the IRS obtained information that allowed it to obtain a freeze of all of his accounts and assets pending the results of the audit. It was at that time that Rodney decided to obtain outside counsel to represent him in the audit.

We entered the picture to represent him. Our attorney contacted Rodney's financial managers to educate them on his financial requirements, and obtained the necessary information to prepare all filings that were and are required. At the end of the audit, Rodney owed the IRS well over half a million dollars, but he was able to avoid going to prison and having all of his assets seized.

Had he had the proper knowledge of his filing requirements as a U.S. citizen, he could have avoided paying excessive penalties and interest. Voluntary disclosure would have been less costly than the costs he incurred in trying to battle the IRS. He learned a valuable lesson from this experience: "Ignorance of the Law is no excuse!"

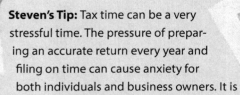

Steven's Tip: Tax time can be a very stressful time. The pressure of preparing an accurate return every year and filing on time can cause anxiety for both individuals and business owners. It is important that if you choose a tax professional to assist you in preparing your tax return that you do so wisely and prudently. In the event that you have anything that looks like, smells like, sounds like or feels like it has "foreign" attached to it, seek assistance. This is the first step in avoiding a possible tax audit.

In the event of an audit, be sure to respond to the IRS notice and have accurate and adequate records available. If you are unsure on how to proceed, seek the advice and assistance of competent and qualified tax professionals. There is plenty in this section to make your head spin. What I have shared is designed to help you make it through the audit process on your own and should be of great assistance. In *examples* and *real life stories*, you read how individuals allowed things to get out of control—either by ignorance or outright defiance—and financially regret it.

As I've said repeatedly throughout this section, if your taxes and/ or financial picture are complicated and there is any possibility of massive fines or even criminal charges—get professional help immediately.

Endnotes

[55] Instructions to Form TDF 90-22.1

[56] Instructions to Form TDF 90-22.1

[57] CCH Master Tax Guide PP2570 (2013)

[58] IRC 6038D

[59] CCH 2570

[60] 1.6038D-6

[61] Notice 2013-10

[62] 6038D

[63] CCH 2570 and IRC 6662(b)(7)

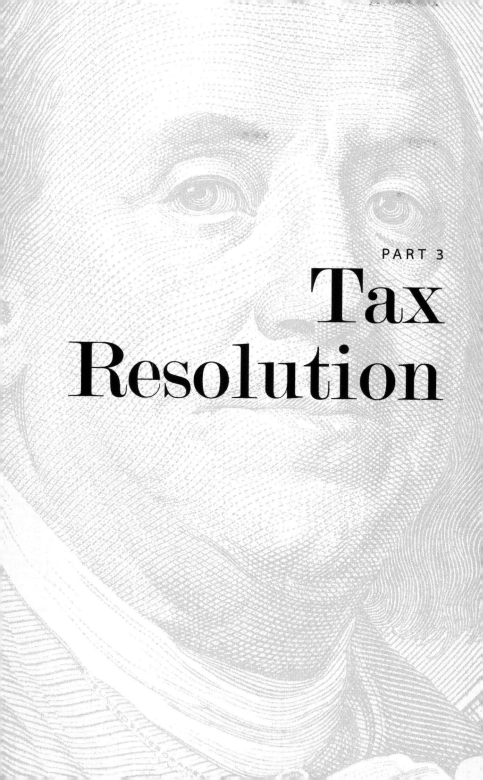

PART 3

Tax Resolution

Inside this chapter

CHAPTER 14

Tax Resolution: The Good, the Bad, the Ugly

Everyone pays taxes to the government in one form or another. Many people fall behind and need to get themselves out of a deep hole. You are not the first person to owe the Internal Revenue Service (IRS) and you will not be the last. However, owing taxes to the IRS is no picnic and it is a lot easier if you have a professional assisting you. This section of *Tax Relief and Tax Resolution* is intended to help inform individuals with tax issues, always keeping in mind that dealing with the IRS is not for the faint of heart.

I have handled thousands of cases and helped my clients save millions of dollars. Throughout the years, I have yelled at, screamed at, cajoled, threatened, and pled with the IRS on behalf of our clients. Believe it or not, the best approach is usually to be nice to whoever you are talking to, while boldly standing up for your rights. Your situation is so common that the IRS has written the Internal Revenue Manual (IRM) that describes how the IRS should operate and what your rights are as a taxpayer. That doesn't mean that you, or I can be lax and assume that the IRS is on "your" side or will alert you if an error has been made that benefits you and not it. If someone does not keep them honest, you will never get half of the results that you are entitled to.

How Do You Handle Dealing With the IRS?

Understand that the IRS is a giant bureaucracy and collection agency. You can get lost very easily in whom to call, which part of the IRS you are talking to, and determining what resolutions you may be eligible for (in fact, you may not have realized that you were even qualified for a resolution). You will get different answers from different individuals because some of the IRS representatives do not know what they are talking about. And more revealing, others do know what they are talking about and are *aware* that you do not.

> When communicating with the IRS, write down the name, the ID number that is given to you that identifies the IRS representative that you have spoken to, the details of the call, and the time and date. When you are dealing with the IRS, make this a practice.

It is even more important to know what you are doing because the IRS is a colossal branch of the government, one that can flip a quiet day to total turbulence with just a certified letter that has its return address on it. You can setup a resolution with the IRS, only to have a manager not put it in place and still have your wages garnished and your bank accounts levied, even though you did everything you were supposed to do. What you thought you had successfully resolved, didn't happen.

It is critical to talk to the right department at the IRS and follow up to make sure the representative you talked to did what they were supposed to do. When you establish a resolution with the IRS, it is recommended that you follow up two weeks later to ensure that your account was successfully resolved. In the Appendices at the back of this book are a variety of tables and charts. The chart in Appendix F shows the various departments of the IRS you may encounter when you call their toll free numbers. Whenever you communicate with the IRS, write down the name, the ID number that is given to you, the details of the call, and the time and date. When you are dealing with the IRS, make this a practice.

Again, the IRS is a giant bureaucracy, but it is possible to navigate it.

The IRS is also a collection agency, very similar to collection agencies that call and harass people who owe any other types of debt. Ironically, with the IRS, the people who have the most information that you need, are also the ones that can start collection activity against you. Meet the Automated Collection System (ACS). Every time you call this department, whoever you get will try to set a deadline for you to do something. If you do not meet the deadline, ACS will take the next step in the collection process.

You are now officially in the "system." The IRS will send you certain letters, with a set number of them before they can garnish your wages, can levy your bank accounts, or take other collection actions against you. Ignoring letters from the IRS only wastes time that you would have had to address your back taxes before the IRS starts taking aggressive collection actions against you.

How Does the IRS Handle Your Case?

Everyone has a Tax Account with the IRS that is based on a Social Security Number (SSN), Individual Tax Identification Number (ITIN) or Employer Identification Number (EIN). Most tax accounts are under the individual taxpayer's SSN but anyone who is not a U.S. Citizen, or are not eligible for an a SSN, but have worked in the U.S. and have paid taxes to the U.S., can apply for and get an ITIN to use with the IRS for tax purposes. Information concerning your case, liabilities, and all collection activity follow your account that is tracked by either your SSN or ITIN. Most Americans have some type of financial transaction that requires the SSN or ITIN—from a credit card, checking or savings account, insurance policy, all the way to employment. All require you to identify yourself numerically. This makes it very hard to hide from the IRS, especially if you use your SSN for other financial transactions, like most taxpayers.

EINs are used by businesses, are specific to the business, and are attached to an individual that created the business formation or applied for the EIN. These numbers are very sensitive and confidential but they are crucial in how the IRS tracks your case. It is important not to have any issues with these numbers, use too many of them, switch numbers needlessly, or use a false number, as any issues with these numbers can prevent the IRS from helping you, and may prevent you from stopping any IRS collection activity against you.

Real Life Story: Anna Maria had used a false social security number (SSN) to obtain work. She had since obtained a valid SSN but was still working under the false social security number. Anna Maria filed her tax returns on time with her valid SSN but her employer was still sending a W-2 under her false SSN. Payroll taxes were submitted under her false SSN. For what she owed the IRS, not only could she not set up an Installment Agreement, she could not obtain a release of the garnishment on her wages. The issue with her account took years to resolve before she had the ability to start negotiating with the IRS collections department to release her wage garnishment.

Your tax account can either be in a *normal status*, a *hold status*, or a *collection status* depending on how the IRS has your account categorized.

Normal Status

Normal is good. If you do not have issues with the IRS, your account should be in a normal status. If you do not owe the IRS and file your tax returns on time, your account will stay in this status.

Hold Status

An account can be in a hold status for various reasons: audit, bankruptcy, appealing any activity by the IRS, and filing an

Offer in Compromise. Any time the IRS cannot pursue collection activity against an individual, their account is placed in a hold status, which also extends out or tolls the expiration date for any debts on the account. Hold statuses can also prevent the release of wage garnishments, bank levies, or other collection activity if they have already been put in place. Ironically, having your account in a hold status can delay or prevent you from resolving your IRS back taxes.

> **Real Life Story:** Beatrice filed for an Offer in Compromise (OIC) with a different company from mine. When her tax account was reviewed by the other attorney, there were no collection issues. In the time it took to submit the offer, the IRS issued a wage garnishment. The offer created a hold on her account which prevented the release of the wage garnishment even though, if successful, the offer would wipe out Beatrice's IRS debt. My firm prevents situations like this by providing a higher level of service to our clients.

Collection Status

If you have not filed your tax returns, or owe the IRS, your account will eventually be placed in a collection status. Unbeknownst to most, you can accelerate the process if you initiate a call innocently, start asking questions, and identify yourself. Calling the IRS can trigger having your account placed in a collection status—basically, you become a "call of interest."

It is wise to be ready to move quickly to resolve your IRS back taxes when you first call them. Once your account is in collection status, the IRS will start to mail collection letters to you. Once they have sent the required number of letters, usually three, the IRS will start to take enforcement action in the form of bank levies and wage garnishments.

One of the worst parts about having your account in a collection status is that the rate of interest and penalties on your tax debt is significantly higher until a resolution is established. Total interest and penalties can be as high as *47.5 percent.*[64]

> Calling the IRS can trigger having your account placed in a collection status.

Moving quickly can save you thousands of dollars in interest and penalties. The goal of any resolution is to get your account out of a collection status and keep it out of the collection status for as long as possible, if not indefinitely.

The IRS Collection Statute Expiration Date (CSED)

Almost all IRS tax debt expires or goes away about 10 years from the date of assessment (the main exception is for fraud), called the Collection Statute Expiration Date (CSED). This means that the IRS has 10 years to collect back taxes from you. The Date of Assessment is normally the day your tax returns were processed by the IRS and the IRS became aware that you owed taxes to them. Various events can extend out when IRS tax debt expires, or you can agree to give the IRS more time to collect from you.

Real Life Story: David owed tens of thousands of dollars
to the IRS. He was going to set up an Installment Agreement with the IRS to pay his debt in full. When one of
our attorneys called the IRS and reviewed his account, he
discovered that approximately $15,000 was set to expire
in seven days. The IRS agent demanded the client pay
the money within seven days. The attorney told the IRS
agent that he would call back in 10 days. He did … on
the tenth day. When the attorney called back, the $15,000
had expired. The door was now opened up to set up an
Installment Agreement for the remaining balance.

Why would someone give the IRS more time to collect
from them and waive their rights? Because they do not know
what their rights are, and when someone does not know what
their rights are, the IRS will ask that people waive their rights
and extend out the CSED. You never have to give the IRS
more time to collect against you, but many people do.

Bankruptcy, audits, appeals, and filing an Offer in
Compromise, are some of the ways the CSED can be extended.
As a rule of thumb, any time that the IRS cannot take collection
activity against you, will normally extend the CSED. Being
prepared to setup a resolution will stop collection activity
while the time goes by on your expiration dates, getting you
closer to not having to worry about the IRS.

Steven's Tip: If there is one single thing to take away from this small and powerful chapter, it is this:

When you are in the a situation that requires tax resolution, get professional help. You are dealing with a powerful collection agency.

Endnotes

64 AccessPointHR.com/_downloads/IRS%2020%20questions-W2%20vs%201099.pdf

Inside this chapter

CHAPTER 15

When the Taxpayer is a Business

Differences between Individual and Business Accounts

Taxpayers who start a new business, or continue to operate an existing business, are faced with the question of what legal form of ownership (entity) should be chosen to hold the business. There are a variety of different entities from which to choose (or the taxpayer can simply hold the assets used in the business as personal assets). The choice of entity can have both tax and non-tax ramifications to the owner/taxpayer (Owner). In general, Owners will wish to choose an entity which both limits their liability for entity debts and avoids taxation at the entity level (double taxation). The decision should be made based on the facts of each case.

Note: Throughout these chapters, when "entity" is used, it refers to the type of business structure you use. The "owner" will be assumed to be you.

Choosing the Type of Business Entity That Works For You

Taxpayers who start a new business, or continue to operate an existing business, are faced with the question of what legal form of ownership ("entity") should be chosen for the business? The two most important considerations for most Owners are:

1. Will the entity offer *limited liability*?

2. Will the entity be subject to "double taxation," or will income and losses *flow-through* to the Owner?

Limited Liability

Limited Liability prevents creditors of the business entity from demanding payment from the individual owner personally, but can demand payment only from the assets of the entity. When this occurs, the entity is said to have *Limited Liability*. If the creditors of the entity may attach the personal assets of the owners of the entity, then the entity does not have limited liability. The C Corporation was originally the major entity type to provide limited liability.

Over the years, this favorable attribute has been adopted by other types of entities as well, giving you more options.

Double Taxation

An entity is subject to *Double Taxation* when the income it earns is taxed once at the entity level, and again when the remainder (after the entity level tax has been paid) is distributed to the owner. For example, if a "C" Corporation earned

$1,000,000 income, the corporation, as a separate entity, would need to calculate its own taxable income ($1,000,000) and pay tax on that amount. The applicable 2014 corporate tax rate is $113,900 + 34 percent over amounts greater than $335,000, the corporation would owe $340,000 to the government. The remaining $660,000 would then again be subject to taxation when it was distributed to the owner/shareholder and taxed at his or her individual tax rate.

Generally speaking, distributions from a corporation's profits are *qualified dividends* subject to a maximum tax rate of 20 percent as of this writing. As a result, the $660,000 distribution would be subject to a maximum $132,000 tax at the shareholder level, making the total tax on the $1,000,000 income equal to $472,000 or roughly 47.2 percent.

"C" Corporations are the major entity form that is subject to double taxation. Entities that are not subject to double taxation are referred to as *flow-through entities* because the income earned by the entity is not subject to tax at the entity level. Instead, it "flows through" to the owners and is taxed as if the owners earned the income directly, regardless of whether they actually receive a distribution.

Let's use the $1,000,000 amount again. If a partnership earned $1,000,000 of income, the partnership would not be subject to tax at the entity level. Instead, the partnership income would be reported directly on the Owner's (or Partners') income tax returns. If each Owner were subject to a 40 percent tax rate, the Owners would be subject to $400,000 of tax in total. Comparing the two entities one can see that the total tax due from a company held in the corporate form is higher than the tax due from the same company held in the partnership form, based on the facts presented.

Limited Liability is almost always a desired characteristic sought by business Owners. In general, flow-through tax treatment is also preferred over double taxation, even if the entity is not expected to earn money in the first few years of operation. A business that loses money in the first years of operation will not be subject to double taxation (because there is no income) but would generally still prefer flow-through taxation because the losses could flow through to the Owners.

For example, if a business were expected to generate a $100,000 loss in its first year of operation, the Owners of a flow-through entity, such as a partnership, would be allowed to report the $100,000 loss directly on their income tax return, sheltering income from other sources. Whereas the owners of a C Corporation, would not be able to use the losses, because a C Corporation is not a flow-through entity and cannot distribute losses.

Allocation of Distributions and Income

Some entities require that distributions be allocated in accordance with the ownership percentage while some entities allow the owners the flexibility to choose (within limits) how the income, losses, and distributions from the entity will be allocated amongst the owners.

One goal of allocating income not in proportion with ownership percentage is to redirect income (for federal income tax purposes) from one owner to another. There could be many reasons for redirecting income from one owner to another:

1. Some owners may have lower effective tax rates than others;

2. Some owners may be tax exempt;

3. Some owners may have net operating losses (or other tax attributes) that are about to expire and which would reduce any income allocated to them; and/or

4. Some owners may want to redirect income to a younger generation family member as part of an estate plan.

Tax Consequences of Distributions

Some entities are required to treat the distribution of appreciated property (property that has increased in value) as a taxable sale for tax purposes, whereas other entities may treat the distribution of appreciated property as a non-taxable distribution. Further, a distribution may be taxed as income to the distributee or treated as a return of capital depending on the type of entity making the distribution.

Social Security and Self-Employment Tax

Each employer has the responsibility to pay for a portion of the Social Security taxes of every employee of the employer. However, a *self-employed* taxpayer in effect pays for both the employer's portion and the employee's portion (because they are treated as both employer and employee).

Social Security taxes are paid on all income below $113,700, while Medicare taxes are paid on all income. During the economic crisis experienced at the end of the recent decade, there was a temporary reduction of the percentage for Social Security taxes withheld during 2011 and 2012 where employees paid a Social Security tax rate of 4.2 percent, while employers paid 6.2 percent. In 2013, the original tax rate was reinstated for employees. Therefore, in 2013, employees paid a rate of 6.2 percent for Social Security taxes and 1.45 percent for Medicare taxes, and the employer also paid the same rate as employees.

> If you switch jobs within a year, you could overpay your Social Security contribution for the year and need to file for a refund of the overpaid amount.

On the other hand, self-employed individuals pay a Social Security tax rate of 12.4 percent, and Medicare taxes of 2.9 percent. The Social Security ceiling has been increased over the years as the Baby Boomers began to retire ($97,500 in 2007; $102,000 in 2008; $106,000 in 2009-2011; $110,000 in 2012; and $113,700 in 2013).

In 2014, Social Security taxes are required on all income below $117,000. However, the Social Security and Medicare tax rates remain unchanged. It's wise to stay abreast of both the percent of withholding and the maximum amount that can be withheld. If you switch jobs within a year, you could overpay your Social Security contribution for the year and need to file for a refund of the amount.

Passive Activity Rules

The *Passive Activity Rules* of Section 469 of the tax code are very complex, but in general, they defer the use of net losses (until disposition) for activities in which the taxpayer did not materially participate: meaning activities which are more like investments than operating businesses. For example, if you invested in a partnership that had large losses due to depreciation of assets (assets that lost value), those losses would likely be subject to the passive activity loss rules because you were not materially participating in the business.

If, on the other hand, you operated a business, any loss as a result of depreciation would not be subject to the passive loss rules because you were actively involved in the business. The choice of entity can affect the application of the passive activity loss rules.

The Art of the Business Entity: The Different Types

There are a myriad of other, more specialized business entities, but these seven are the most common choices that businesses take:

1. Sole Proprietorship (SP)

A *Sole Proprietorship* (SP) is a business conducted in one owner's separate capacity and does not require the creation of a separate entity. If you choose to act as a sole proprietor, you are deemed to own each asset directly, even though it is used for business purposes. All income earned is deemed to be earned by you, the owner. As such there is no separate entity income tax form to file and there is no distribution. The income from a Sole Proprietorship will generally be reported on Schedule C of your income tax return (Form 1040).

Allocation and Distribution of Income. All income earned is deemed to be earned directly by you. As a result, there is no ability to allocate, or redirect income.

Social Security and Unemployment Tax. Income earned through a *Sole Proprietorship* is subject to self-employment tax—meaning you pay the full amount of the 15.3 percent on all income after expenses are reported on your Schedule C.

Passive Activity Loss Rules. The Passive Activity Rules apply to all individuals. A Sole Proprietorship is generally an operating business and generates active income or loss, and not passive income or loss, and thus is not subject to the Passive Activity Loss Rules. An individual, however, may have passive losses from other investments that cannot offset active gains generated by the Sole Proprietorship.

2. General Partnership (GP)

A *General Partnership* (GP) is the association of two or more persons (which for this purpose can include entities and individuals— called partners) who carry on an activity for the purpose of making a profit. In general, there are no restrictions on either the number or types of partners, and a partner may be a foreign person, trust, estate, or S Corporation. A GP is managed by all the partners in accordance with their ownership interest although a GP may elect certain managing partners if desired.

Like all partnerships, a GP is a flow-through entity for tax purposes. It files a separate tax return, but does not pay any tax. If you are a partner, the tax flows-through to you and the other partners, and is reported directly on each partner's personal income tax return. A GP does not provide limited liability to any partner.

Allocation and Distribution of Income. The owners of a partnership may allocate distributions and income (and items of loss) in any manner they determine, and not in accordance with ownership percentages, provided the allocations have *substantial economic effect*.

"Simple" is not what a substantial economic effect is. It's a very complicated term, but in general, it means that the allocations chosen by the partners for tax purposes must comply with economic consequences of the allocations. For example, if one partner is allocated all of the partnership losses for tax purposes, the amount of partnership assets that partner would receive upon dissolution must be reduced by the amount of losses taken, in order for the allocation to have substantial economic effect.

Distributions. Distributions of *property* are not treated as taxable sales by the GP. By definition, a partnership is a flow-through entity. Therefore, each partner recognizes their distributive share of income as if earned directly by the partner, regardless of whether a distribution is actually made. As a result, a distribution from the GP to a partner is generally not a taxable event. The partner will take a basis (starting value) in the property received equal to the GP's basis in the property.

Social Security and Unemployment Tax. A partner's share of distributive *income* from a GP is subject to self-employment taxes which includes income, social security, and in some cases, unemployment tax.

Passive Activity Loss Rules. A partner's share of distributive income from a GP is treated as if it was earned directly by the partner. The passive activity rules apply to this income in the same manner as any other income earned by the partner.

3. Limited Partnerships (LP)

A *Limited Partnership* is a partnership organized under a specific provision of state law, which has at least one *general partner* and one or more *limited partners*. In general, under state statute, the LPs cannot actively conduct the business of the partnership. The GP(s) remains liable for the debts of the partnership. The limited partner's liability for partnership debts is limited to the capital contributed by that limited partner. If you contributed/invested $10,000 to a LP, your liability/risk is limited to $10,000. Thus, some of the partners, i.e., the LPs are afforded the benefit of limited liability, which exposes the GP(s) to greater liability. Because an LP has no restriction on partners, the GP may be an entity with limited liability such as a C Corporation. Like all partnerships, an LP is a flow-through entity.

Allocation and Distribution of Income. The GP(s) of a limited partnership may allocate distributions and income (and items of loss) in any manner they determine, and not in accordance with ownership percentages, provided the allocations have *substantial economic effect*.

Distributions. Distributions of *property* are not treated as taxable sales by the GP. By definition, a partnership is a flow-through entity. Therefore, each partner recognizes their distributive share of income as if earned directly by the partner, regardless of whether a distribution is actually made. As a result, a distribution from the GP to any partner is generally not a taxable event. The limited partner will take a basis (starting value) in the property received equal to the GP's basis in the property.

Social Security and Unemployment Tax. Income earned by a GP in a LP is subject to self-employment tax; however, a limited partner's share of distributive income is not subject to self-employment tax because a limited partner's distributive share of income would not be related to employment activities.

Passive Activity Rules. A LP is deemed to not materially participate in the partnership (because of the restriction on actively conducting the business) and may be subject to the passive activity loss restrictions.

4. Limited Liability Partnership (LLP)

Similar to a LP, a *Limited Liability Partnership* (LLP) is different from a LP. In a LLP, the limited partners may actively conduct the partnership's business under state law. Because of that, the limited partners are afforded only modified limited liability. If you are a limited partner in a LLP, you are not liable for any debts of the entity caused by the wrongful acts of other partners. Each limited partner is personally liable for the debts of the partnership caused by his or her own wrongful acts. A LLP is a flow-through entity.

Allocation and Distribution of Income. The GPs of a LLP may allocate distributions and income (and items of loss) in any manner they determine, and not in accordance with ownership percentages, provided the allocations have *substantial economic effect.*

Distributions. Distributions of *property* are not treated as taxable sales by the GP. By definition, a partnership is a flow-through entity. Therefore, each partner recognizes their distributive share of income as if earned directly by the partner, regardless of whether a distribution is actually made. As a result, a distribution from the GP to any partner is generally not a taxable event. The limited partner will take a basis (starting value) in the property received equal to the GP's basis in the property.

Social Security and Self-Employment Tax. A limited partner in a LLP may actively participate. The distributive share of partnership income to the limited liability partner may be subject to self-employment tax.

Passive Activity Rules. There has been much controversy in the application of the passive activity rules by the IRS in relation to LLPs. The IRS will generally treat LLPs similarly to LPs. In the cases of *Garnett v. Commissioner, 132 TC No. 19 (2009)* and *Thompson v. United States, 2009-2 USTC ¶50,501 (2009)),* the courts determined that LLPs should be treated similarly to general partners when applying the passive activity rules.

5. Regular C Corporation (C Corp)

A *C Corporation* (C Corp) is organized as a separate entity under state law and is taxed as a separate entity. Because it is a separate entity (not a flow-through entity), a C Corporation is subject to double taxation. One feature of a C Corporation is that it may be operated by a Board of Directors, who is elected by the owners (shareholders) but, who need not be owners/shareholders of the corporation. A shareholder has no power to speak for the corporation merely by being a shareholder. Also, shareholders of a C Corporation have limited liability.

Allocation and Distribution of Income. A C Corporation must distribute assets based on the shares of stock held by the shareholder. There is no ability to allocate income or distributions among the same class of stockholders. However, a C Corporation may issue different classes of stock. Different classes of stock may be entitled to different levels of distributions. Therefore, there is some ability to allocate income and distributions between different classes of stockholders.

Distributions. Distributions received by an owner/shareholder of a C Corporation are taxed either as dividends or as a return of capital depending on the C Corporation's prior earnings. Dividends are often treated as Qualified Dividends which are currently subject to a maximum rate of taxation of 20 percent. Distributions of appreciated property are treated as taxable sales and gain is recognized at the entity level. If services are provided by a shareholder to the C Corporation, and no salary is reported, the IRS could re-characterize the distribution as salary. Also, if the corporation reports an unreasonable amount of salary paid to a shareholder, the salary may be re-characterized as a distribution.

Social Security and Unemployment Tax. Distributions from a C Corporation are not subject to self-employment tax.

Passive Activity Rules. A C Corporation is generally not subject to the passive activity loss limitations. Certain types of C Corporations, such as personal service corporations (engaged in the practice of personal services such as law, medicine, accounting, actuarial services, architecture, etc.) and closely held corporations (corporations in which five or fewer people own 50 percent or more of the corporation) generally are subject to the passive activity rules.

6. S Corporation (S Corp)

An *S Corporation* (S Corp) is a corporation that meets certain requirements (listed below) that make it eligible to elect "S" status according to Subchapter S of Chapter 1 of the Internal Revenue Code. The effect of S status is that the S Corporation is essentially a flow-through entity and not subject to double taxation. In order to be eligible to elect "S" status, the corporation must:

1. Be a domestic corporation;

2. Have less than 100 shareholders;

3. Not have any shareholders who are not individuals (although certain trusts such as grantor trusts may qualify as shareholders);

4. Not have any non-resident alien shareholders;

5. Have only one class of stock;

6. Not be an ineligible corporation (a certain type of business, such as an insurance company, that is prohibited from making the "S" election).

S Corporation shareholders enjoy limited liability, and as mentioned above, an S Corporation is a flow-through entity for tax purposes.

Allocation and Distribution of Income. An S Corporation is permitted to have only one class of stock. Accordingly, allocating income among the shareholders other than on the basis of their proportionate ownership interests is not permitted if the S corporation status is to be maintained.

Distributions. The S Corporation is a flow-through entity and like all partnerships, distributions received are generally not taxable events. However, like a C Corporation, and un-like a partnership (flow-through entity), distributions of appreciated property are treated as taxable sales and cause the S Corporation to recognize gain (which flows-through to the individual shareholders).

Social Security and Unemployment Tax. Like a C Corporation, distributions from an S Corporation to a shareholder are not subject to self-employment tax. (And thus losses that pass-through do not reduce self-employment tax.[65]

As a reminder to all shareholders, the IRS has the ability to re-characterize distributions as salary. For example, let's say you actively participate in S Corporation operations (valued at $50,000 which could be attributed to your skill and the work you provided to the corporation) and receive $100,000 of distributions during the year and no salary. The IRS could re-characterize your *distribution* by reducing the distribution to $50,000, and reclassify the other $50,000 as *salary*. In addition, the salary could be subject to self-employment tax.

Passive Activity Rules. The shareholders in an S Corporation may be subject to the *Passive Activity Loss Rules* at the shareholder level. Make sure you get accounting and/or legal advice so that you don't run afoul of the Passive Activity Loss Rules.

7. Limited Liability Company (LLC)[66]

A *Limited Liability Company* (LLC) is an entity defined under state law which generally provides limited liability to all of its owners in the same way a corporation does.

Because LLCs are defined under state law, each state may have its own unique set of additional requirements for qualifying as a LLC. As per the *check the box* regulations, discussed below, a LLC may elect to be taxed as a corporation (double taxation) or as a flow-through entity for tax purposes (no double taxation).

Because flow-through taxation is generally desired, the vast majority of LLCs elect flow-through status and it is assumed herein that a LLC is a flow-through entity unless specifically noted. Unlike an S Corporation, an LLC usually has no restrictions on the number or types of allowable owners and a LLC may also have only one member (called a *Single*

Member LLC). The owners of an LLC are usually referred to as *Members* or *Partners*.

Allocation and Distribution of Income. The partners of a LLC may allocate distributions and income (and items of loss) in any manner they determine, and not in accordance with ownership percentages, provided the allocations have *substantial economic effect.*

Distributions. Distributions of *property* are not treated as taxable sales by the GP. Most LLCs are a flow-through entity. Therefore, each partner recognizes their distributive share of income as if earned directly by the partner, regardless of whether a distribution is actually made. As a result, a distribution from the GP to any partner is generally not a taxable event. The limited partner will take a basis (starting value) in the property received equal to the GP's basis in the property.

Social Security and Unemployment Tax. Whether a partner/member's distributive share of a LLC's income is treated as self-employment income is not entirely determined. In general, the characterization will depend on the partner/member's level of activity in the LLC. If the partner/member actively participates in running the LLC or is personally liable for the LLC's debts, then it is likely that partner/member's income will be self-employment income.

If the partner/member acts more like a limited partner and does not participate in running the LLC, then it is likely that partner/member's income will not be self-employment income.

A Single Member LLC is taxed as a Sole Proprietorship and the single member will be treated like a GP and all net income will be self-employment income.

Note: If the LLC elects to be taxed as a corporation, then, like a C Corporation, distributions will not be subject to self-employment tax, even if the LLC is a true single member LLC.

Passive Activity Rules. The LLC is subject to the same rules as a GP, assuming the LLC elects to be taxed as a partnership. *Note:* An LLC electing to be taxed as a corporation will be subject to the same rules as a C Corporation.

Check-the-Box

Whatever form of business you elect to operate in, you will *check-the-box* on your tax return. Make sure that you mark the appropriate one. Any business that is incorporated by filing papers with the Secretary of State (of a State) must be taxed as a corporation. There are also certain types of businesses (such as an insurance company and certain foreign entities) that are automatically taxed as a corporation.

In general, any other unincorporated business, may choose which taxation scheme (*double taxation* or *flow-through*) is desired. Because the vast majority of entities would prefer flow-through, if no choice is made, the default position is flow-through. An entity that would like to be taxed as a C Corporation (double taxation) may elect to flow-through as well.

If you elect one type of entity, are you stuck with it forever? No. "Entities" may change a status from one entity to another by filing the appropriate forms with the Secretary of State of the state in which the business was established, and in some instances, the Internal Revenue Service. Within your state, there may be a nominal fee to reclassify it—it's easily done online in most cases.

Once an entity changes its status (other than its initial election), it generally may not change again for 60 months unless you meet the exceptions including if there is a change in ownership. Again, this is a situation where the wise business owner gets professional advice and files all forms that are necessary with the change.

In general, limited liability and flow-through taxation are desired and are the most important factors in choosing an entity form in which to hold a business. As a result, the LLC is currently the most popular form of entity chosen for qualifying businesses. The S Corporation also provides both limited liability and flow-through taxation. A S Corporation, generally has many more restrictions on ownership, and is less flexible than an LLC.

Do You Need to Obtain an Employer Identification Number (EIN) for Your Business?

Individuals who own business commonly ask, "Do I need to have a business *Employer Identification Number* (EIN)?" The answer is Yes.

Any Business or Self-employed individual that files any kind of Federal tax return needs to file for and obtain an EIN. This includes truck drivers (Form 2290 Heavy Highway Use Tax), Farmers (944 Agricultural Employee Taxes), any business that employs at least one W-2 wage earner, partnerships, corporations, and any other income taxes not reported on the Form 1040. Small businesses that report their income on a Schedule C and do not have W-2 employees do not have to obtain an EIN, but it is best to consult a tax professional for guidance on whether obtaining an EIN would be beneficial.

> **Real Life Example:** Charlene had a Revenue Officer assigned to her case because she owed payroll taxes for one part-time employee at her daycare center that she operated from her home. The IRS was demanding she make quarterly tax filings, deposits, and pay her debts in full within two years because it was a payroll case. One of our attorneys suggested that the part-time employee at the daycare could be paid as a 1099 employee on a part-time basis. To Charlene's relief, the IRS accepted the change and the client's account was placed in a currently not-collectible status where she was not required to make any monthly payments to the IRS for at least two years.

An EIN is treated much the same as a *Social Security Number* (SSN) or *Individual Taxpayer Identification Number* (ITIN), but is only handled by the business departments at the IRS. It is much more likely for a business to have a Revenue Officer assigned to their account and engage in onsite inspections. If there is a personal tax debt, the IRS closes down businesses every day of the week despite the economy.

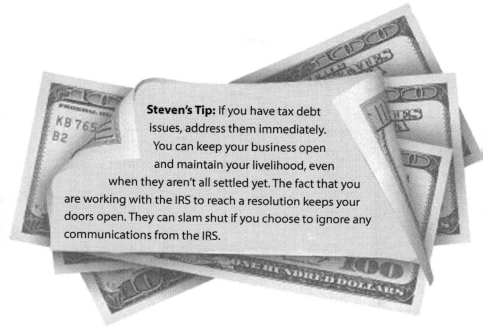

Steven's Tip: If you have tax debt issues, address them immediately. You can keep your business open and maintain your livelihood, even when they aren't all settled yet. The fact that you are working with the IRS to reach a resolution keeps your doors open. They can slam shut if you choose to ignore any communications from the IRS.

Endnotes

[65] CCH PP 48,894

[66] BNA 700-3RD T.M., II-A

Inside this chapter

CHAPTER 16

Making the Call to Resolve My Debt

You owe the IRS money. Maybe just a little; maybe a significant amount. You want to end the cloud over your head and move on. Are there key steps to take to get you on track so you can negotiate effectively with the IRS? Yes, there are; read on. Within are the most common situations that occur between you, the taxpayer, and the IRS when moneys are owed.

What You Need to Do Before the IRS Will Work With You (Compliance)

There are two things you need to do before the IRS will assist you in most cases:

- First, you need to file all required tax returns.

- Second, you need to make sure you are paying sufficient current taxes so that you will not owe again in the future.

This is called *Compliance* by the IRS. It means that you are current with your ongoing tax requirements. The first question to ask yourself before you go forward is:

Have you filed all the Tax Returns you need to?

You need to determine where you are. What tax return years, if any, are missing? Are they just "missing" as in you can't get your hands on them; or are they "missing" meaning that they were never filed? You may need to have them all filed before you first call the IRS. It is important to make the most of it and get all the information you need so that you can meet the deadlines set by IRS. This allows you to be prepared to make further progress on your case on the next call.

> You cannot get a refund for filing tax returns if the tax years are more than three years old.

The IRS will tell you if there are any tax returns you need to file. Normally, it should only ask for you to file missing tax returns for the last six (6) years. Technically, the IRS cannot ask you to file any missing tax returns if you did not have a filing requirement that year. If the IRS records do not show you made sufficient income in a given year, you should not have to file that tax return.

You cannot get a refund for filing tax returns if the tax years are more than three (3) years old. Even if you do not have a filing requirement, it might be a good idea to file more recent tax returns if you think you will get a refund.

Substitute for Returns (SFR) Are Not Your Friend

One terrible thing the IRS will do to taxpayers that do not file their own tax returns is to file the return on the taxpayer's behalf. When the IRS files the return on your behalf, those returns are called *Substitute for Returns* (SFR). It doesn't know what deductions you are entitled to claim, what credits you may have claim to, or if you have additional dependents. What you can expect if the IRS does file a SFR on your behalf, is that it won't be to your benefit.

The IRS usually takes a few years to do this and so the expiration date is usually much later for these tax years, and the tax debts are usually much higher. Don't expect this to be a "friendly" filing. This is because the IRS files in the worst possible way for the taxpayer.

When you call the IRS, you can ask if any tax returns were filed by the IRS as *Substitute for Returns*. Even if you cannot get a tax refund it might be worth it to file original returns for those years to claim the deductions you are entitled to and lower your tax bill. The good news is that once you have filed all your required tax returns, you are half way to being Compliant.

Paying Estimated Tax Payments (ETPs)

Most taxpayers receive a W-2 wage earner and have taxes withheld from each paycheck. Their employer sends the withheld taxes to the IRS for their employees. The IRS requires that everyone who will owe taxes make periodic payments through the year to make sure taxpayers will not owe the IRS at the end of the year. This helps taxpayers from owing a large sum when they file their tax returns the following year. It is too difficult for the IRS to make sure all individual taxpayers pay throughout the year.

In order to resolve your tax debt, you may have to provide proof that you are paying enough current taxes so you will not owe again at the end of the current tax year. You do that either by demonstrating withholding through your paychecks or copies of quarterly payments you are making.

Determining if a W-2 Wage Earner has Sufficient Withholdings

Even if you are a W-2 wage earner, meaning that your employer deducts taxes from your income, you might not have enough taxes withheld from your paycheck to make sure you do not owe taxes at the end of the year. The IRS might insist that you change the number of exemptions you claim on your W-4 to increase your withholding with your employer before agreeing to setup a resolution for your tax debt.

If you do not, the IRS can also send a *Lock-in Letter* that locks in the number of exemptions or deductions to zero. This will increase the taxes withheld from each paycheck but it will most likely ensure that you will not owe the IRS at the end of the tax year.

On the flip side, it is possible you will overpay your current taxes and the IRS will most likely keep any tax refunds until your back taxes are paid in full.

Determining if You Are a 1099 Independent Contractor

The easiest way to tell if you are a W-2 wage earner or a 1099/self-employed independent contractor is if your employer withholds Federal Income taxes, Social Security taxes, and Medicare taxes. If your employer does not withhold these taxes from your wages then you are likely classified as a 1099 independent contractor and will receive a Form 1099 from your employer instead of a W-2 to prepare your tax return at the end of the year.

Most 1099 independent contractors do not have any tax withholding from their earnings which is why many 1099 independent contractors end up owing taxes at the end of the year. A 1099 independent contractor should discuss his/her taxes with a tax professional in order to ensure that they pay adequate Estimate Tax Payments (ETPs) as required. It is recommended that you either pay taxes throughout the year in the form of tax deposits, or deposit the same funds into a bank account set aside for that purpose, so that if you owe taxes at the end of the year, the funds to pay the taxes owed will be readily available.

If you are a 1099 independent contractor and owe taxes for multiple years, the IRS will frequently require you to make quarterly *Estimated Tax Deposits* to the IRS in order to not owe in future tax years.

The IRS can also require a 1099 independent contractor to make multiple tax deposits to demonstrate that he or she is dedicated to not owing past taxes again. As quarterly payments are only due every three months, it might take six to nine months for you to show the IRS you will stay up-to-date on the current year tax deposits. This is a common reason why a taxpayer might have to wait to setup a resolution. It might also prevent the release of wage garnishments and bank levies for months.

Tax Obligations for Business Income

Most business income/profit is subjected to two levels of taxation, at the business level and again after income has been distributed to the owners, or shareholders, etc. In the same manner as a 1099 independent contractor, a business needs to make Estimated *Tax Payments* or *Deposits* to avoid owing taxes at the end of the tax year. The IRS is a lot more likely to demand regular quarterly (or more frequent) payments to assure the IRS the business will not owe taxes in the current tax year or in the future.

Similar to a 1099 independent contractor, the IRS will commonly require businesses to show that they are committed to not owing the IRS by making regular quarterly payments for at least two, but usually three quarters. If a business or individual has not been making payments, it might take six to nine months to show the IRS that they are willing to stay compliant and not owe the IRS again.

Note: This requirement can prevent a resolution for a business until it is too late, causing the business to shut down due to garnishments on business income, clients, and levies on bank accounts.

Determining Who is Required to Pay Payroll Taxes

Payroll Taxes are the taxes that are withheld from the checks of W-2 wage earners by an employer. The employer is required by law to submit the amounts withheld from their employees' paycheck: and the employer's portion of Social Security and Medicare taxes. The IRS does not see or does not treat these taxes as taxes on a business, but on the employees. All businesses have a fiduciary duty to pay their employees' taxes to the IRS.

As a result, when a business falls behind on payroll taxes, the IRS treats the business like it stole from its employees. As a result, the IRS will typically only give businesses one opportunity to get current on past due payroll taxes. That means a business may only have one opportunity to set up an *Installment Agreement*. If it defaults because the business owes payroll taxes again, the business normally has three choices:

1. pay the tax debt in full;

2. file for bankruptcy; or

3. go out of business.

It is possible to obtain a second chance for a business, but it is very difficult.

Real Life Story: Elmer contacted my firm when the assigned IRS Revenue Officer had seized $140,000 from his business bank accounts. The business needed some of those funds to stay open, and needed the garnishments released on its clients and vendors. I jumped in the middle of the case and got about $70,000 immediately released. It took another six months of fighting the IRS and an appeal to the regional supervisor to get a second Installment Agreement put in place, and a second chance for his business.

The IRS normally will not place a business in a *Currently Not Collectible* status or consider an *Offer in Compromise* while the business is still in operation. Normally, a business will only have up to two years to pay the debt in full on an *Installment Agreement*.

If a business can terminate their ongoing payroll tax liability, or stop having W-2 employees, their case will be treated like any other case. Warning: a business needs to be careful not to classify employees that should be W-2 employees as 1099 independent contractors as the IRS can contest and reverse misclassifications of employees.

What to Do If You Are Levied or Garnished by the IRS

If your bank accounts have been levied, or your *wages garnished*, or your business accounts levied, you need to move quickly. The quicker you set up a resolution on your account, the sooner you will stop incurring a high punitive interest rate while your account is in a collection

> Once a bank receives a *Notice of Levy*, all funds held by the bank for accounts connected to the SSN or ITIN at the time the levy is received by the bank will be frozen.

status, and the sooner you will be able to release the *Bank Levy* or *Garnishment*.

What to do When a Bank Account is Levied

The IRS will use your SSN or ITIN to find your bank accounts. All banks have to report the SSNs or ITINs that are used to open accounts to the IRS. Once the IRS has sent three *Notice of Intent to Levy* letters, they can start collection activity. Normally only one letter can be sent every 30 days. Once a bank receives a *Notice of Levy*, all funds held by the bank for accounts connected to the SSN or ITIN at the time the levy is received by the bank will be frozen.

If your bank account receives a deposit after the levy has been received by his/her bank, the later deposit should not be frozen too, but banks tend to be cautious and sometimes freeze funds they should not.

Do I have 21 days to respond?

A taxpayer only has 21 days from the date the bank received the levy to get the IRS to issue a *release of levy* to the bank. After 21 days, the bank will send the seized funds to the IRS. At that point, it is very difficult to get any funds returned. To get seized funds returned, you would have to show the funds in the account did not legally belong to you, or a liable spouse.

How could this happen? Easily. If you were placed as a second authorized user for someone else's account that is not liable for the tax debt. Remember, the IRS is using a SSN and an ITIN to seek and attach bank accounts. If yours show up on an account with someone else, it can create a sticky problem.

The Heightened Hardship Standard

Normally, you would have to show that your expenses exceed your income, or set up an *Installment Agreement* to get a *Wage Garnishment* released, or other collection activity. As a bank levy is a one-time event, to release a bank levy before the 21 days has passed, the IRS requires proof that the bank levy itself places you in an *extreme hardship*.

Examples of qualifying situations are missed mortgage payments, rent payments, car payments, overdue utility bills, or other vital bills that you need to pay or suffer undue hardship. The IRS will normally release just the amount you need to pay the bills you are behind on which is called a *partial release* if the bills do not add up to more than the amount seized.

Real Life Story: Frederica had a Jaguar automobile and a business. She also had about $20,000 levied in her bank accounts. It was hard to argue that someone driving a Jaguar was in a "financial hardship." Through some creative arguments and proof the client was behind on important bills, my firm was able to release $7,000. I was worried it would not be enough, but it was what the client needed to pay her bills and she was very grateful.

Lastly, it is important to get the fax number for the *bank's levy department* so that once the IRS agrees to release all or part of the funds seized, they can fax a release directly to the correct department at the bank. Otherwise, the IRS will mail the release, which might not get to the bank before the 21 days pass and the funds are sent to the IRS anyway.

Note: It is better to prevent bank levies before they hit by moving quickly to resolve your case.

Wage Garnishments ... What They Are and What To Do

Wage Garnishments can be more painful than bank levies. Normally, they continue to take a portion of your paycheck until the debt is paid in full, a resolution is arranged, or the debt is satisfied in some other manner. A wage garnishment is a deduction of a certain amount from your paycheck each pay period based on the *IRS Levy Exemption Table* (*See* Appendix G for IRS Levy Exemption Chart).

Avoiding Wage Garnishments

Ignoring any communications from the IRS is not a smart thing to do. The best way to deal with *Wage Garnishments* is to avoid them in the first place by responding to the three *Notice of Intent to Levy* letters the IRS will send every 30 days before they start seizing your assets. Responding with professional help is recommended.

Setting up a resolution with the IRS will prevent further collection activity as long as you maintain their *Compliance* and payments when required.

What Employers do When a Notice of Garnishment is Received

If your wages are garnished, your employer will receive a *Notice of Levy* from the IRS. You must respond to your Payroll department immediately. Why? Because if you don't, the number of withholding allowances (exemptions) you claimed prior to the *Notice of Levy* are at risk. As part of a wage garnishment is a request for how many dependents you can claim. If you do not respond, the wage garnishment will go into effect with zero dependents, including none for yourself.

This means you will have more of your wages garnished if you do not respond, meaning even less money to you each pay period. As a taxpayer, you can at least claim yourself.

Do not try to convince your employer not to impose the Wage Garnishment because the employer can become liable for the garnishment and additional penalties if they do not comply with the law. Once a garnishment is in place, the only way to reduce or release it is to set up a resolution for your case.

Releasing a Wage Garnishment

To get your wage garnishment released, you first must be compliant, or close to being compliant, to obtain a resolution. You will also need the fax number for your payroll department so the IRS can fax a *Release of Levy* directly to your employer's payroll department. Once a resolution is negotiated, you will need to request that the IRS agent send the fax, which is normally done within 24 hours. If you do not provide a fax number, then the IRS will mail the release of levy to your employer which may take 10 to 14 days before it is received by your employer.

Tax Liens ... the What and the How

A *Tax Lien* is a notice to other creditors that the IRS has a certain priority to any assets you might have, normally real estate, and may also attach to your credit. They are filed with your local County Recorder's office. Usually within 30 days, they are reported to the credit bureaus (Experian, TransUnion and Equifax) as well. The IRS does not file tax liens for every tax debt, and depending on the resolution, might not file a tax lien at all.

Releasing Tax Liens

The easiest way to release a Tax Lien is to pay off the tax debt in full. Make sure you keep copies of the notice that states the tax lien has been released—you may need this to prove to a lender it is no longer valid.

You can also file a *Collection Due Process (CDP) Hearing* request in order to contest the filing of the tax lien. However, as long as you owe the tax debt, a CDP is usually not a successful way to release a tax lien.

A successful *Offer in Compromise* will also release the tax lien after the program is completed. If you arrange a *Streamlined Installment Agreement* to pay your taxes in full within six years, the IRS might not file a tax lien even though you owe the IRS. Lastly, once a tax debt expires, you can request that the tax lien be removed.

Tax Liens Affect Your Credit

A tax lien shows up on a taxpayer's credit report just like any other unpaid or delinquent debt. The tax lien will continue to show on a credit report until the debt is resolved or the tax debt expires. Make sure you follow up with the major credit bureaus (Experian, TransUnion, and Equifax) to ensure that the tax lien has been removed. If it hasn't, notify the reporting bureau that the lien has been removed. Annually, you can get a free copy of your credit report without a charge. Take advantage of this. A good source to start is at*AnnualCreditReport.com.*

The IRS Seizure of your Assets

One of the fears of many when they get into tax trouble is the fear of seizure: will the IRS swoop in and take everything you have? To answer a frequently asked question: Can the IRS seize assets?—the answer is: Yes, it can. The reality is that the IRS prefers not to do so. Instead, its strategy is *to threaten* to seize assets in order to force you to sell them before the IRS auctions them off for you ... at whatever they can get in the shortest period of time and regardless of its "true" value.

Seizing assets requires paperwork and legal approval before the IRS can take possession of your property. However, the IRS does seize assets and holds regular auctions to recoup what they can from seized property.

Avoiding Seizure Starts With You

You can have your property seized by the IRS if you ignore their letters, phone calls, and try to hide assets. It is a hassle for the IRS to seize your assets, but if you make your case difficult enough, the IRS agent assigned to your case will return the favor.

The single best way to avoid seizure of property is to stop collection activity by the IRS by setting up a resolution for your IRS tax debt. There are resolutions that will allow you to avoid selling your property and/or seizure by the IRS.

> If you transfer title or sell assets to friends, family, or acquaintances for less than the fair market value, the IRS might treat the sale as a fraud and hold you accountable for the fair market value of the assets.

Liquidating Assets Before Seizure Occurs

If you have an asset that the IRS is trying to seize and you cannot protect your asset through setting up a resolution, it is always better to sell the asset as long as the asset is sold for full value. If this is your strategy, don't wait until the last minute to implement your plan. In almost all sales initiated by you, you will get more for your asset than the IRS will at auction. Those moneys can then be used to reduce your tax debt. When seizure becomes the IRS' option, know that it is less likely to work with you and approve a resolution favorable for you.

Warning: If you transfer title or sell assets to friends, family, or acquaintances for less than the fair market value, the IRS might treat the sale as a fraud and hold you accountable for the fair market value of the asset. The IRS discounts the value of most items for *Quick Sale* by reducing the value of an asset by 80 percent of the fair market value for vehicles, to

50 percent (this percentage may vary) for stocks, bonds, and other investment assets.

You can normally obtain a successful resolution that will satisfy an IRS agent by listing assets with a broker, real estate agent, or third party for sale.

Substituting Assets for Other Uses

You may be wondering if you can use your assets for other uses so the IRS won't take them. The answer is maybe. If you use your assets for the production of income, they can be exempted from seizure or sale by the IRS. The IRS normally will not seize your primary vehicle or home but other vehicles, equipment, or tools can be exempted from seizure if they are actively being used to generate your income for you.

Assets used for necessary living expenses can also be exempted from seizure, but persuasive facts are usually needed for assets aside from a home and vehicle. Assets needed for medical needs can be very persuasive but need to be supported by a good story and proof.

Real Life Story: George started out with $80,000 in his bank account when he first contacted our firm. One of our attorneys had to fight with the IRS to show that he needed the money due to a recent kidney transplant. The IRS agreed to place his account in a Currently Not-Collectible status because the attorney showed the IRS that the client was using the money for his post operational care.

When you contact the IRS, you will be asking for assistance from it. It is important to be very aware that the IRS, like any collection agency, will be doing their best to collect information from you to take collection activity against you during your call. They will ask for bank information, your employment information, who lives in your home, and other sensitive information that the IRS can use to seize your assets and collect on the tax debt.

The IRS will also try to set deadlines for you to take action to address any problems with your tax debt. For example, if you need to file your 1040 income taxes for 2011, the IRS will normally give you a deadline of 14 to 30 days to file that tax return. If you do not meet that deadline and contact the IRS again to inform them that you have met the deadline, the IRS computers will show that you have missed a deadline. It can take the next step toward taking collection activity.

This may only be a letter, but it can also be a bank levy. Regardless, once you start making contact with the IRS, it is very important to follow through until your tax matter is resolved. Don't miss a deadline. Anytime you communicate with the IRS over the phone or at an IRS office, make sure you document the time, place, who you spoke with, their IRS employee # (you will get it as soon as you start talking with someone on the phone), and the content of the communication.

Steven's Tip:
Document, document, document.

Inside this chapter

CHAPTER 17

Will the IRS Shut Down Your Business?

The previous chapter looked at the elements of resolving your debt to bring you into compliance. For a business owner, dealing with the IRS takes your time—time that could be critical in a business that could be on shaky ground. With that said, it is rare that the IRS actually comes and places a lock on the front door of a business, but it can happen.

Businesses usually go out of business for three main reasons:

1. There is a decline in business activity;

2. Moneys are low due to bank levies and garnishments of business partners, vendors, clients, etc.;

3. The owner decides to close the business up—age and health are the most common reasons.

> If you have a business in trouble and the IRS is breathing down your neck, you need a professional handling your case. Now, not later!

Looking at the first two, business cases with high balances usually have an IRS

Revenue Officer (RO) assigned. Once a Revenue Officer starts taking collection action, strong intervention is usually needed to allow the business to get back on track and to set up a Resolution.

Preventing the IRS from Closing Your Business

You can prevent the IRS from closing your business. To save your livelihood, swift action needs to take place. Over my career, I have released millions of dollars that were seized by bank levies by the IRS. What is clear, especially at this level, if you have a business in trouble and the IRS is breathing down your neck, you need a professional handling your case. Now, not later. Hiring one will buy your business a little time. But, and it is a significant "but," the clock is against a business, especially one with payroll tax debts.

To save your business, it is extremely important to get *compliant* as soon as possible and work to set up a resolution. Once your clients grasp that your business is having all of its income taken by the IRS, they will go elsewhere. They know that you are in trouble.

How do they find out? A variety of ways—from other customers talking about you; from what appears to be an interruption in your business (employees let go, hours reduced, you are not unavailable, etc.). They may also discover the news about the business owing the IRS through public records.

When the IRS files a lien against a business, a copy is filed with the county and is a public record. Depending on the popularity of your business, the media may also publicize the company's tax problems with the IRS. If you provide a product or service, clients may leave because they have no assurance that their orders will be completed. Moneys they pay in advance to your business will be diverted to the IRS instead.

Then there are the accounts receivable. They will often go unpaid as your clients will expect the business to close shortly, so why pay a doomed business! Once your bank accounts are seized, merchant services garnished, and vendors and account receivables garnished, you will not be able to keep your business running. That is why the IRS normally does not have to place locks on doors. The collection activity kills businesses more efficiently, a type of tool that is "invisible to the naked eye" but very effective indeed.

Over the years, I have saved businesses in these types of situations, but many businesses do not make it when they procrastinate and put off dealing with their IRS back taxes. Getting on top of the situation quickly and with professional help is the best way to get your business out of a collection status and stop levies and enforcement.

Payroll Employees and Liabilities

Even if your business has Payroll Liabilities, if *your business ceases* to have W-2 wage earners/payroll employees, the concern that you will continue to owe payroll liabilities *stops*. Doing so resolves a lot of compliance issues. Your business can then qualify for a Currently Not Collectible or an Offer.

There are some ways to legitimately stop having payroll issues, but if your employees really are W-2 employees then it will not help your business to try to change the characterization of your employees. Your assigned Revenue Officer might even over-rule your attempt to change how you classify employees if done incorrectly.

Differences Between 1099 Independent Contractor and W-2 Employees

The test for who qualifies as a 1099 versus a W-2 employee is a fact driven analysis that has some gray area. Some of that has already been covered in a previous chapter. If your business is the type of business that has a few employees, as in one or two, that might qualify as 1099 independent contractor, it might be in the best interest of your business to change its classification provided it meets the requirements of a 1099 independent contractor (see previous section on misclassification of employees).

> **Real Life Story:** Howard owed just under a $100,000 to the IRS in payroll taxes. He had a Revenue Officer assigned that was looking to close down his business. Howard worked full time at another job and his business was a side project with one employee who pretty much ran the business and was very independent. Ironically, Howard's employee had asked to be paid as a W-2 wage earner so he wouldn't have tax withholding problems at the end of the year and it was his boss who was up to his eyes in tax problems instead.
>
> Because his employee was so independent, working without the guidance of Howard, the IRS approved reclassifying him as a 1099 independent contractor. The result was that all the tax debt was then frozen in a *Currently Not Collectible* status for two years. Howard could breathe and got counseling on how to document his new status as a 1099 worker and how to pay his taxes when due since he was now "self-employed" and responsible for paying any taxes due.

Can the IRS force you to have W-2 employees?

If you have multiple employees that do not function like Independent Contractors, do not try to classify them as such. If your business is in trouble, your Revenue Officer will likely review any changes in characterization. A mischaracterization will only cause your business more trouble. If you are unsure about how to classify your employees, you should consult a Tax or Employment Attorney for advice.

If You are in Trouble, is Bankruptcy an Option?

Filing for Bankruptcy protection is usually the last effort of a business to stay in operation. Filing for Bankruptcy will do the following for the business:

1. Stop all IRS collection activity after the date the Bankruptcy petition is filed; and

2. Release garnishments on merchant services, new account receivables, clients, etc.

In other words, you can breathe. But it's temporary. There are strings attached and a few are pitfalls in filing for Bankruptcy protection as well. They include:

1. A Bankruptcy trustee will try to take whatever assets she can to satisfy your business' creditors;

2. Not all tax debt is dischargeable in Bankruptcy; and

3. Most payroll tax debt is not dischargeable.

If your business survives a bankruptcy, it will have a chance to setup a payment plan in your Bankruptcy proceedings to address any *un-dischargeable debt*.

Steven's Tip: If you are considering Bankruptcy protection, consult a Bankruptcy professional. This is advisable sooner versus later. For businesses, make sure you work with someone who is well-versed in business bankruptcies.

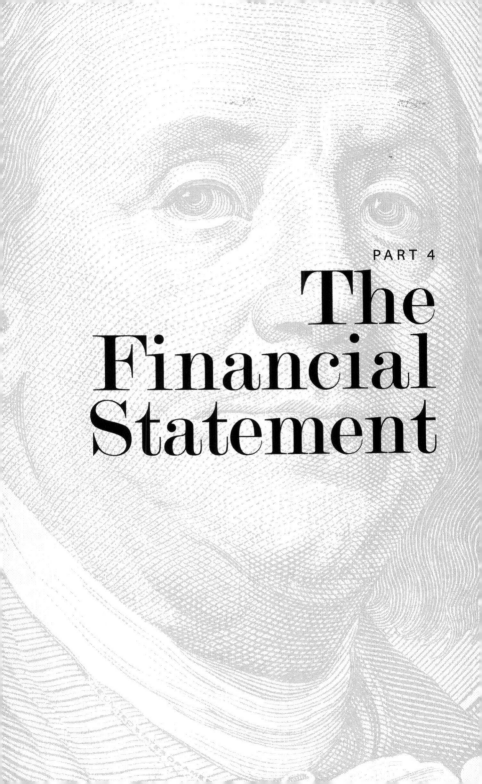

PART 4

The Financial Statement

Inside this chapter

CHAPTER 18

Yours and Ours ... Assets and the IRS

One of the biggest questions you may have is: *Will the IRS seize my assets?*

Let's start by defining what assets are. They include vehicles, homes, financial instruments, or any item of value you can legally access. So, yes, the IRS can seize your assets if you don't pay your tax obligations. But, just as the IRS can also send you to jail, they will only do so for extreme cases.

In the end, the IRS does not want you in jail where you will cost more in taxpayer money than they will get from you. In the same manner, seizing assets is usually time consuming difficult and the IRS will normally sell seized assets at an auction for a fraction of their true value.

The IRS normally seizes assets when a taxpayer has no immediate need for the asset.

Examples of this are boats (unless you live on one), RVs, quads, and other recreational vehicles. Time shares normally cannot be auctioned off as they often have little to no fair market value. The IRS also will only do forced seizures of property when a taxpayer refuses to cooperate with the IRS for an extended period of time.

Real Life Story: Kendra worked in real estate and owned her primary home and a second home in a posh suburban area. She knew that the IRS was demanding she liquidate the property within a few months. Kendra wanted to wait until the market rebounded after the market crashed in 2008. The longer she waited, the more impatient the IRS got and the worse the real estate market became. She decided to ignore her assigned Revenue Officer and the letters she received from her. Whenever the IRS got close to seizing her second house, Kendra would file an appeal, ask for an *Offer in Compromise,* or a *Collection Due Process Hearing.*

Her Revenue Officer got so irritated with Kendra's game playing that she not only went after her second home, but after her business and livelihood as well.

Being difficult with the IRS beyond reason made a bad situation worse for Kendra. To avoid becoming a "Kendra," you need to know what the IRS is requiring in order to obtain a resolution. Ideally, the IRS would like you to write a check for the amount owed and be done with it. Most likely, you aren't in a position to do that, at least, not yet. With that said, what the IRS is looking for is information—information that will start with identifying what your assets are.

The Treasure Trove

Your financial statement is an essential factor in working out any resolution with the IRS. There is a lot of information contained within it that you are required to supply. Within this section, you will find a series of questions that my offices routinely hear throughout the tax resolution process. The information becomes a treasure trove that the IRS uses to make decisions as it works with you.

What information will the IRS request from me?

To setup a resolution with the IRS, there are two main categories of information you will want to review to see what resolution you might be eligible for: *Asset Information* and your *Income and Expenses*.

Assets are ...

Any personal property or real property that you own is an Asset. The IRS treats each asset category a little differently. The *Fair Market Valuation* (FMV) for most assets can be based on commercially accepted and available sources such as *Zillow.com* for real estate and *KBB.com* (Kelly Blue Book website) for vehicles. In most cases, the IRS will normally take a taxpayer's valuation of his or her assets as long as the valuation is reasonable.

Typically, most taxpayers tend to over-estimate the value of their assets. When dealing with the IRS, always give the true estimate of your asset rather than trying to over-estimate the value because it may affect your eligibility for various resolutions.

Is your real estate an asset?

If you are like most taxpayers, real estate will be the most valuable asset you own and the most important. This category includes all kinds of real estate such as a house, land, time-shares, undeveloped lots, rental property, etc.

Will the IRS seize your home?

As I mentioned earlier, the IRS does not like to seize assets unless they have to. In most cases, it will not seize a primary residence, but it can. The IRS is more likely to ask you to mortgage a home that is fully paid for. Alternatively, the IRS can ask you to sell your primary residence if it is too far above normal living standards as defined by the *IRS National Standards* which varies by county and state. The IRS National Standards are predetermined amounts that the IRS determines are the maximum amount a taxpayer may spend on certain expenses that are considered reasonable.

What if you own your home?

If you own your home, the IRS takes an 80 percent Quick Sale Value (QSV) of the FMV of your home to see if you have equity in your home.

> **Example:** Albert owns a home worth $400,000 that carries a mortgage of $320,000. Eighty percent of the FMV of $400,000 is $320,000 (**$400,000 x .8 = $320,000**). While the home has a QSV of $320,000, $320,000 is also owed on the home. As a result, there is no equity in Albert's home (**$320,000 (QSV) -$320,000 (loan) = $0**).

Today, if you are like many homeowners, you will not have substantial equity in your primary residence. If you do, it is usually not difficult to show the IRS that you cannot obtain a loan on the equity in the home due to your personal financial situation; the current higher lending requirements of the financial intuitions also make obtaining a loan more difficult.

If you can access the equity in your home, you can use those funds to pay down your IRS debt or use a resolution option that does not require you to present your asset information to the IRS like a *Streamlined Installment Agreement* (SIA) which allows taxpayers to make monthly payments for six years in order to pay off their tax debt in full and does not require disclosure of your income or assets if you owe less than $25,000. If you owe more than $25,000, but not more than $50,000, you may be required to disclose your income and assets prior to establishing a *Streamlined Installment Agreement*.

Will the IRS seize other properties you own?

The IRS can seize other properties but will only do so if there is substantial equity to justify requiring liquidation of the property. It will prefer that you list your property for sale if required to satisfy your tax debt.

Is your car an asset?

The second most valuable asset for many taxpayers is their vehicle. We are a society where four wheels is the primary, and in some cases, the only mode of transportation. Again the IRS does not like to seize assets, including motor vehicles, but they will, and do, when taxpayers do not cooperate with the IRS to resolve their back tax liabilities.

What if your car is paid off?

If your primary vehicle is paid in full, the IRS will not require that you liquidate it, unless it is a luxury item. The FMV of any vehicle will be added to an Offer amount. It will be the amount you can reasonably expect to obtain if you were to sell the vehicle to a prudent buyer. Having a lot of vehicles, even older vehicles might make a resolution more expensive. Disposing of cars to relatives or signing away title is not a good idea as the IRS will do a title search and see any suspicious recent changes.

Can you buy a new car?

You can buy a new car, especially if you have an older car that is having repair issues. In 2013, the IRS allowed up to $517 per month as a car payment. In 2014, that number will increase. If you are planning to buy a newer vehicle, doing so might actually help your eligibility for a resolution.

Can you own a nice car?

Yes you can, but you have some guidelines. Per the IRS, a taxpayer can own any vehicle desired, but if a taxpayer is asking for a resolution, it does not help if the taxpayer is driving a new Jaguar, Mercedes, BMW or other luxurious vehicles. A reasonable vehicle can be obtained at a monthly payment of $517 per month or less—and a nice one at that! Also, owning a vehicle that has high equity may prevent you from qualifying for an *Offer in Compromise*, something that you don't want to leave off your option plate in dealing with the IRS.

What about extra cars, boats, or RVs?

The IRS will allow expenses for one vehicle per adult listed as the primary and secondary (basically spouses) on the tax return filed with the IRS. It will not allow expenses for a third vehicle for a teenage son, older parents, etc. Normally, the IRS will not have an issue if an extra vehicle is owned, unless the vehicle has a lot of equity (classic vehicle, custom job, etc.). Recreational vehicles, boats, motorcycles, quads, etc., might have to be sold as they are considered as unnecessary assets, unless there is a valid reason that you need these assets besides recreation.

Real Life Story: Darrell was divorced and owned two vehicles. He drove one and his 16-year-old son drove the other. The IRS only gave him credit for one vehicle as his son was a dependent on his tax return, and not a joint filer. Darrell didn't get credit for the other vehicle expense.

Older vehicles, even recreational vehicles that are either non-operational, need work, or have a low FMV are often not an issue due to little or no equity in the vehicles.

Is your bank account an asset?

Most taxpayers have bank accounts. The money available in your bank account is also considered an asset. Many employers commonly deposit employees' wages directly into a bank account. If the IRS levies your bank account (as mentioned in an earlier chapter, it has the capability of knowing where you bank because of the Social Security Number), it can clear out your bank account quickly, even the money you intended to be used to pay bills.

Will the IRS seize the money in your bank account if you tell them about it?

If your account is in the Collections Department at the IRS, it is very possible that the IRS will *levy* your bank accounts if you tell it where you are banking. As noted above, the ability to track you using your Social Security Number (SSN) isn't difficult. The important thing to remember when dealing with the IRS is to get holds placed on your tax account every time you call, or to work very quickly to accomplish what you need to do in order to resolve your case efficiently to get your account out of a collection status.

Telling the IRS about any asset can lead to the IRS seizing your asset if you do not move quickly to resolve your case. However, do not attempt to hide your bank account(s) from the IRS. If asked by the IRS, be truthful about all of your assets, including your bank account(s).

Can you hide your money from the IRS?

Yes, but only for a short time, and it is highly recommended that you do not attempt to hide assets from the IRS. Any bank account requires a SSN to open an account. The IRS can use your SSN to search for your bank accounts, no matter which financial institution you use. Cash assets are the easiest for the IRS to seize if they are discovered. The law prohibits hiding assets from the IRS, and it can make your case more difficult to resolve.

Can you just open new accounts to keep the IRS from finding out about your bank?

You can shuffle funds between banks. With that said, it is one of the easiest ways to annoy the IRS and encourage it to take more collection activity against you. Bank levies can be issued to multiple banks at the same time, which might result in more funds being seized and multiple charges at multiple banks. Banks usually charge a fee each time a bank levy needs to be processed, regardless of the funds in the account.

Is your retirement account an asset?

Outside of a home, retirement accounts are the next largest asset for most taxpayers. You may have one, or several. Included are 401k accounts, pensions, IRA's, accounts using annuities, whole life insurance plans, etc. The kind of retirement plan you have can affect how the IRS treats an asset. If you haven't made a list of places where you have worked in the past that included some type of a profit or pension sharing plan, this is the time to do it.

Will you have to liquidate your retirement?

The IRS will frequently request that you liquidate (cash out) a retirement or savings account if the funds in the account can be readily accessed and pay off your debt. However, it can be argued that the IRS should ignore an asset if it is producing regular income for a taxpayer that is needed to meet the taxpayer's necessities.

If the funds cannot be accessed, the IRS will not require that you liquidate your retirement account, but will require proof that you are prevented from accessing the account.

Example: Jack has a 401k with about $250,000 in the account. The IRS would normally ask him to liquidate the account, but in this case, he is 68 and pays part of his bills by making regular monthly withdrawals of $1,000 to supplement his social security income. Because of this, the IRS did not require Jack to liquidate his 401K.

Is paying into your retirement account an allowable expense?

The answer to this question has good news and not so good news to it. The IRS will allow you to put money towards a 401k or a retirement plan, but normally, will *not allow you a credit* of your monthly deposits as an expense. The IRS will only allow payments toward a retirement plan if it is a mandatory retirement plan that the employee cannot opt out of. Then it's an allowable expense. In other words, it must be *mandated* and required by your employer.

Union members and government workers usually have mandatory retirement plans that employees must contribute to. If you can show the IRS that you are required to contribute to a retirement plan as a condition of your employment, or that you do not have a choice to opt out, the IRS will allow the monthly contribution as an expense. If a taxpayer has a loan on a 401k account, they can get credit for paying the loan off.

What if you cannot access your retirement account?

Even if the IRS requests that a taxpayer liquidate a retirement account or other asset, if you can show that you cannot access those funds or retirement account, the IRS cannot insist you liquidate the asset.

Examples of some accounts the IRS typically cannot access are pension plans, trusts not in your control, or investment accounts that do not allow you to access the funds. To find out if you can access an account, you should read the fine print on the contract or agreement, or call the account manager. Having that information upfront is helpful in any negotiation.

Are investments treated as assets?

When you have investments, the IRS clearly considers them as assets. They are, though, treated differently than your retirement accounts because you can most likely access the funds in your investment accounts. The IRS normally reduces the assessed value of an investment by 20 to 50 percent using a quick sale value. This anticipates transaction costs and/or market fluctuations that can reduce the take home value you might receive when liquidating any investment.

Do you have to sell your investments?

Whether or not you need to actually liquidate/sell your investment depends on whether a good reason can be provided to the IRS as to why the client needs the asset. If the need is for necessary living expenses such as paying a mortgage or for rent, paying for medical expenses or other vital expenses, the IRS can be convinced to leave your asset alone. A college fund for your child is an example of a "non-necessary" expense because of the other options available for paying for your child's education.

How can you protect your assets?

The best way to protect your assets is to establish a resolution with the IRS. The sooner, the better.

However, if you have *substantial assets* (value of assets exceed your tax debt), you should seek a resolution that would not require disclosure of your assets. If you owe less than $50,000, you can set up a *Streamlined Installment Agreement* (SIA) to pay the balance of tax debt in full within six years and you will not be required to disclose your assets.

Even if you owe more than $50,000, you can make a lump sum payment, or multiple payments to get your balance below $50,000. This will allow you to qualify for the Streamlined Installment Agreement. Streamline Installment Agreements that are established for balances below $25,000 do not require disclosure of your income or assets.

Above $25,000, but below $50,000 may require disclosure of your income and assets, but will generally not be affected if you demonstrate an ability to pay the monthly payment amount requested by the IRS.

What about life insurance—is it an asset?

It may be. The two basic types of life insurance are *Whole Life Insurance* and *Term Life Insurance*. One will be treated as an asset, the other as an expense, and may also qualify as an allowable expense. It starts with the differences of a whole life and term insurance policy.

What is the difference between Whole Life and Term Insurance?

Typically, whole life insurance costs a lot more than term life insurance, especially in the early years of the policy. It builds cash value that you can receive at the end of the policy, and normally, you can borrow from the cash value upon request. Whole life will stay in force as long as you keep paying the premiums. The IRS treats these policies just like other retirement accounts because of the cash value that accumulates annually within the policy.

Because the IRS treats whole life insurance policies like other retirement accounts, the IRS does not give taxpayers credit for monthly payments to maintain a whole life policy as an allowable expense. The IRS can, and often does, request that cash values built up as part of a whole life policy be borrowed against or liquidated to reduce a taxpayer's tax debt.

Term life insurance is for a specific period of time and stays in force during the period as long as you pay the premiums. When the period of time is up, so is the insurance coverage. If you were to die before the time expires, your beneficiaries will receive the death benefit amount. If you live and the policy expires, you get nothing—there is no accumulated, unlike the cash value that a whole life policy creates.

You may be thinking, why get the one without the cash? It's a good question. First, it's a lot less in cost in the early years, so a family can purchase more coverage. If the primary breadwinner dies, his or her beneficiaries would have a cash settlement to take care of everyday living needs for a few years. The IRS treats it as a necessity and considers it a wise financial planning tool.

The IRS will allow monthly payments toward a reasonable term life insurance policy as an allowable expense in its financial analysis. A term life insurance policy of two million dollars might be considered too extravagant to qualify as an allowable expense. As there is no cash value in any term life policy, there is no asset value for the IRS to liquidate. For that reason, it is not treated as an asset by the IRS.

Real Life Story: Ward had a whole life insurance policy with MetLife and paid $200 monthly. The vested cash value was $25,000 and his policy allowed him to access the vested cash value. He only owed the IRS $15,000 in back taxes. When Ward reported to the IRS that he could access $25,000 from the whole life insurance, the IRS requested that he pay the entire $15,000 because he had the money to do so. The IRS also disallowed the monthly payment on the whole life insurance because it was not a reasonable and necessary expense.

Ward then hired me—he wanted to retain the full value of his whole life insurance and didn't realize he had other options. I contacted the IRS and negotiated a Streamlined Installment Agreement so he didn't have to disclose his assets, and could continue to make monthly payments rather than liquidating his whole life insurance policy.

Note: When you are unsure about your assets and the impact that they might have on your case, seek the assistance of a professional because disclosing more information than necessary may have dire consequences.

> **Example:** Now in the same example, if Ward's life insurance was a term life insurance policy valued at $25,000 payable upon death, the IRS would not have requested that he attempt to liquidate it—it knows that there is no value to it while he is alive. Also, the monthly payments made by him on it would be allowed by the IRS as an allowable monthly expense.

Are your household furnishings considered assets?

It's always a good idea to define a common term. For household furnishings, think of any item used to furnish your home or needed for personal use (furniture, electronics, and appliances, etc.). The IRS generally accepts the value you report, unless they are articles of great value such as antiques, jewelry, artwork, or collector's items.

Rarely does the IRS ask for the value of household furnishings to establish a *Currently Not Collectible* (CNC) or *Installment Agreement* (IA) unless the value of these items exceeds $10,000. However, when reviewing an Offer in Compromise, the IRS will require a reporting of household furnishings and personal effects if the total value exceeds the levy exemption of $7,900.

The Levy exemptions are updated annually by the IRS. When determining the *Quick Sale Value* (QSV) of an item, it's common to assume that you will receive 80 percent of the value. The following calculation will be used: QSV = FMV x

0.8. For example, if you have a couch that was purchased for $2,000, it would have a QSV of $1,600 ($2,000 x.8 =$1,600).

What do you need to disclose to the IRS?

The items that you should disclose as household furnishings will depend on the type of resolution that you are trying to obtain with the IRS. If under $10,000 in value, you will most likely not be required to disclose the furnishings. If you have items that *exceed* $10,000 in value, you must disclose them to the IRS (that includes antiques, jewelry, art work, or collector's items). The IRS may require that these items be liquidated to either reduce or pay off your tax liability.

When submitting an Offer in Compromise, if the total value of your household furnishings exceeds the levy exception of $7,900, then you would be required to disclose these items to the IRS. If you use any books or tools within your trade or business that are valued over the levy exemption of $3,950, they must also be reported when submitting your Offer in Compromise.

Is the IRS going to inspect your home?

The IRS has the discretion to inspect the assets reported in order to determine whether the values reported are true and accurate. Whether the IRS will utilize its discretion to inspect your assets will be based on the facts and circumstances of your case. In most cases involving a currently not collectible or installment agreement negotiation with the IRS customer service lines, personal inspection is not likely to occur. In cases involving an IRS Revenue Officer, home or business inspections are more common.

When the IRS has reason to believe that the valuation of assets or the information provided has been fabricated, it is likely that your home or business will be personally inspected by a revenue officer. It is important that you remain honest when dealing with the IRS. Providing any false information can have dire consequences.

Real Life Story: Josephine recently purchased a home and bought furniture and other household items in order to enhance the home's decorum. The furniture, appliances, and electronics combined had a QSV of $7,000. However, she also had a Picasso painting that she had inherited from her deceased grandmother with a QSV of $15,000 that she hung over the fireplace. When Josephine submitted her Offer in Compromise, she thought that she would not have to include the painting because she did not purchase the painting.

The IRS had a different opinion. It determined that because the painting was a work of art she owned and valued at an amount over the $7,900 levy exemption, it needed to be included in her Offer. This resulted in an increase of her *Offer in Compromise* by $14,100 (**$7000 + $15,000 − $7,900 = $14,100**). The IRS did not inspect Josephine's home because it was able to obtain the value of the Picasso painting via the internet, and did not suspect that she was hiding other assets.

Do you have other items that may be considered assets? There are other items besides the usual household furnishings that you may be required to disclose to the IRS. Whether an item should be disclosed will depend on the resolution that you are trying to establish with the IRS. If it is an item of value, it is likely an asset. Whether you are required to disclose these assets will depend on the resolution that you are trying to establish with the IRS.

Are trade or business tools considered assets?

Any trade tools or business items that are used as a regular part of your trade or business to produce income are considered assets. These could include vehicles, electronics, tools, equipment, etc.

Whether these items are required to be disclosed will depend on the type of resolution you are seeking and the department within the IRS that has control over your case. Generally, when a business owes less than $10,000 in back taxes, the Business ACS department will have control over your case. When negotiating with Business ACS, your business assets will generally not be required if you intend to establish a Streamlined Installment Agreement. If you request a Currently Not Collectible, then you will be required to disclose your business assets.

When a business owes more than $10,000 in back taxes, an IRS Revenue Officer may be assigned to the case. In this instance, he or she may request a financial statement on the Form 433-B—it requires you to disclose your business assets. Generally, the revenue officer will not seek to liquidate necessary business assets when liquidating such assets would hinder the business from operating, or from producing income.

However, if the revenue officer seeks to shut your business down completely, all assets, whether income producing or not, are fair game. They may be seized and liquidated in order to satisfy your tax debt. Such actions usually will not occur when a business demonstrates viability and an ability to pay the taxes owed if allowed to continue to operate.

Sometimes a business or self-employed individual may submit an Offer in Compromise. In these instances, the business/self-employed individual will be required to disclose the business assets. In determining their value, the IRS will use the QSV formula, (QSV= FMV x 0.8 [80 percent]).

There is also a Business Levy Exemption of $3,950 that applies to the total value of business assets for self-employed individuals. The exemption does not apply to Corporations, and does not apply to business vehicles of self- employed individuals. As a result, business assets of a self-employed individual with a total value of $3,950 or less would be excluded from the Offer. When the total value of business assets exceeds $3,950, the amount remaining after deducting $3,950 will be included in the Offer.

> **Example:** Barney owns a pool cleaning business. The total value of his tools and supplies used to clean pools is $5,000. When submitting his Offer in Compromise, he offered $50 (**$5000 x 0.8 – $3,950 = $50**) in addition to the QSV of his personal assets.

Is your jewelry an asset?

Generally, jewelry is not required to be disclosed unless its value is such that if liquidated, it may significantly reduce the back taxes you owe to the IRS. If your jewelry in conjunction with your other personal assets is valued over $10,000, you may be required to disclose this to the IRS depending on the resolution that you are trying to establish with the IRS.

When filing your Offer in Compromise, you will be required to disclose the value of jewelry along with your other assets. The levy exemption would apply allowing $7,900 of your total assets to be excluded from the Offer.

> **Real Life Story:** When Kathie's mother passed away, she left her wedding ring valued at $10,000. Kathie now owes the IRS $9,000 in back taxes. She was unsure whether to inform the IRS about the ring because she did not want to be forced to sell her mother's ring. Because the ring is valued at more than her IRS tax debt, she should disclose the ring to the IRS.
>
> There is another option. Kathie may choose to establish a Streamlined Installment Agreement since her balance is below $25,000 so that she would not have to disclose her assets and the treasured ring. If she tried to obtain a Currently Not Collectible, Installment Agreement or Offer in Compromise, she would be required to report the ring to the IRS.

Is art considered an asset?

The term "art" includes paintings, antiques, and other objects classified as Art. Count them in your asset column. In general, art valued at $10,000 or more should be disclosed to the IRS if the resolution involves disclosure of your financial information such as a Currently Not Collectible or Installment Agreement. When submitting an Offer in Compromise, you will be required to disclose the artwork as an asset, but it would be subject to the $7,900 Levy exemption.

Example: Using the previous example where Josephine inherited a Picasso painting valued at $15,000 from her deceased grandmother, if she was negotiating a Currently Not Collectible or Installment Agreement, she would be required to disclose the painting because it is valued at over $10,000.

What other miscellaneous items can be considered as assets?

Other items classified as *personal effects* include collector's items such as coin collections, stamp collection, baseball cards, or a rock collection, etc. These items may require an appraisal in order to determine the value of these items. Generally, such assets would require disclosure if the total value exceeds $10,000 or if the value is sufficient to drastically reduce your tax debt or pay off your tax debt. Disclosure of such items is not common when negotiating a Currently Not Collectible or Installment Agreement with ACS.

When dealing with Revenue Officers, you may be required to liquidate your collection to reduce or pay off your tax debt. When submitting an Offer in Compromise, you would be required to disclose these assets, but the levy exemption of $7,900 would also apply.

Example: Clifford was given a Jackie Robinson baseball card for his 5th birthday. Now 30, he recently had the card appraised. To his surprise, it has a value of $14,000 in today's market. Clifford owes the IRS $100,000 and has a Revenue Officer assigned to his case. When the Revenue Officer reviewed his financial statement on the Form 433-A, she noticed the baseball card and its value. Clifford was required to sell the baseball card in order to bring down the balance of his tax debt. If he didn't, his request for an installment Agreement would be denied.

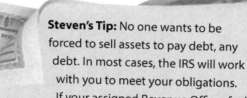

Steven's Tip: No one wants to be forced to sell assets to pay debt, any debt. In most cases, the IRS will work with you to meet your obligations.

If your assigned Revenue Officer feels that you are holding back and not disclosing your true assets, there are consequences that you may not like.

Before you get to that point, get some help. And know what your assets are, all of them, along with their value. Work with professionals who are skilled in dealing with the IRS Offer in Compromise and Settlement areas. This is not the time to be working with someone who is green and new to the tax resolution area. This is the time that you want them to do the talking.

Inside this chapter

CHAPTER 19

Income Sources

Being clear as to what are your *income sources* and what your *expenses* are is fundamental in not only reporting your tax forms, but in dealing with any types of issues with the IRS. It is important to understand how your income and expenses will be calculated, and the effect that both items have on your case. There are various ways in which the IRS may determine your income, and various expenses that the IRS will allow or disallow.

Understanding how it determines and calculates them creates the foundation in establishing a resolution.

This chapter and the next will explore the wide world of income sources, both within the work-related environment and outside of it, as well as expenses connected to it.

What is Income?

For IRS purposes, income is monetary wages, salaries, tips or any compensation received from an employer, self-employment, social security, pension, retirement, disability, interest, investments, alimony, child support, rental property, agricultural subsidies, unemployment, distributions, gambling winnings, oil credits, rent subsidies, judgments, inheritance, etc. In some cases, you may have received money from relatives or friends on a regular basis and thought of them as "gifts."

The IRS may think otherwise. If it determines that these "gifts" have been received consistently, such as on a monthly basis, it may declare them as income. It is important to understand how your income will be calculated because it will determine the outcome of your case.

Are You a W-2 Wage Earner?

W-2 wages are received by individuals who typically work for an employer as an hourly or salaried employee. You are considered a W-2 employee if your employer provides you with a paycheck stub that demonstrates deductions for federal and/or taxes from your income. It is very important to review your paycheck stub or form that indicates your pay period, gross pay for that period, and an itemization of whatever amounts are withheld and what they are. Some also have an accumulation of the total amounts paid year-to-date (YTD).

It's wise that you have sufficient taxes deducted from your income on a regular basis to ensure that you won't have a tax filing surprise stating you owe money. As a general rule, the exemptions you claim for your income should be less than or equal to the total exemptions that you receive when you file your annual income tax return.

Real Life Story: Eleanor was a W-2 employee with two children. When she filed her 2012 income tax return, she received a total of three exemptions. In reviewing her paycheck stub, my offices realized that she had 99 exemptions listed, not three. As a result, insufficient taxes were being withheld. In fact, no taxes were being withheld and Eleanor would have a significant shortfall in paying what she owed.

We advised her to reduce the number to three (or less) so that adequate taxes would be withheld and prevent her from owing the IRS in the future.

When calculating your income, the IRS will first determine your monthly *gross income*. Gross income is the income you earn prior to any deductions being withheld. If you are a W-2 employee, it is calculated by one of two ways: it will be based on your year-to-date income, or it will be based on an average of your income, determined by your pay frequency (weekly, bi-weekly, semi-monthly, or monthly).

You should always calculate it by using both calculations in order to determine which calculation is most favorable to your case. Ideally, select the calculation that provides you with the lowest monthly gross income. **Caution:** it may be a battle at times to get the IRS to accept the method that you have chosen, so it is a good idea to review your income based on both methods. This will allow you to be prepared for the worst case scenario. Let's look at both methods in greater detail.

Calculating Your Income Based on the *Year-to-Date Method* (YTD)

As the term implies, you would calculate your income by using the YTD income provided on your paycheck stub divided by the number of months worked.

Formula:

Monthly Income = YTD income ÷ by the number of months worked

The IRS may also divide the YTD income by the number of pay periods worked up to the date reported on your paycheck stub multiplied by your pay frequency.

Formula:

Monthly Income = YTD income ÷ by the number of pay periods x pay frequency

The YTD method should not be used if you did not work at least 6 months for the year, or if you did not start working from January of that year. Otherwise, using the Year-to-Date Method would produce an incorrect calculation of your income.

Example: Anne worked for her employer for over two years. Her current paycheck stub is dated June 30, 2012, and is paid semi-monthly on the 15th and 30th of every month, meaning she gets two paychecks per month. Her YTD total income reported on her paycheck stub was $25,000.

Using the Formula #1: Monthly Income = YTD ÷ number of months, the following is determined:

$25,000 (YTD) ÷ 6 = $4,166.67 (number of months through June) arriving at $4,166.67 for Anne's monthly gross income.

Using the Formula #2: Monthly Income = YTD ÷ number of pay periods x pay frequency, we would have the following:
$4,166.67 = $25,000 (YTD) ÷ 12 (pay periods since paid twice per month (2 x 6 = 12)) **x2** (semi-monthly pay frequency). Anne's monthly gross income is **$4,166.67.**

As you can see, by the examples, the two YTD calculations resulted in the same answer. These are simply two different ways of determining your monthly income based on your YTD income.

Calculating Your Income Based on Last 3 Paystubs

Another method used to calculate your monthly gross income is the *average income method* (AIM). This method should be used when you have worked less than six months for the year, or when your income is often inconsistent. Using your three most recent pay check stubs, you would determine the average monthly gross income. You may use more paystubs if it would create a lower monthly income or present a more accurate calculation of your monthly income. The paystubs used must also be consecutive, meaning that each pay period immediately follows another.

Prior to using this method, it is important to understand how each pay period is calculated by the IRS. Each pay period is assigned a multiplier that will be used to determine your monthly income. The table below provides the multipliers for each pay period:

IRS Pay Frequency Multiplier Table	
Pay Frequency	**Multiplier**
Weekly	4.3
Bi-Weekly	2.17
Semi-Weekly	2
Monthly	1

Source: IRS Publiciation F433a

Using the table, you would then determine your pay frequency. This is often labeled directly on your paystub, or presented to you at the time of hire.

Which Pay Period Are You?

Paychecks usually are paid one of four ways: weekly, bi-weekly, semi-monthly and monthly.

Weekly: you receive a weekly paycheck, usually on the same day each week for a total of 52 checks each year.

Bi-Weekly: you receive a paycheck every other week usually on a specific day for a total of 26 checks each year.

Semi-Monthly: you receive a paycheck twice a month usually on two specific days each month for a total of 24 checks each year.

Monthly: you receive a paycheck once a month usually on a specific day for a total of 12 checks each year.

Calculating Your Average Monthly Gross Income

Beginning with three consecutive paystubs, you can easily calculate your monthly gross income based on an average of the three. Add the gross income reported on each paystub, divide the total by the number of paystubs, and then multiply that total by the multiplier designated for your pay frequency from the table above.

Monthly Gross Income =
(paystub 1 + paystub 2 + paystub 3) ÷ 3 (total number of paystubs) x (Pay Frequency Multiplier)

Example: Mary Margaret is paid weekly and submitted the three paystubs dated: 3/7/2013, 3/14/2013, 3/21/2013. The gross income on 3/7/2013 was $500. The gross income on 3/14/2013 was $650 and on 3/21/2013, $550.

Step 1: Add the gross income of each pay check: **$500 + $650 + $550 = $1,700.**

Step 2: Divide the total gross income by the total number of pay checks: **$1,700 ÷ 3 = $566.67.**

Step 3: Multiply the total in Step 2 by the pay frequency multiplier (weekly = 4.3): **$566.67 x 4.3 = $2,436.68.**

Result: Mary Margaret's monthly gross income is **$2,436.68.**

> Knowing your opponent's strategy helps you anticipate their attack and to be prepared to counter-strike.

The IRS also has a second method for calculating your monthly gross income; it is by taking an average of three or more of your paystubs. The alternate method adds the gross income of each paystub, then divide by the number of paystubs, then multiplies by the number of weeks you would be paid per year, and then divide by 12 (number of months in a year) in order to determine your monthly gross income (**Formula**: monthly gross income = (paystub1 + paystub2 + paystub3) ÷ (total number of paystubs) x (number of weeks paid annually) ÷ (12)).

> **Example:** Using the same income provided in the example above by Mary Margaret, the following is arrived at:
>
> **Step 1:** Add the gross income of each pay check: **$500 + $650 + $550 = $1,700**
>
> **Step 2:** Divide the total gross income by the total number of pay checks: **$1,700 ÷ 3 = $566.67**
>
> **Step 3:** Multiply the total in Step 2 by 52 (since she is paid weekly and receives a paycheck every week for the year, she would be paid for a total of 52 weeks; **$566.67 x 52 = $29,466.84**
>
> **Step 4:** Divide the total provided in Step 3 by 12 (number of months in one year): **$29,466.84 ÷ 12 = $2,455.57**
>
> **Result:** Mary Margaret's monthly gross income is **$2,455.57**

As you can see, the second example is different—the monthly gross income determined by using both methods is not the same. The alternate method actually produced a higher monthly income of $2,455.57, from that of the multiplier method of $2,436.68, a difference of $18.89.

Sometimes the method used determines your eligibility for your desired resolution. As a result, it is important that you try both methods in order to determine whether one calculation could prevent you from being eligible for your desired resolution. This will help you decide on what arguments you can make in favor of the calculation method you prefer, and what counter arguments the IRS may make in support of the other method. Knowing your opponent's strategy helps you anticipate their attack and to be prepared to counter-strike. So always be prepared to battle when negotiating with the IRS.

1099's, Income and Expenses

Individuals that are classified as independent contractors or self-employed would receive a statement of their income at the end of the year on a Form 1099 if they were paid $600 or more for that tax year. You are considered an independent contractor or self-employed if you were required to sign an independent contractor agreement and no taxes were deducted from your income. You may also be classified as a 1099 individual if any of the following applies (*see* also section on Misclassification of Employees for IRS factors for determining W-2 or 1099 Independent Contractor in Chapter 11, *Common Mistakes You Can Avoid*):

1. You receive at least $10 in royalties or broker payments in lieu of dividends or tax-exempt interest;

2. You receive at least $600 in rents, services (including parts and materials), prizes and awards, other income

payments, medical and health care payments, crop insurance proceeds, or cash paid from a notional principal contract to an individual, partnership, or estate;

3. If you receive any fishing boat proceeds; or

4. You're an Attorney who received gross proceeds of $600[67]

It is important to understand how to calculate your income as a 1099 independent contractor when negotiating a resolution with the IRS. All income is calculated using one of these three methods:

- Year-to-date income (YTD);

- Average Income based on your last three paystubs; and

- Profit/Loss Statement.

You should use the method that provides you with the lowest gross monthly income calculation. Make sure you perform all three calculations in order to be prepared for counter arguments by the IRS, and to understand how each calculation affects the resolution that you are seeking.

Calculating Your 1099 Income Using the Year-to-Date Method

The Year-to-Date (YTD) method calculates your monthly gross income by dividing the year-to-date total provided by your income statement, by the number of months worked (monthly gross income = YTD income ÷ number of months worked). An independent contractor or self-employed individual may receive an income or commission statement from a company or individual that provides an accounting of earnings based on a specified pay frequency, or at the end of the year on a Form 1099 (this is reported as non-employee compensation).

> **Example:** Paula worked as an independent contractor for the entire year and received a 1099 at the end of the year from Company A. The 1099 reported her gross earnings/non-employee compensation for the year was $36,000. Using the YTD formula, she would arrive at the following: $3,000 (monthly gross income) = $36,000 (YTD income) ÷12 (number of months in one year). As a result, Paula's monthly gross income is $3,000.

Calculating Your 1099 Income Using Your Last 3 Paystubs

The *Average Income Method* (AIM) used to calculate W-2 income could also be used to calculate the average monthly gross income for a 1099 individual. The AIM method requires that the average monthly gross income be determined by three or more consecutive paystubs in order to insure accuracy. Then you would add the gross income reported on each income statement; divide the total by the number of pay periods, and finally multiply the new total by the multiplier designated for your pay frequency (Monthly Gross Income = (paystub1 + paystub2 + paystub3…) ÷ (total number of paystubs) x (Pay Frequency Multiplier).

Example: Roger is paid monthly and submitted three income paystubs dated: 3/1/2013, 4/1/2013, 5/1/2013. The gross income on 3/1/2013 was $5,000. The gross income on 4/1/2013 was $6,500 and for 5/1/2013, $5,500.

Step 1: Add the gross income of each statement: **$5,000 + $6,500 + $5,500 = $17,000.**

Step 2: Divide the total gross income by the total number of pay checks: **$17,000 ÷ 3 = $5,666.67.**

Step 3: Multiply the total in Step 2 by the pay frequency multiplier (monthly = 1): **$5,666.67 ÷1 = $5,666.67.**

Result: Roger's average monthly gross income is **$5,666.67.**

When an independent contractor or self-employed individual reports inconsistent income annually, the IRS may also utilize an alternate method to calculate the average monthly gross income by taking an average of the Adjusted Gross Income (AGI) for three or more consecutive years as reported on the Federal Income Tax Return or Form 1040.

In Roger's case, he really didn't make $5,666.67 every month. In fact, it was far from it. Roger is what would be called "cyclical"—he only makes his income within a limited period of time each year. The alternate method will be truer to his cash flow. Read on.

The alternate method adds the AGI of each year, then divides by the number of years used, and then divides by 12 (number of months in a year) in order to determine the true average monthly gross income (**Formula:** (AGI1 + AGI2 + AGI3) ÷ (total number of years) ÷ (12 months)).

> **Example:** Using the example provided above for Roger, assume that the figures reported were his AGI for three consecutive years: Year 1 = $5,000, Year 2 = $6,500, and Year 3 = $5,500. Using these figures, his picture changes and looks like this:
>
> **Step 1:** Add the AGI of each year:
> **$5,000 + $6,500 + $5,500 = $17,000**
>
> **Step 2:** Divide the total AGI income by the total number of years: **$17,000 ÷ 3 = $5,666.67**
>
> **Step 3:** Divide the total provided in Step 2 by 12 (number of months in one year):
> **$5,667.67 ÷ 12 = $472.22**
>
> **Result:** Roger's average monthly gross income is **$472.22,** significantly different from the previous method. The true monthly amount of $472.22 is a far cry from $5,666.67.

It is important to calculate your income based on these methods in order to determine which method is most favorable to your case and to also be able to anticipate counter arguments, or alternate determinations that may be made by the IRS.

Business Expenses That Are Allowable to Deduct From Income

An independent contractor or self-employed individual may also incur various expenses that are required in order to perform their job. As a result, the IRS allows him or her to deduct allowable business expenses in order to off-set their gross monthly income. Allowable business expenses are those incurred as a regular part of performing your job. Such expenses may include the following:[68]

Advertising

Car & Truck Expenses

Commissions & Fees

Contract Labor

Employee benefit programs

Insurance (other than health)

Interest (paid to banks, loans, etc.)

Legal & Professional Services

Office Expense

Pension & Profit-Sharing Plans

Rent or Lease (vehicles, equipment, etc.)

Repairs & Maintenance

Supplies

Taxes and Licenses

Travel, Meals and Entertainment

Utilities

Wages

Other

Most Items listed on the IRS Schedule C are allowed to be deducted as business expenses with the exception of depreciation and business use of home.

Calculating your new income

After determining the average gross monthly income, you would then determine your average monthly business expenses. The same methods discussed previously may be used in order to determine your average monthly business expenses. You may use your Schedule C filed with your Form 1040 in order to determine your average monthly business expenses using the YTD method. You may also use the AIM method by using receipts of business expenses that you incurred.

> Your income is one of the most, if not the most important factor, when negotiating with the IRS as it will have a great effect on your eligibility for various resolutions.

When you have determined your average monthly income and expenses, you are now ready to calculate your monthly net income. When negotiating with the IRS, you should always use your *monthly net income* when asked for your monthly income, if you incur any business expenses.

Your monthly net income is calculated by first determining your average monthly gross income and then subtracting your total monthly business expenses.

Formula:

Net Income = Average Monthly Gross Income – Total Monthly Business Expenses

Example: Douglas was an independent contractor at a real estate firm. He reported the following income and expenses:

Gross Monthly Income = $5,000
Office Rent = $500
Gas = $200
Supplies = $300
Dry Cleaning = $100
Utilities = $150
Telephone = $100
Meals = $300
Total Monthly Expenses = $1,650

Using the **Net Income Formula** you would arrive at the following: **$3,350 = $5,000** (gross monthly income) **– $1,650** (total monthly expenses). As a result, Douglas' monthly net income = **$3,350.**

It is important to note that Douglas claimed $200 in expenses for gas in the example provided above. The IRS has a no "Double Dipping" rule that would prevent him from claiming the IRS allowance for transportation expense when completing the Form 433-A or Form 433-F Financial Statement since he already listed gas as a business expense.

He should determine whether his reported gas expense is greater or less than the IRS allowance for transportation. If Douglas' reported amount is less than the IRS allowance, he should elect to accept the IRS allowance, and exclude the gas expense when calculating his net income. This would cause the net income to increase by $200 to $3,550. However, if his reported amount for gas was greater than the IRS allowance, he should elect to keep the net income calculation as originally stated.

If you are an independent contractor or self-employed, it is important that you claim any business expenses that you incur so that you may accurately report your monthly net income. Your income is one of the most, if not the most important factor when negotiating with the IRS as it will have a great effect on your eligibility for various resolutions.

Calculating Your Business Income Using a Profit & Loss Statement

The IRS also allows for businesses, independent contractors and the self-employed to calculate the average monthly gross income or monthly net income by preparing a profit and loss statement—a financial statement that provides the business income and expenses for a specified period of time. Also known as a P&L, it resembles a Schedule C that is filed along with the Form 1040 for businesses, independent contractors, or self-employed individuals.[69]

It may be used as the income statement in place of the 1099 or other statement of incomes. It's recommended because of the ease in determining the monthly net income using the YTD or AIM methods.

Double Dipping

The IRS has a no **"double dipping"** rule that prevent

independent contractors or self-employed individuals from claiming an IRS allowance for a given expense if that expense was already claimed on the profit/loss statement. For example, in the previous example, Douglas claimed a gas expense of $200 when calculating his monthly net income. As a result, he could not claim the IRS allowance for transportation expense on the Form 433-A or 433-F Financial Statement. It would have been *double dipping*. Not only does double dipping open you up for an audit, you may mistakenly believe that you are eligible for a specific resolution, but when the mistake is corrected, you may no longer be eligible.

Real Life Story: Quinn was self-employed, and filed an Offer in Compromise with the IRS in the amount of $1,000. Based on her profit/loss statement, Quinn's monthly net income was $3,500. Her total allowable expenses were $3,800, and total equity in assets amounted to $1,000. However, she claimed an automobile lease expense of $450 per month on her profit/loss statement and also on her 433-A.

Quinn was double dipping because she claimed the IRS allowance for automobile payments as well as deducting the automobile payments as a business expense. Because of this, the IRS reduced her allowable expenses to $3,350. As a result, she was no longer experiencing a hardship and had a net disposable income of $150. The IRS determined that she could fully pay her IRS tax debt, and rejected her Offer.

The Dos and Don'ts of Deducting Personal Expenses to Reduce Your Income

It always sounds so simple, yet gets complicated for many. When calculating any *business expenses*, it is important that you do not mingle *personal expenses* with them. Business expenses are the costs incurred in operating your business or performing your job. Any other costs incurred that are not related to operating your business or performing your job are personal.

Let's say you claim paying for an office as a business expense. If you do not work out of your home, you cannot claim a part of your mortgage as a legitimate expense. If you did have a home office, you would then apply a percentage of the mortgage based on what percentage of the home is used for exclusive business purposes.

Do not attempt to reduce your monthly net income by trying to include personal or fraudulent expenses. The wise taxpayer provides true and accurate information to the IRS. Self-employed and 1099 individuals are more likely to be audited than the W-2 taxpayer—always keep that in mind. If it is discovered that you provided false and inaccurate information, the consequences will not be favorable.

Your Social Security Income

Social Security isn't just retirement income that many believe it is. It includes retirement, disability, and survivor benefits that are paid by the Social Security Administration on a monthly basis. By definition, Social Security income does not need to be reported as income for tax purposes. Many recipients who use it as the primary source of income do not owe taxes because their taxable income is too low to be taxed. **Note:** Tax payers with pensions, or retirements, can owe taxes for SSI. If payments are deducted for Medicare, and/or supplemental Medicare programs, these payments may be claimed on the Form 433-A or 433-F as medical insurance or health care payments.

The amount received is usually increased by a few percentage points at the beginning of the year as indicated by the Social Security Administration, with the new amount paid out on the same day monthly. Because of this, the annual Social Security Statement would be sufficient in order to calculate the monthly gross income, or the SSA 1099 Form that is provided at the end of every year to all recipients. If using the SSA to calculate the monthly gross income, you would use the YTD method: Monthly Income = YTD ÷ 12 (number of months per year).

When calculating your income as a recipient, it is important to use the gross benefit amount before any deductions are made. This is required even when deductions are made for overpayment or for Medicare benefits. Remember, Medicare payments may be allowed as health care or health insurance expenses. Also, any overpayments that are being repaid may be claimed as a secured payment expense.

Example 1: Terrance received Social Security income in the amount of $1,000 monthly. After deductions for

Medicare, $850 is directly deposited into his bank account. Based on this information, his monthly gross income would be $1,000 and he would also be allowed to claim the $150 deducted for Medicare as a health insurance expense.

Example 2: Terrance received an SSA 1099 for 2012 reporting an annual income of $12,000 and Medicare deductions of $1,800. Based on this information, he would use the YTD method (Monthly Gross Income = YTD ÷ 12) in order to figure his monthly gross income and utilizes this formula, **$1,000 = $12,000 ÷ 12.** As a result T's monthly gross income is **$1,000.**

With the YTD formula, his monthly health insurance expense is determined by: **$1800 ÷ 12 = $150.** As a result, his monthly health insurance expense is **$150.**

Annuity Income

Created by the insurance industry, an *annuity* is a fixed amount received annually by an individual for a specified number of years or term. It is seeded with either a lump sum investment by the policy holder (that would be you) or, over a period, other amounts are added—sometimes monthly during the span of a career—others much like an investment. Any additional funds are stopped once an annuity policy is annuitized, meaning you have decided that you want to begin to withdraw money, typically monthly or annually. When there is no definite end, it is also called a perpetuity ...

Individuals receiving moneys often end up owing the IRS because they fail to realize that a portion or the entire annuity may be taxable. It may be partially taxable if received from an employer-sponsored retirement plan in which you made contributions. Annuities are fully taxable at a rate of 20 percent or a rate based on your Form W-4P if you did not contribute to the plan, no contributions were withheld from your salary or income, or you received all of your contributions tax free in previous years.[70]

If you receive certain annuity payments prior to age 59½, you may also be subject to an additional 10 percent tax unless the distribution qualifies for an exemption. You are exempt from the additional penalty if you receive a distribution after separation from the company, you are permanently and totally disabled, distribution was payable upon death to beneficiary, or the distribution was made after separation from service after reaching age 55.[71]

Payments should be calculated using either the AIM or YTD method depending on the pay frequency or income statement used. If the income statement used is the 1099R, the YTD method should be used. You may also use AIM to calculate the monthly gross income by using one month's annuity statement if paid the same amount monthly, or the three most recent annuity statements depending on the pay frequency.

Example: Aaron receives annuity payments in the amount of $1,500 every month and is payable until his death. At that time, all payments will cease. Using the

AIM Formula:

Monthly gross income =

(Paystub 1+ paystub 2 + paystub 3) ÷

(number of paystubs) x pay frequency)

the following is verified: **$1,500 = $4,500 ÷ 3 x 1.**

As a result, A's monthly gross income is **$1,500.**

Calculating your pension income

Retirement pensions are also considered income and recipients are typically paid the same amount on a monthly basis. Some retirement pensions are taxable while others may be exempt from taxation. The two most common pensions that recipients are exempt from are railroad retirement benefits and Social Security (which is sometimes called a retirement pension). If you receive any other type of retirement benefits, you will likely be required to pay federal taxes. You would utilize the AIM or YTD methods previously used in order to determine the gross monthly pension income.

Calculating other types of income

Other forms of income include unemployment, distributions, interest, alimony, and child support. The frequency of payment for each of these items may vary. As a result, you would utilize the AIM or YTD methods when applicable in order to calculate your monthly gross income.

Unemployment

Contrary to popular belief, unemployment income is fully taxable. Too many times individuals owe moneys to the IRS because they believed it was not taxable income. If you are receiving it, I would recommend that you elect to have federal taxes withheld. Typically, it's paid on a bi-weekly basis at a fixed amount. As a result, you would use the AIM in order to calculate your unemployment income.

Distributions

Think taxable—*distributions* include interest payments, dividends, royalties, 401K distribution, or any other distribution requested from a financial plan. They are considered income and are taxable by the IRS. You often must request that the payer deduct federal taxes, otherwise you would be required to make ETPs (estimated tax payments) similar to 1099 employees. The frequency may vary. Some may be fixed regular payments, sporadic, or on an as-needed basis. As a result, the YTD Method is preferable when calculating your income.

Alimony

Received as a fixed monthly or lump sum payment, alimony is made to an ex-spouse that was ordered by a court of law. Any payments received are subject to IRS taxation. If you are a payer of alimony, it is an allowable expense. The payer of alimony is not likely to withhold taxes for the recipient, and as a result, the recipient should make regular ETPs similar to 1099 individuals. Alimony is usually received on a monthly basis at a fixed amount. As a result, AIM is the preferable method for calculating alimony income.

Child Support

The good news is that child support payments you receive are not taxable income on your annual 1040. The bad news is that it is considered income for purposes of negotiating with the IRS during the tax resolution process.

For the payer of child support, he or she may claim it as an allowable monthly expense on the Form 433-A or 433-F. The pay frequency of payments is often determined by the pay frequency of the payer. As a result, AIM is the preferable method for calculating child support income.

Steven's Tip: Income is income. In 95 percent of income cases, it will be taxable. In situations, such as with distributions of IRAs, retirement and annuity, the payer will often designate which portion is taxable and which is not on the 1099P Form sent out at the beginning of each year. I can't stress enough, do not assume that something is not taxable or not considered income. This is where you need some advice, especially if you are in a tax resolution situation.

Endnotes

[67] IRS.gov/uac/Form-1099-MISC,-Miscellaneous-Income

[68] IRS.gov/pub/irs-pdf/f1040sc.pdf

[69] IRS.gov/taxtopics/tc410.html

[70] IRS.gov/taxtopics/tc410.html

[71] IRS.gov/taxtopics/tc410.html

Inside this chapter

CHAPTER 20

Expenses and Payments

I n order to add a level of fairness and reasonableness in
evaluating the financial circumstances of individuals, the
IRS developed *National Standards*. They are predetermined
amounts that the IRS will permit for certain allowables, for
food, clothing, and miscellaneous items. The standards are
determined by the IRS from the Bureau of Labor Statistics
(BLS) Consumer Expenditure Survey (CES) which collects
information from the nation's households and families on
their buying habits (expenditures), income, and household
characteristics.[72] The list of standards is updated periodically
to account for inflation and other economic changes and
varies by state and county.

By developing these standards, the IRS seeks to determine
the average dollar amount spent for these common expenses
by region, state, and county. The amount predetermined for
these expenses are typically the maximum that the IRS would
allow an individual to claim without requiring proof of the
expenses or substantiation. In some cases, the IRS may allow
a deviation if it determines that the standards are insufficient

to sustain the basic living expenses of the individual or household.

Any deviations from the standard will require proof or substantiation of the amount claimed and a determination of whether a deviation is reasonable based on the facts and circumstances.[73]

The IRS only allows certain *living expenses* that it deems to be necessary for the health and well-being of individuals and/or the production of income through the Necessary Expense Test (NET).[74] The most common expenses include:

1. food, clothing, and miscellaneous items

2. health insurance

3. out-of-pocket health care

4. housing and utilities (cable, internet, etc.)

5. transportation

6. taxes

7. court ordered payment

8. term life insurance

9. mandatory retirement

10. student loans

11. child care

12. non-reimbursed expenses

13. other secured debts. In order for the expense to be allowed, it must past NET—the Necessary Expense Test.

Allowable Expenses vs. Actual Expenses

It's not uncommon for the average taxpayer to cross the line and claim an expense as a deduction when it's either quite gray or non-allowable. In tax resolution, there are further definitions between what is allowable and *what is not*.

Expenses must pass the NET: the IRS' Necessary Expense Test

Allowable expenses are those that meet the NET requiring that the expense be n ecessary for the health and welfare of the individual, or for the production of income. An expense may be allowable but a portion of the amount may be disallowed if it exceeds the national standards or determined to be unreasonable. The IRS does allow deviations under some circumstances, depending on the type of resolution being sought.

When negotiating a *Currently Not Collectible* or *Installment Agreement*, the IRS will generally allow a deviation from the national standards when the expense passes the NET and proof of payment of the expense is provided. When negotiating an *Offer in Compromise*, the IRS will only allow a deviation from the national standards for out-of-pocket health care expenses, but will not allow a deviation for anything else on the list.

Actual expenses are all expenses being paid by an individual and also include payments for allowable expenses that exceed the national standards. Any expenses paid must pass the NET in order to be allowable. Some actual expenses that are typically disallowed are expenses for voluntary retirement, whole life insurance, unsecured debt, and charitable contributions.

When the actual expense is allowable and below the set standard, the IRS will allow the full amount claimed by the individual. If the actual expense is allowable but exceeds the designated amount, the IRS may allow a deviation in both *Installment Agreement* and *Currently Not Collectible* cases but not in an *Offer in Compromise*.

In some cases, when an individual owes more than $100,000, the IRS may not allow a deviation from the national standards even when the expense passes the NET or when proof is provided. Understanding which expenses and the amounts that will be allowed are important in order to determine which resolutions you are eligible for and determining the likely outcome of your case.

> **Real Life Story:** Francine owned a dog that was constantly sick and would incur large medical bills in caring for this dog. She wanted to have the medical bills paid for her dog included as a medical expense on her form 433-A because it exceeded the national standard allowed of $60 and would make her a *Currently Not Collectible* candidate.
>
> The IRS did not allow her request. It does not allow medical bills paid for pets because having a pet is not a necessity in most cases. If Francine's dog was a seeing-eye dog that was necessary for her daily living needs or some other type of valid medical assistance animal, perhaps an argument could have been made that the dog was a necessity. Her beloved dog was classified as a "pet" and all medical payments were not allowed.

In the example above, Francine's medical bills incurred while caring for her dog was an actual expense, but it was not an allowable expense because it did not pass the NET, the Necessary Expense Test. Despite the actual amount being spent by her, the IRS only allowed the national standard of $60 for out-of-pocket medical expenses.

Start With Who's Who on Your Tax Return

In order to determine which national standards are applicable to your case, you must first determine how many members are in your household. The members of your household will be determined by the number of exemptions claimed on your Form 1040 Federal Income Tax Return. For example, if you claimed two exemptions in 2012, the IRS will determine that you have two individuals residing in your household. If you have other individuals living in your household that you would like to have considered, you will likely be required to provide proof of the other individuals residing in your household, and explain why they were not claimed on your Form 1040.

Whether you will be allowed to increase your expenses will depend on the type of resolution you are seeking. When negotiating a *Currently Not Collectible* or *Installment Agreement*, it may be easier to obtain an increase in exemptions. However, when negotiating an *Offer in Compromise*, the IRS generally will not allow a deviation in exemptions unless the increase is due to a newborn baby, or proof can be provided that you will claim the other individuals on your next Form 1040.

Example: Understanding how the exemptions you claim affects your case is important because the dollar amount of expenses allowed by the national standards increases as the number of exemptions claimed increases. For example, the national standard for food, clothing, and miscellaneous expenses for a household of one individual was $583[75] but increased to $1,092[76] for a household of two individuals. The more that you claim, legitimately of course, the higher your allowable expenses will be. **Note:** National Standards are subject to change. It's wise to do an Internet search for the latest updates.

Your Tax Debt Liability

Not all individuals claimed on your Form 1040 as dependents are liable for your tax debt. *Your spouse* will be held liable for your tax debt if you filed jointly on your Form 1040 that resulted in taxes being owed to the IRS. Other dependents or household members you provide as a part of your financial statement on the Form 433-A or 433-F will not be held liable for your tax debt.

> Having members of your household with income that you do not claim as dependents may affect your eligibility for the resolution that you are seeking.

Income ... Whose and What?

If other members in your household have income, whether you claim them as dependents or not, it matters if these individuals have their own income. If they have income of their own, the IRS will pro-rate the shared expenses based on your income (*see* the section on pro-ration). Pro-ration is also done when one spouse owes the IRS but the other does not, and they both live in the same home. Having members of your household with income that you do not claim as dependents may affect your eligibility for the resolution that you are seeking.

> **Example:** Joe and Anna are married but they file their tax returns separately using the Married Filing Separately status. Joe owes the IRS every year, while Anna does not. As a result, she refuses to file her returns as Married Filing Jointly with her husband. Because the couple does not file joint returns, when Joe wanted to resolve his tax problems, the IRS performed a pro-ration on the household income and shared expenses in order to determine whether he was eligible for a *Currently Not Collectible Status*.
>
> Joe's monthly income was $3,000 while Anna's monthly income was $2,000. As a result, the IRS performed a pro-ration using the following steps:
>
> 1. Add all household income together in order to obtain the total household income: **$3,000 + $2,000 = $5,000.**
>
> 2. Divide the income of the individual negotiating a resolution by the total household income in order to determine their portion of household expenses: **$3,000** (Joe's income) **÷ $5,000** (Total Household Income) = **60%.**

3. Multiply shared expenses (like housing and utilities, and in some cases food) by the percentage in order to determine the individual's portion. If the monthly housing and utilities expenses were a total of $2,000, Joe's share would be **$2,000 x .60 = $1,200**. As a result, the IRS would allow Joe to claim housing and utilities expenses of $1,200 instead of the full $2,000 because Anna is expected to cover some of the shared household expenses.

In this example, if they had children who also earned income, their income would be included in the calculation of the total household income in order to determine Joe's portion of the shared household expenses.

If there are other household members earning income living with you that did not file taxes with you as a spouse, immediately consult a professional in dealing with the IRS. These cases are very complicated and require careful analysis to ensure you are treated fairly.

Housing and Utilities

Housing and Utilities Expenses are grouped together by the IRS into one standard expense and are allowable expenses. These expenses includes: Mortgage or rent, property taxes, interest, insurance, maintenance, repairs, gas, electric, water, heating oil, garbage collection, residential telephone service, cell phone service, cable television, and Internet service.[77]

The standards for housing and utilities are derived from the U.S. Census Bureau, American Community Survey and BLS data, and are arranged by state and county. The national standard for the housing and utilities expense is the maximum amount that the IRS will allow in most cases. In working with the IRS for a resolution, you will normally not be allowed to claim greater than what the national standard states, even when your true expenses exceed it.

As discussed previously, the IRS will accept an amount claimed if it is less than or equal to the national standard of your county. Any deviations you request above the standard will require substantiation by the IRS and may be allowed when negotiating a *Currently Not Collectible and Installment Agreement*, but will generally not be allowed when negotiating an *Offer in Compromise*. The amount allowed by the national standard will increase as the number of exemptions claimed on your Form 1040 increases or as your household size increases.

For example, the national standard for housing and utilities of Sacramento County, California, for a household of one individual is $1,904,[78] and increases to $2,237[79] for a household of two individuals. You are only allowed to claim housing and utilities expenses for your primary place of residence.

Example: Eldon is single with no dependents and no other members in his household. He lives in Sacramento County, California, and reported the following housing and utilities expenses:

- rent = $1,000
- electricity = $150

- gas = $50

- water = $25

- trash = $25

- basic telephone = $50

- cell phone = $150

for a total housing and utilities expense of $1,450. Based on this information, Eldon would be allowed to claim the full amount of housing and utilities expenses of $1,450 since it is less than the national standard of $1,904.

Note: If Eldon's total housing and utilities expenses had exceeded the national standard of $1,904, he would have been allowed to claim only the maximum of $1,904.

Mixing Housing, Utility, and Business Expenses

One of the most common items my offices come across is the intermingling of personal and business expenses. In a word: don't. It leads to confusion and tax reporting trouble. The IRS does not allow *Double Dipping*, an all too common mistake made by 1099 or self-employed individuals.

If you work from home and claim some of the housing and utilities expenses on your profit/loss statement, you cannot claim the full amounts a second time on your Form 433-A or Form 433-F. You would need to *pro-rate* this expense by determining how much of the housing and utilities expenses are caused by the business and what portion was used for personal use. You may only claim the portion caused by personal use on your Form 433-A or Form 433-F (review Chapter 19, *Income Sources*, on double dipping for further details).

Transportation Expenses

You need transportation, which is definitely an allowable expense. Not only is it necessary for the health and welfare of your household, it is necessary for the production of income in the great majority of American households. The two types of transportation allowed by the IRS are personal vehicles and public transportation. In most cases, the IRS will not allow an individual to claim expenses for personal vehicles and public transportation at the same time unless the person can show that they actually incur this expense on a regular basis. It mainly occurs in metropolitan areas.

There are exceptions that can be made but the argument must be reasonable. The national standards for transportation consists of nationwide figures for monthly loan or lease payments referred to as ownership costs and monthly operating costs broken down by census region and metropolitan statistical area (MSA).[80]

Ownership Expenses

Your payments for a lease or purchase of a vehicle come under ownership expenses. You will be allowed them for one vehicle each for the primary and secondary on a tax account (husband or wife) with a maximum of two allowed per household, including married couples. A single individual will only be allowed to claim ownership expenses for one vehicle, even in cases where the single individual may own more than one vehicle.

The national standard is set for ownership costs of $517 for one vehicle and $1,034[81] for two vehicles. These figures will not vary regardless of the state or county averages and are the maximum allowed by the IRS. The IRS will allow the lesser of the actual ownership cost or the national standard. However, when negotiating a *Currently Not Collectible* or *Installment Agreement*, the IRS may allow a deviation for the actual amount claimed even when it exceeds the national standard so long as it is determined to be reasonable, and you are able to provide proof of your actual expense. When negotiating an *Offer in Compromise*, the IRS will not allow any deviations from the national standard for ownership costs above the national standard.

> **Example:** Harvey and Winifred are married and have two vehicles that they are currently financing. The vehicle driven by Harvey has a monthly payment of $600, while the vehicle driven by Winifred has a monthly payment of $450. Based on this information, they can only claim $967 because Harvey can only claim the maximum of $517 while Winifred will claim the $450 (actual amount spent), arriving at **$517 + $450 = $967.**

> **Note:** Notice that the IRS will not add the two payments and then determine if they are below the standard of

$1,034 for two vehicles. The IRS will assess each payment individually in order to determine what portion will be allowed for each, and then add them together. Harvey and Winifred would not get the full maximum of $1,034 even though their combined expenses or $600 and $450 total $1,050, exceeding the national standard of $1,034. Do not make the mistake of adding the two payments together first then compare it to the standard because as you can see with Harvey and Winifred's example, they paid out an amount greater than the amount that the IRS will actually allow.

> Claim no more than the national standard allows.

In addition to lease and automobile payments, vehicles have operating expenses. They include the cost of gas, insurance, non-reimbursed parking and tolls, and maintenance and repair of the vehicle. Unlike vehicle ownership costs which remain the same regardless of state or county, operating costs vary and are determined by the region and metropolitan area.

The IRS will allow individuals to claim the lesser of their actual operating expense or the national standard for their location. For example, the national standard for the Northeast region is $278[82] for one vehicle and $556[83] for two vehicles. Therefore, an individual living in the Northeast region can claim a maximum of $278 if single or $556 if married and has two vehicles.

Older Vehicles Created Additional Expenses

In *Offer in Compromise* cases, if you own and use a vehicle that is at least six years old and has over 75,000 miles on it, you are allowed an additional operational expense of $200. The IRS rationale for allowing the additional $200 is because older vehicles will require more maintenance and repair than newer vehicles. This amount does not vary by region or metropolitan area. You are allowed to claim the maximum *even* if your actual expenses are less. But, if your actual operational expenses are greater, you will not be allowed to claim it.

> **Example:** Gregory is single and lives in the Northeast region. He has a 1999 Chevy Corvette with a total mileage of 120,000 and owns it free and clear, with no payments and no lease. His monthly costs are: gas = $200, insurance = $150, repairs and maintenance = $300 for total operating costs of $650. He is submitting an *Offer in Compromise* to settle his IRS tax debt.
>
> Using the national standard for his region, he is allotted $278 for his operating expenses. Gregory would also be allowed to claim the additional $200 (ownership notwithstanding) in operational expenses because his vehicle is over six years old and exceeds 75,000 in miles. As a result, he would claim a maximum operational expense of $478 ($278 + 200) and not the actual cost he reported of $650.

> **Note:** If Gregory had negotiated a *Currently Not Collectible* or *Installment Agreement* instead, he may have been allowed to deviate from the standard and claim the full

$650 if he could prove that he pays that amount every month and the IRS accepts his explanation as reasonable. If it is determined to be unreasonable, the maximum amount allowed would be $278 because the additional operational expense of $200 for an older vehicle is only allowed within *Offer in Compromise* cases.

Public Transportation Expenses

If you use public transportation, such as taxis, buses, trains, ferries, trolleys, etc., the national standard for public transportation applies nationwide and does not vary by region or metropolitan area. The Bureau of Labor Statistics sets the national standard amount for public transportation at $182[84]. Even if you spend less than the national standard, you will be allowed to claim the maximum if you *don't own* a vehicle or claim vehicle expenses on the Form 433-A. You will not be able to claim more than the national standard without being required to provide substantiation and a reasonable explanation that the IRS accepts. This amount will cover your entire household and not increase or decrease—per household.

The IRS generally will not allow an individual to claim both the vehicle expenses and public transportation. In some cases, it may allow a deviation from this rule when necessary for the health and welfare of the household, or for the production of income. If this is allowed, only the actual amounts can be claimed. This exception is rare and will only be considered in *Currently Not Collectible* and *Installment Agreement* cases.

Health Care Costs

The IRS considers your health care costs allowable and a necessary expense. These would include both health insurance and out-of-pocket expenses such as: prescription drugs, medical visits, co-pays, and medical supplies (eye glasses, contact lenses, etc.).[85] It will also allow the actual cost of health insurance and out-of-pocket expenses claimed, provided that you are able to prove the amounts that you claim.

If you do not have proof of your expense and purpose, the national standard for out-of-pocket health care costs will be used. It does not vary by state or county but does vary by age. The national standard for out-of-pocket health care cost for individuals under age 65 is $60, increasing to $144 for individuals over the age of 65. The national standard was determined from the Medical Expenditure Panel Survey data.[86]

Health Insurance

Your health insurance includes the cost of medical, dental, and vision insurance which are your typical health insurance expenses. The IRS will allow the actual amount claimed but may request substantiation. When negotiating a *Currently Not Collectible* or *Installment Agreement*, it may accept the actual amount claimed if it appears reasonable. If you are negotiating an *Offer in Compromise*, the IRS will request substantiation of your health insurance expenses via medical statements, cancelled checks, and/or bank or credit statements.

Out-of-Pocket Payments for Medical Bills and Supplies

The standard out-of-pocket health care cost is the maximum amount an individual is allowed to claim without being required to provide substantiation. The standard amount is per individual and should be calculated by multiplying the standard amount by the number of members in the household (standard out-of-pocket cost times the number of members in household).

If you are single with no dependents and under age 65, you would be given $60 as your out-of-pocket health care costs automatically. A household of two individuals under the age of 65 would receive $120 total in out-of-pocket health care costs. Or, if a household has one individual over age 65 and the other under 65, it would be allocated $204 (**$144 + $60 = $204**). The IRS will allow a deviation from the standard if substantiation is provided and the explanation is reasonable. Elective procedures including plastic surgery or cosmetic dental work are typically not allowed—they are not considered a necessary expense and do not pass NET … the Necessary Expense Test.

Court Ordered Payments

For any court ordered payments, the IRS will accept the actual amount claimed—it will request a copy of the court order and proof of your most recent payment, however. The payment must be ordered by a court of law and cannot be voluntary in order to be allowed by the IRS. Typically, court ordered payments include child support payments, alimony payments, judgments, etc.

Child Support Payments

Child support payments are allowable if ordered by a court of law. If you voluntarily pay them without a court order, they are not allowable … but they can be claimed under the child care expense. To clarify, the IRS will request a copy of the court order in order to verify that the payment is not voluntary, and that the amount claimed is the actual amount ordered by the court. If you volunteer payments or add extra amounts in additional payments not ordered by the court, they will not be allowed.

If you are in arrears in child support, payments will be allowed as a court ordered payment.

Proof of Dependent Children

The IRS wants to know when your dependent obligations end. It will request the age of the child or children that you provide child support to in order to determine your commitment period. The result is that it could negatively affect your case as the IRS will seek to determine whether you will still be eligible for a *Currently Not Collectible* when the obligation ends, or whether an *Installment Agreement* will be in place. And, if an *Installment Agreement*, the payments will increase by the amount previously paid for child support once the obligation ends.

If you are negotiating a *Currently Not Collectible,* you may have your financial statement reevaluated once the child support obligation ends in order to determine whether you can afford it, and transition to an *Installment Agreement.*

When negotiating an *Offer in Comp*romise, the end date of your child support obligations will also determine whether you will be able to pay off your IRS tax debt after the obligation ends, if it is determined to present a retired debt issue (*see* section on retired debt for further details in Chapter 24, *Bankruptcy, Retired Debt, Spouses and Ex-Spouses*).

Alimony Payments

The IRS will allow monthly alimony payments as an allowable expense only when ordered by a court of law. Voluntary payments made to a spouse in a separate agreement not ordered by the court will not be allowed—there are exceptions, however. You will need a copy of the court order to verify that the alimony was actually ordered by a court of law, the amount to be paid, and the terms of the alimony payments.

Some alimony payments are payable for a specified length of time, while others are continuous until the death of either party or until the recipient remarries. When the alimony obligation ends is important because it will determine whether you remain on a *Currently Not Collectible* or whether your *Installment Agreement* payment increases. When the alimony obligation ends, it could also affect your eligibility for an *Offer in Compromise* if it presents a retired debt issue (*see* section on retired debt in Chapter 24, *Bankruptcy, Retired Debt, Spouses and Ex-Spouses.*)

Judgment Payments

The IRS will allow judgment payments ordered by a court of law so long as the payments are *continuous* or *periodic*. It will not allow a single lump sum payment as an allowable expense. Whether a judgment payment is allowed will also depend on the type of judgment ordered by the court.

Court orders on traffic fines, restitution, or other governmental matters are typically allowed by the IRS. A civil judgment obtained on non-secured payments is generally not allowed. The IRS may accept monthly payments made on secured and non-secured civil judgments for *Currently Not Collectible* or *Installment Agreement* cases, but not for an *Offer in Compromise*.

Child and Dependent Care Expenses

As a taxpayer, it is safe to assume that your basic child or dependent care expenses will come under the allowable expense category ... but, they must pass the NET (the Necessary Expense Test) in order to be allowed by the IRS. In order for the child or dependent care expenses to be allowed, the child or dependent care must be necessary because of your employment. The IRS will require substantiation for expenses in order for it to be allowed.

For a case where a couple is married and claiming expenses, it will *only allow* child or dependent care expenses when both parents are employed. If one parent is unemployed, this expense will not be allowed. In home care for disabled children or an adult will be allowed as an allowable monthly expense so long as such care is necessary and meets the NET.

The IRS will not allow payments for college tuition or life insurance for children unless they were court ordered.

Note: when negotiating an *Offer in Compromise*, the IRS will not allow tuition or life insurance payments for children even if court ordered.

Remember ... expenses must pass the NET: the IRS' Necessary Expense Test.

Current Tax Payments

Your current tax payments are allowable expenses and include Federal Income Tax, Social Security, Medicare, and State and Local taxes. The IRS will allow the actual amount deducted from your paystub as a W-2 employee for Federal income tax and state and local taxes, but will automatically calculate the amounts for Social Security and Medicare taxes. You would calculate your current taxes using either AIM or YTD methods.

Current taxes will also include estimated tax payments (ETPs) if you are self-employed or a 1099 taxpayer who is required to make ETPs either monthly or quarterly. The IRS will allow the actual amount claimed if verified internally. If you do not make ETPs, (the IRS will verify internally if you are), you will not be given credit for the current taxes that you should be paying. If the IRS has no record of any payments credited to your account via your Social Security Number, any amount claimed will not be allowed.

Secured Debts and Mandatory Payments

All secured debts are allowable expenses. The actual amount claimed will be allowed as long as the payment is necessary and reasonable. It must be secured by collateral. You will be required to substantiate the need for payment. These debts include: student loans, loans with collateral such as cars, real estate, or other physical property, state installment agreements, and non-reimbursed work-related expenses/payments such as union dues, mandatory retirement payments, tools, uniforms, and other equipment required for work.

Unsecured Loans and Payments

Unsecured loans or debts such as credit card payments or personal loans are usually not allowed by the IRS. In some cases, it may allow credit card payments when negotiating a Currently Not Collectible or Installment Agreement. The IRS does not allow such payments for an Offer in Compromise.

Student Loan Payments

Your student loans are allowable expenses, but must be owed to the federal government in order to be allowed. The IRS may allow student loan payments if provided by a private lender not contracted through the federal government. It will need your most recent student loan statement that shows the total amount owed and proof that the monthly payment has been made. If you are not current with your payments, no credit will be given.

The end date of your student loan payments can also affect whether you will remain on a Currently Not Collectible, whether your Installment Agreement increases in the future, or whether you are eligible for an Offer in Compromise if it presents a retired debt issue discussed in Chapter 24, *Bankruptcy, Separation, Divorce, and Debt.*

State Tax Debt Payment Plans

The IRS will allow the actual amount claimed for State Debt Payment Plans. It will require a copy of the state installment agreement and proof that the payments are being made. The ending of the state installment agreement may also affect whether you remain on a *Currently Not Collectible*, whether your *Installment Agreement* will increase in the future, or whether there is a retired debt issue that affects your eligibility for an *Offer in Compromise*. Again, refer to *Chapter 24.*

Work Related Expenses

Your expenses that are work-related will be allowed by the IRS so long as they are mandatory. The most common work related expenses are union dues, mandatory retirement, tools, uniform, and equipment.

Make sure you review the list in the preceding chapter that identifies the business related expenses. You may be spending money in areas, forgetting that they are necessary for your work.

The IRS will not allow voluntary payments such as payments on a 401K plan, stocks, or other voluntary investment plans, savings, or annuities.

Endnotes

[72] IRS.gov/Individuals/Collection-Financial-Standards

[73] IRS.gov/Individuals/Collection-Financial-Standards

[74] IRS.gov/Businesses/Small-Businesses-&-Self-Employed/National-Standards:-Food,-Clothing-and-other-Items

[75] IRS.gov/Businesses/Small-Businesses-&-Self-Employed/National-Standards:-Food,-Clothing-and-other-Items

[76] IRS.gov/Individuals/Collection-Financial-Standards

[77] IRS.gov/Individuals/Collection-Financial-Standards

[78] IRS.gov/Businesses/Small-Businesses-&-Self-Employed/California---Local-Standards:-Housing-and-Utilities

[79] IRS.gov/Businesses/Small-Businesses-&-Self-Employed/California---Local-Standards:-Housing-and-Utilities

[80] IRS.gov/Businesses/Small-Businesses-&-Self-Employed/Local-Standards:-Transportation

[81] IRS.gov/Businesses/Small-Businesses-&-Self-Employed/Local-Standards:-Transportation

[82] IRS.gov/Businesses/Small-Businesses-&-Self-Employed/Local-Standards:-Transportation

[83] IRS.gov/Businesses/Small-Businesses-&-Self-Employed/Local-Standards:-Transportation

[84] IRS.gov/Businesses/Small-Businesses-&-Self-Employed/Local-Standards:-Transportation

[85] IRS.gov/Businesses/Small-Businesses-&-Self-Employed/National-Standards:--Out-of-Pocket-Health-Care

[86] IRS.gov/Businesses/Small-Businesses-&-Self-Employed/National-Standards:--Out-of-Pocket-Health-Care

Inside this chapter

CHAPTER 21

Resolutions, Offers, and Agreements

I f a business is dealing with the IRS over unpaid taxes, it is not uncommon for the business to have other financial problems as well. If you are an individual dealing with the IRS over unpaid taxes, it is also not uncommon for you or your business to have other financial problems as well. It's similar, but with differences.

For a business, you will need to demonstrate that your business can handle an *Installment Agreement,* by completing the Form 433-B. This form is similar to the Form 433-A or 433-F that individuals would complete and submit. Within it, you would list the business assets, income, and expenses. The key questions that the IRS wants to know:

- Is the business viable?

- Is there positive cash flow?

- Could the business meet the payment commitments if an Agreement was granted?

If negotiating an Installment Agreement is not successful and the business demonstrates that it is operating at a loss, the IRS may, instead, grant a business a Currently Not Collectible status and allow it to continue to operate and revive itself, or it may choose to close the business and liquidate its remaining assets. Businesses will normally only be granted this status if there are no ongoing payroll obligations.

One way to side-step providing a financial statement is to request a Streamlined Installment Agreement. If your business owes $25,000 or less to the IRS, a financial statement is not required.

Seizable Assets

Outside of a Streamlined Installment Agreement, as a business owner, you must provide the financial statement contained on the Form 433-B. It will reveal to the IRS all the assets owned by the business. When it is viable and can demonstrate the ability to correct its past practices that caused the IRS tax debt, the IRS is not likely to seek a seizure of your business assets.

Contrary to what many believe, the IRS does not seek to put companies out of business unless the company demonstrates an inability to continue operation, or a consistent disregard of the United States Tax Codes and regulations. If a business demonstrates that it is not viable and consistently operates at a loss, the IRS will seek to close the business and liquidate its remaining assets. Notice and appeal rights will be given to the business prior to the final sale/auction of any assets.

The IRS may also request that businesses such as Corporations (C-CORP), Partnerships, Limited Liability Companies (LLC), and S-Corporations (S-CORP) submit financial statements on the Form 433-B when requesting resolutions. These would include an In-Business Currently Not Collectible, Installment Agreement, or Offer in Compromise resolutions.

> To submit an Offer in Compromise, the business must be closed. A business financial statement is usually not needed for a Streamlined Installment Agreement—although a Revenue Officer may request one in order to verify whether the business is able to afford the payments.

Identifying the Right Resolution For You and Your Business

There are generally four ways to resolve your IRS tax debt:

- Streamlined Installment Agreement (SIA)
- Installment Agreement (IA)
- Currently Non Collectible (CNC)
- Offer in Compromise (OIC)

Every individual or business owing the IRS will usually be eligible for at least one of the four resolutions. Prior to negotiating any agreement with the IRS, it is important that you are compliant. That means all tax returns for the last six years for individuals, and *all* un-filed returns for businesses must be filed or have the filing requirement closed, meaning that you do not have a requirement to file, or the tax year is beyond the IRS filing statute that they are not requiring that you file. For a Currently Not Collectible, the IRS may make an exception to this rule. My recommendation is that you don't risk a rejection of your request. File all necessary returns so that you can have all of the balances resolved at the same time.

Note: When you or your business is in a resolution status, the IRS requires that you file all future returns on time. It will seize all refunds due your business and apply it to the tax debt until the tax debt is paid in full. If you file a tax return that has a balance due, you will be required to pay that balance in full when you file. Otherwise, the new tax debt may default any resolution you you previously established with the IRS.

Streamlined Installment Agreements

Streamlined Installment Agreements (SIA) are determined based on the amount owed, and no financial statements are required. Under the *IRS Fresh Start* initiative, the criteria for an SIA has recently changed. There are now two types of Streamlined Installment Agreements with different requirements available to individuals:

1. Less than $25,000 owed, or
2. More than $25,000 owed but less than $50,000.

Businesses may also qualify for the In-Business Trust Fund Express Installment Agreement, also known as an In-Business Streamlined Installment Agreement. Individuals or businesses that would like to avoid having a tax lien filed should consider this approach, as it is the best option to prevent the IRS from filing tax liens.

When you negotiate a SIA over the telephone, these types of agreements are approved right away if all terms are met, and do not require managerial approval. You will then receive written confirmation in the mail within two weeks.

Individuals or businesses that would like to avoid having a tax lien filed should consider a Streamlined Installment Agreement Installment Agreement—it is the best option to prevent the IRS from filing tax liens against the business or oneself.

Owing Less than $25,000 is a Must

In order to qualify for the Streamlined Installment Agreement of $25,000 or less, you must truly owe $25,000 or less of the assessed balance (interest and penalties don't count but are usually included) when the agreement is put into place. Not a dollar over. If you do, you can pay down the difference to bring you at or below the ceiling level.

The tax debt must be paid in full within 72 months or prior to the Collection Statute Expiration Date (CSED), whichever is earlier. Your monthly payment amount will be calculated by dividing your total liability by 72 months or the number of months remaining under the CSED (**Formula: Monthly Payment = tax debt ÷ 72 months**).

You should also consider multiplying the payment amount calculated by 1.2 in order to estimate the cost for interest and penalties. Under this agreement, all interest and penalties will continue to accrue (**Interest Formula: Monthly Payment = tax debt ÷ 72 (months) x 1.2**).

Example 1: Howie owed $23,000 and wanted to set up a Streamlined Installment Agreement. The CSED date is beyond 72 months. Based on this information, his SIA monthly payment amount would be calculated as follows:

$23,000 ÷ 72 = $319.44, or $320

(*Note*: IRS will not round down, only up).

If Howie wanted to account for interest, the payment would be calculated as follows:

$23,000 ÷ 72 x 1.2 = $384.

Example 2: Using the information provided above for Howie, let's assume that the CSED date expired in 48 months. As a result, he does not have 72 months to pay the balance in full, only 48 months. The calculation would be as follows:

$23,000 ÷ 48 (number of months remaining in CSED) = $479.16 or $480.

If Howie wanted to account for interest, the payment would be calculated as follows:

$23,000 ÷ 48 x 1.2 = $575.

A Fresh Start: Owing From $25,001 to $50,000

Under the Fresh Start Program, individuals may now qualify for a Streamlined Installment Agreement if the amount owed in back taxes is between $25,001 and $50,000. The debt must be paid within 72 months or before the Collection Statute Expiration Date (CSED), whichever is earlier.

The same calculation used for $25,000 or less would be used to determine your monthly payment for the $50,000 or less agreement. Penalties and interest will also continue to accrue. The difference between this type of Streamlined Installment Agreement and the maximum $25,000 agreement is that you will be required to provide a limited financial statement in order to demonstrate that you have the ability to make monthly payments. You will also be required to enter into a direct debit installment meaning that the IRS will automatically deduct your monthly installment payment from your bank account or wages.

Your Eligibility if You Have a Business

Your business is eligible for these agreements (IBTF - EXPRESS IA) *If it is compliant with all filing requirements* (all business returns must be filed), and the business owes $25,000 or less. Businesses owing more than $25,000 may pay down the balance in order to qualify for this type of resolution.

Typically, the IRS will not require a financial statement for this type of agreement. When you are in this situation, you need to think of the IRS as a financial institution and you are seeking a loan. Most loan officers are not going to approve the loan unless there are some assurances that the debt will be paid. In this case, don't be surprised when negotiating with an IRS Revenue Officer that he or she requests that you complete a financial statement or Form 433-B in order to demonstrate that the business has the ability to make the required monthly payments.

You have to pay the balance owed in full within 24 months or the CSED, whichever is earlier. If the business owes between $10,000 and $25,000, it must also authorize a direct debit installment agreement as well, deducting the payments directly from your bank account. To calculate the monthly payment, the following formula should be used: Monthly payment = tax debt ÷ 24 months (or months remaining prior to CSED). To account for the penalties and interest, you should also multiply the monthly payment by 1.2 as interest and penalties will continue to accrue (**Monthly payment = tax debt ÷ 24 (or CSED) x 1.2**).

> **Example:** Heidi's Bar & Grill is an S-Corp owing $12,000 in IRS tax debt and is compliant. It would like to enter into a Streamlined Installment Agreement. Heidi's payment would be calculated as follows: **$12,000 ÷ 24 = $500**. To calculate for penalties and interest, Heidi's Bar & Grill's payment would be calculated as follows: **$12,000 ÷ 24 x 1.2 = $600**.

Installment Agreements

If you can't pay the amount proposed from a Streamlined Installment Agreement, you have another option. Installment Agreements (IA) may be requested for any balance owed if the individual or business cannot pay or does not qualify for a SIA if individual debt exceeds $50,000 or business debt exceeds $25,000. For this, you would have to supply a detailed financial statement on the Form 433-A or 433-F for individuals and 433-B for businesses in order to determine your ability to pay. The remaining net income, after all allowable expenses are deducted from the gross income, will determine your monthly payment. Generally, the IRS will file a tax lien when an IA is accepted and the balance owed is $10,000 or more.

There are two types of installment agreements:

• Full-Pay Installment Agreement
• Partial-Pay Installment Agreement

Under a Full-Pay Installment Agreement, the IRS is required to accept the amount shown on the financial statement provided you substantiate any items that the IRS may require. You *may offer to pay more* than the financial statement shows, but the IRS will not accept less than the amount shown on the financial statement. If negotiated over the telephone with an IRS agent, the agreement may be submitted to a manager after your financials are taken, with a determination typically made within two weeks. You would be given a date to call again in order to check on the status of the Installment Agreement.

If you do not receive a confirmation in the mail within two weeks that your Installment Agreement was approved, contact the IRS again to check on the status. Sometimes there may be delays, or the representative may have failed to correctly submit your request, so always call back within two weeks if you do not receive confirmation in the mail that your agreement was approved.

> Once you have exhausted the maximum hold time, you will not be granted future holds.

Full-Pay Installment Agreements

If you agree to pay your debt in full, it will be done under a Full-Pay Installment Agreement, meaning you will pay what you owe over a period of agreed upon time. The IRS will not require a financial statement and it will estimate your pay-off amount based on both 30 and 60 days by using a payoff calculator.

It will then grant you an initial 60 day hold in order for you to obtain the funds necessary to pay off the entire debt. An additional 60 days may be allowed upon showing that you have made efforts to obtain the funds and will likely have them within the next 60 days. The maximum time given for you to pay your debt in full is 120 days—four months.

Caution: Failure to meet the terms of your agreement may cause the IRS to file a tax lien on your credit and assets, along with any other collection action it may deem appropriate. Once you have exhausted the maximum hold time, you would not be granted future holds. *It's not wise to request the full hold time from the beginning—120 days can go by quickly, and if you exhaust all of the time available, you can expect rapid collection action to be taken against you by the IRS.*

Partial-Pay Installment Agreements

After completing your financial statement, it will be determined which agreement will work best for you with the Partial-Pay Installment Agreement, the monthly payment amount will likely not fully payoff the tax debt owed. Now there's a new twist. The IRS cannot refuse to accept the Installment Agreement because the amount proposed will not fully payoff the tax debt. This is because it must accept the amount shown on your financial statement. If you state that you will pay a higher amount than what your financial statement indicates, that's up to you—remember, you don't have to.

As mentioned previously, the IRS will not accept less than the amount shown on the financial statement. For a Partial-Pay installment Agreement, the IRS will request substantiation of all items that exceed the national standards, and may allow a deviation if the expense is reasonable. The IRS may also file a tax lien on your credit and assets.

How Your Account Gets Reviewed After an Agreement is Confirmed

The IRS may review an account at some point in the future. For that to happen, you must do something to get its attention. Events that may trigger a review of your account are:

1. Increase in income demonstrated by your income tax return;

2. Default of the agreement because a new balance is owed, or two or more payments were missed;

3. An expense claimed has expired such as car loan, student loan, mortgage, etc.;

4. CSED date is approaching; and

5. Unfiled tax returns.

Absent any of the above occurring, the IRS is not likely to review your account.

Currently Not Collectible

Financial hardships happen—the IRS recognizes that some individuals or businesses may not be able to afford monthly payments due to a variety of legitimate hardship reasons. It may temporarily suspend all collection action by notating the account as Currently Not Collectible or CNC. To move into this status, the IRS will require a financial statement on the Form 433-A, or 433-F for individuals and the Form 433-B for businesses.

> The most effective way to have a levy or garnishment released is by being in a Currently Not-Collectible status.

In order to be eligible for this resolution, you must demonstrate that you have no income remaining after all allowable expenses have been deducted from your gross income. In other words, you either break even, or are negative every month. The IRS is also likely to file a tax lien against your credit and/or assets if this status is approved. If you negotiate a Currently Not-Collectible over the telephone, the agent is almost always required to submit the case to a manager for approval, and you will be required to call back in two weeks in order to check on the status.

If you have a current levy on your bank account or a wage garnishment, the IRS will typically remove it by granting a release immediately if no substantiation is required. This is the most effective way to have a levy or garnishment released. You may also negotiate a levy release, even if you are not compliant. But, it is recommended that you obtain compliance so that you may resolve your entire tax debt if multiple years are involved, rather than having to contact the IRS several times for each tax year. While your account is in this status, the IRS will keep any refunds due in the future until your account is paid in full or until the CSED expires absolving all of your back taxes.

Time Allowed for Currently Not-Collectible Status

If you or your business are in a Currently Not-Collectible position, you will remain in that status for at least 2 years, so long as your financial situation remains the same. Typically, the IRS may review your account every two years in order to determine whether you are still eligible. There are also some events that may hasten its review of your account, including:

- increase in income
- new tax debt
- close to CSED (Collection Statue Expiration Date)- review should not be be done within two years of negotiation
- unfiled income tax return

Absent these events, the IRS is not likely to review your account, and you may remain in a Currently Not-Collectible status until the CSED expires. If the IRS requires your updated financial information, you should receive a notice in the mail. In some cases, individuals who have been placed in this status never pay any money toward their IRS tax debt other than any tax refunds due.

Note: The IRS will seize all refunds due while a balance is owed even though your account is placed in an SIA, IA, or CNC status. In an OIC, discussed below, the IRS will keep the refund for the year in which the OIC is accepted, and all subsequent refunds will be released to you.

Offer in Compromise

A settlement that you propose to the IRS in order to resolve your tax debt by paying less than the amount owed is called an Offer in Compromise (OIC). This resolution is available to both individuals and businesses that cannot full pay their tax debt, where doing so would create a financial hardship.

If filed for a business, it must be closed, no longer have a filing requirement for that tax type, or no longer operating to qualify. When evaluating your offer, the IRS will determine your eligibility based on several factors, including:

- ability to pay
- income
- expenses
- equity in assets

The IRS generally accepts your Offer in Compromise when the amount offered is the most that it can expect to collect before the CSEDs.

Prior to submitting an OIC, you must be compliant with all filing requirements, and cannot have a case in bankruptcy. If you have a case pending in bankruptcy court, the IRS will terminate your request.

Note: If you are in bankruptcy or considering it, *do not file* an Offer in Compromise until your case has been resolved in bankruptcy court and the bankruptcy hold has been lifted from your account, or file for bankruptcy after your case has been closed by the IRS. This can take up to six months after a discharge.

Eligibility and Qualifying

In order to determine your eligibility, you must first determine your ability to pay back your tax debt. Before the CSEDs, a financial statement must be completed in order to determine whether you have disposable income (money left over after paying all necessary expenses), or sufficient equity in assets to liquidate to pay your tax debt in full by the CSEDs.

Steps to Determine Your Ability to Pay

Prior to accepting your submission, the IRS will first determine your ability to pay off your tax debt in full. It looks at special circumstances that may exist in your case including:

- health
- education
- occupation
- ability to borrow, etc.

If there are special circumstances that exist in your case, the IRS may determine that you do not have the ability to pay off your tax debt in full. If so, the IRS proceeds to evaluate your financial statement (433-A OIC or 433-B OIC).

Disclosure of Income and Expenses

Offers in Compromise mandate that you complete a financial statement on the Form 433-A OIC for individuals and Form 433-B OIC for businesses. The financial statement forms require that you provide your employment information, assets, income, and expenses.

The financial statement will request your monthly gross income and monthly allowable expenses. Your monthly gross income should be calculated based on your current wage and income information. However, you may also use your wage and income information from the previous year if you expect to earn the same amount or less. The IRS will verify your income based on the prior year's return. If there are any deficiencies in income, the IRS will likely request substantiation of your income. Please *see* the section on Income Calculation for details on how to accurately calculate your income found in Chapter 19, *Income Sources*.

Your monthly expenses will be based on the IRS allowable expenses such as:

- Food, Clothing, and Miscellaneous items
- Housing and Utilities
- Vehicle Ownership and Operational Costs
- Health Care
- Court Ordered Payments
- Current Taxes
- Term Life Insurance
- Mandatory Retirement
- Student Loans, and other secured debt
- Non-reimbursed work-related expenses
- Child Care Expenses

See section on allowable expenses for further details in Chapter 20, *Expenses and Payments*.

The IRS will then determine whether you have sufficient income to pay off your tax debt in full by subtracting your allowable expenses from your monthly gross income. The IRS will determine that you are experiencing a hardship if you have more expenses than income (you end up with a negative number after subtracting allowable expenses from income).

When this happens, your offer amount will be determined solely from your equity in assets. If you have a positive number after subtracting your allowable expenses from your income, the IRS will then perform a Future Income (FI) calculation in order to determine whether you have the ability to pay off your tax debt in full by making monthly payments. If the total debt can be paid by the CSEDs or by the equity in assets, the Offer will be rejected. The amount that FI will add to your final Offer will vary depending on the type of OIC that you submit.

It is important to note the IRS uses two calculations when reviewing an Offer in Compromise:

- Whether the taxpayer or business will be able to pay the balance in full by the CSEDs.

- What the Reasonable Collection Potential (RCP) is for the taxpayer or business.

1. To determine whether a taxpayer or business can pay the balance in full, the IRS will take the monthly available Future Income (FI) if any, multiplied by the months remaining until the CSEDs and then add any equity in assets. If the total is equal to or greater than the total tax debt owed, the Offer In Compromise will

be rejected based on an ability to pay the debt in full before the tax debts expire or CSEDs.

Successful Offers meet the following criteria:
- (Monthly available FI) x (# of Months left until CSEDs) + equity in assets (FI x Months left until CSEDs + equity in assets must be less than the tax debt owed.

Example: John has $200 after his allowable expenses each month and $5,000 in equity in his car.

($200 positive cash flow) x (120 – most possible months before debts expire) + $5,000 in equity < tax owed.

$24,000 + $5,000 = $29,000. As long as this taxpayer owes *more* than $29,000 his Offer in Compromise should be accepted. This is *not* the amount of his Offer or RCP, just the calculation the IRS used to determine if a taxpayer can pay the tax debt in full before the CSEDs.

2. In determining the amount of the Offer In Compromise, it depends on what kind of Offer the taxpayer is submitting to the IRS. There are two types of Offer in Compromises:

- Lump Sum Cash Offer in Compromise
- Short-Term Periodic Payment Offer in Compromise

The first, the Lump Sum Cash Offer in Compromise, requires that you pay off the proposed offer amount within five months or less of the acceptance of the Offer. The second, a Short-Term Periodic Payment Offer in Compromise gives more time. It requires that the proposed offer amount be paid off within 24 months or less (see section below on what should I submit with the forms for further details).

When the Lump Sum method is submitted, the future income will be calculated based on a term of 12 months (**FI = net positive amount x 12 months**), while the longer Short-Term Period Payment method is 24 months (**FI = net positive amount x 24 months**). If the resulting amount is greater than or equal to the tax debt owed to the IRS, your Offer in Compromise will be rejected.

> **Real Life Example 1:** Jeb owed the IRS $20,000 and had no assets. He submitted a Lump Sum Cash Offer in Compromise of $200. After subtracting his allowable monthly expenses from his monthly gross income, he had a positive income of $50.
>
> With the information provided, his offer amount should be calculated as follows: **$600 = $50 x 12**. Based on this information, the IRS determined that Jeb's offer amount should be increased to a total of $600. He was happy to accept the increased amount because he did not have to pay the full $20,000 tax debt and was given five months to pay the offer amount in full.
>
> **Note:** Notice that the IRS did not reject Jeb's Offer in Compromise—the reason why it was not rejected is because his future income would not fully pay off his entire tax debt of $20,000.
>
> In cases such as this one, the IRS will make a counter offer and provide you with a table showing how they obtained and arrived at its calculations.

Real Life Example 2: Abby submitted a Short-Term Periodic Payment Offer in Compromise in the amount of $4,800 in order to settle an IRS tax debt of $100,000. She had no assets. When her offer was submitted, she was required to make an initial payment of $200 (**$4,800** (offer amount) **÷ 24** (24 months of payment required in STP Offer) = **$200**) and would be required to continue making monthly payments of $200 until the $4,800 was paid in full.

By the time the IRS had reviewed the offer, 10 months had already passed. This meant that Abby had already paid $2,000. After reviewing her income and expenses, the IRS determined that she had a positive income remaining of $200.

Using the Short Term Periodic Calculation, it calculated Abby's future income as follows: **$4800 = $200 x 24** (months in the Short-Term Periodic Payment Offer in Compromise). The IRS accepted her Offer in Compromise as it was submitted because it agreed with her figures reported on the financial statement originally submitted.

Note: The IRS may also calculate future income based on the number of months remaining in the CSED or by 120 months.

When the CSED date is less than the number of months allotted by the Lump Sum Cash Offer in Compromise of 12 months, or the Short-Term Periodic Payment Offer in Compromise of 24 months, the IRS *MUST* base its future income calculation based on the number of months remaining under the CSED.

Example: Using the example of Jeb previously, who submitted an Offer in Compromise of $200 but was increased to $600 using a future income calculation of 12 months, assume that his tax debt will expire in 8 months. Since 8 is less than 12 months, the IRS would then calculate his future income as follows: **$50 x 8 = $400.**

As a result, Jeb's Offer in Compromise should then be increased from $200 to $400 instead of $600 that was previously calculated. In this instance, the IRS would then make a counter offer of $400.

Note: If the IRS had calculated Jeb's future income by 120 months, which is far greater than 12 months or the CSED of 8 months, his future income would have been $6,000 ($50 x 120). While he would still have an acceptable Offer in Compromise since $6,000 is less than the tax debt of $12,000; the IRS's counter offer is far greater than what he initially proposed. In some cases, this calculation causes the IRS to reject offers that should have been accepted. If this happens to you, remember to cite *IRM § 5.9.8.5.25.*

> *Internal Revenue Manual § 5.9.8.5.2.5* states that future income should be calculated based on the number of months designated for the type of Offer in Compromise, or the CSED, whichever is **less**.

Equity in Assets

After determining your gross monthly income and expenses, you will then need to determine your equity in assets—the amount you can reasonably expect to collect from an asset if sold or liquidated.

Cash on hand and Bank accounts have a $1,000 exemption.
Note: This exemption only applies to individual bank accounts.
They are valued at the average monthly balance remaining
after you have paid all of your necessary expenses. Other
financial accounts such as IRA, Stocks, Bonds, etc., are
calculated based on the terms of the asset account. If no terms
are provided, you would calculate the values of these assets
as well as any real estate you own and other personal assets
by calculating the Quick Sale Value (QSV) of your assets.

The formula for determining the QSV of your assets is as
follows:

**QSV = FMV times 80 percent minus loan balance
(when applicable),** or

QSV = FMV x .80 – loan balance

Also remember that there is an IRS levy exemption for
personal effects and business tools (see section in Chapter 18,
Household furnishings or Trade and Business Tools for further
details.)

You will determine the QSV of your assets individually,
then add the values obtained together in order to obtain your
total equity in assets. If the total value of your equity in assets
when combined with your future income equals or exceeds your
IRS tax debt, you are not eligible for an Offer in Compromise.

Real Life Example 1: Wallace came to me in order to
determine whether he could negotiate with the IRS and
if so, what would he be eligible for, as he owed the IRS
approximately $50,000. After reviewing his financial
statement, it was clear that he had a negative income.

Wallace only owned a vehicle with a FMV of $13,000 and an outstanding loan balance of $5,000. Based on this information, his QSV for the vehicle would be calculated as follows: **$13,000 x 0.80 – $5,000 = $1,860** (adjusted for the $3,540 vehicle exemption). As a result, the QSV or equity in his only asset is $1,860. **Note:** In order for the vehicle exemption to apply, the vehicle must be used for work, the production of income, and/or the welfare of the taxpayer(s).

We next calculated Wallace's offer amount. Adding the equity in his assets to his future income, it was determined that he did not have a positive income remaining and, therefore, he would have no future income. Wallace's calculation is as follows: **$0 + $1,860 = $1,860**

As a result, he submitted an Offer in Compromise of $1,860 in order to settle his tax debt of $50,000.

Real Life Example 2: Rosella owed the IRS approximately $11,000 and hired my firm to determine her eligibility for an Offer in Compromise. She owned a luxurious vehicle with an FMV of $45,000 and also her home with an FMV of $500,000. The home had an outstanding loan balance of $350,000. Using this information, we first calculated the QSV of her vehicle:

$45,000 x .80 – 0 = $36,000 – $3,450 = $32,550

The QSV of her home was calculated as follows:

$500,000 x .80 - 350,000 = $50,000

Adding the QSV of her vehicle to the QSV of the home, we determined her equity in assets at $82,550.

Without reviewing Rosella's income and expenses, it was readily apparent that she was not eligible for an Offer in Compromise because her equity in assets of $82,550 exceeded her IRS tax debt of $11,000. Instead, my offices established a Streamlined Installment Agreement. This way, she didn't have to disclose her assets and avoided liens being filed on her credit and assets.

Applying for an Offer in Compromise

After verifying that all of your required tax returns have been filed, you need to contact the IRS in order to determine what tax forms and years you owe balances for individually. The next step is to determine your eligibility for an Offer in Compromise and the offer amount by completing your financial statement on the Form 433-A OIC for individuals, and 433-B OIC if filing on behalf of a business that has an EIN number.

After completing the Form 656 Offer in Compromise Form, attach the appropriate fees (see section on fees below for explanation) and mail the required verification documents requested by the Form 433-A OIC or 433-B OIC to the appropriate address via certified mail or postage that has a way to track the documents you send to the IRS. **Note:** You may also use the Form 433-A or 433-B.

There are only two locations where you send your Offer in Compromise unless submitting an Offer to directly to a Revenue Officer assigned to your case: the Memphis IRS Center in Memphis, Tennessee or the Brookhaven IRS Center in Holtsville, New York. Each services assigned states as follows:

If you reside in: AK, AL, AR, AZ, CO, FL, GA, HI, ID, KY, LA, MS, MT, NC, NM, NV, OK, OR, SC, TN, TX, UT, WA, WI, WY

Mail your application to:
Memphis IRS Center COIC Unit
P.O. Box 30803, AMC
Memphis, TN 38130-0803
Phone: 866-790-7117

If you reside in: CA, CT, DE, IA, IL, IN, KS, MA, MD, ME, MI, MN, MO, ND, NE, NH, NY, OH, PA, RI, SD, VT, VA, WV; DC, PR, or a foreign address

Mail your application to:
Brookhaven IRS Center COIC Unit
P.O. Box 9007
Holtsville, NY 11742-9007
Phone: 866-611-6191

When your Offer in Compromise is received by the IRS, you will be sent a letter confirming receipt. In some cases, you may be given a tentative date in which the IRS will contact you to discuss your case. If you do not receive a letter of confirmation within 30 days after submission, you should contact the location where you mailed it to confirm that it was received. If you mail your Offer in Compromise to the wrong address, do not be alarmed or worried. The IRS will forward the package to the appropriate location, although it will most likely result in further delays of your case.

Fees for an Offer in Compromise

When submitting an Offer in Compromise, it is important that you attach the appropriate fees. There is a non-refundable processing fee of $186 and a 20 percent deposit of your offer amount if you are submitting a Lump Sum Cash Offer in Compromise, or the first periodic payment if submitting a Short-Term Periodic Payment Offer in Compromise.

With a Short-Term Periodic Payment Offer in Compromise, you are required to continue making the monthly payment amount determined for 24 months and cannot miss one month. If you do, the IRS may return or reject your offer for failure to meet the terms of the agreement. The deposits are non-refundable, and will be applied to your offer amount if the offer is accepted in order to determine your remaining balance. If it is rejected, the amounts paid in will be applied to your oldest tax year, or the year you designate on the Form 656.

If you meet the low income guidelines established by the IRS, you may not be required to pay the $186 processing fee.[87] Keep this in mind: approval of the low income waiver is made solely by the IRS. If the IRS denies the waiver, you will be notified that you are required to pay the $186 processing fee, and be given a strict deadline in which the fee must be paid.

When in doubt, it is best to submit the $186 processing fee as this may delay your case. Each fee must be paid separately on a check or money order, and made payable to *United States Treasury*. Be sure to include your name, Social Security Number, past year's owed, what type, and address to ensure that your fees will be applied to the correct account.

Caution: Be sure to include the appropriate fees or fee waiver with your forms. Failure to do so will cause an automatic return of your Offer in Compromise. Always double check your documents and forms to ensure that you have attached everything that is required in order to avoid possible delays.

Decision Time Frames

Once you submit your Offer in Compromise, you will then be on the schedule of the IRS, although there is no set time for when the IRS will review yours. Within the IRS' Streamlined Process, you will receive a tentative contact date in the mail. An Offer Examiner (OE) is then assigned to your case and will determine whether your Offer in Compromise is acceptable.

The IRS attempts to review all cases within two years. The usual time frame is six months to a year prior to receiving a decision or being contacted by an OE. You may also receive periodic notifications from the IRS, so it is very important that you check your mail daily.

The IRS may also send a letter notifying you that a lien may be filed while the OIC is being reviewed in order to protect the Government's interest.

Returned and Rejected Offers in Compromise

There are two dreadful notices to receive in the mail from the IRS after submitting an Offer in Compromise. They are the *Offer Returned Letter* and the *Offer Rejected Letter* with the "returned" one being the worse.

The IRS sends a returned offer letter when your initial Offer in Compromise is inadequate or incomplete. This may mean one or more of the following:

- you were not compliant with your previous tax filings;

- you did not include a required form or payment;

- you have a case pending in bankruptcy;

- you waived your right to appeal the decision; or

- you failed to respond to the appeal notice within the specified time frame.

A returned offer is final, and cannot be appealed. You would be instructed to submit a new Offer in Compromise if you wish to have your offer to be considered. Any deposits or periodic payments made will either be applied to the oldest tax year in which you owe back taxes, or the tax year that you specified on the Form 656.

> During this process, it's critical you pay attention to dates and respond within the allocated time frames.

A rejection letter is sent when the OE does not agree with the figures you have provided and has either made a counter offer, or has determined that you are not eligible for an Offer in Compromise. The rejection letter will include the calculations made by the IRS showing how the determination was made. *A rejection letter is not final*, so you will either be given 14 days in which you can respond with your own analysis, or 30 days in which to file an appeal. It is important that you respond within the allotted time frame.

Failure to do so will result in the IRS closing your Offer in Compromise and sending an *Offer in Compromise return letter* which *cannot be appealed*. Any deposits or periodic payments made will either be applied to the oldest tax year in which you owe back taxes, or the tax year that you specified on the Form 656. After you respond to the analysis, the OE may either agree with your calculations or arguments, or may make revisions and provide a counter offer, or disagree completely.

If an agreement is reached between you and the OE, he or she will inform you that they will recommend the offer for acceptance. If an agreement could not be reached, you will be sent a rejection letter in the mail. At that point, you will have 30 days in which to file an appeal.

Note: During this process, it's critical you pay attention to dates and respond within the allocated time frames.

Response Times and Deadlines

The IRS may request other substantiation by sending a request letter in the mail. It is important that you check your mail often after submitting an OIC in order to ensure that you receive any correspondence sent by the IRS. If you receive a request letter from the IRS, it is critical that you respond within the time allotted. The deadlines set by the IRS are very strict, and at times may be very tight as they allow little time in which to respond. Once an OE is assigned to your case, you may receive a phone call from the OE requesting information or a call back by a certain deadline.

An OE may also send a 10-Day Notice in the mail requesting that you contact them within 10 days from the date of the letter. It is important that you do not miss any deadlines set by the IRS as it could result in your Offer in Compromise being returned. As mentioned previously, returned offers cannot be appealed.

Appealing a Rejected Offer in Compromise

When you receive an *Offer in Compromise Rejection letter* in the mail, you will be given 30 days in which to file an appeal. If you desire reconsideration, you should complete and submit Form 13711 *Request for Appeal of Offer in Compromise* that should be included with your rejection letter. If this form is not included with your rejection letter, you may call your OE and request that one be mailed to you, or you may download the form by visiting the IRS website at:

IRS.gov/pub/irs-pdf/f13711.pdf

On Form 13711, you will be given an opportunity to explain the items that you are disputing, and provide additional information that you wish to have considered. You would submit the completed Form 13711 to the OE assigned to your case within the 30-day deadline. The OE will then submit the appeal request to the IRS appeals department.

After the OE submits the appeal request, he or she will

> Appealing an Offer in Compromise is the last and final step in the process, and the decision made by the Appeals Officer is the last and final decision.

no longer be assigned to your case. You will receive a letter confirming receipt of your appeal request by the appeals department. If you have not received a letter confirming receipt of your appeal request within 30 days of submitting, you should contact the original OE and confirm that your request was forwarded. As an additional follow-up, also contact the appeals department to confirm that they have received your request.

Once an Appeals Officer (AO) is assigned, you may be contacted via telephone to discuss the appeal, or receive a letter requesting contact or additional information from the AO. Again, it is important that you respond within the deadline provided in order to avoid having your OIC returned. Once the Appeals Officer makes a determination on your appeals request, that decision will be final and cannot be appealed.

Appealing your Offer in Compromise is the last and final step in the process, and the decision made by the AO is the last and final decision.

Post Approval of your Offer in Compromise

If you are approved, you will receive a letter in the mail confirming acceptance and the terms of the agreement.

- If you submitted a Lump Sum Cash Offer in Compromise, you will be given five months from the date of the acceptance letter to pay the remaining offer amount.
- If you submitted a Short-Term Periodic Payment Offer in Compromise, you will continue to make your monthly periodic payments until you have made a total of 24 total payments.

Note: You must pay the remaining balance on your Offer in Compromise within the time frame allowed. Otherwise, the IRS may reverse it and reinstate the previous tax debt.

As part of the terms, the IRS will retain the refund for the tax year the Offer in Compromise is accepted. For example, if it was accepted in 2014 and you are due a refund that year, the IRS will retain all of it and apply it towards your tax debt. All future refunds will be released to you.

In addition, you will be placed on a five year probation that requires you to file all income tax returns on time with no balances due. If you file a return showing taxes due, you will be required to pay the taxes due in full at the time of filing. If you don't, the IRS will reverse your Offer in Compromise and reinstate your previous tax debt.

Dissipated Assets

The IRS frowns on assets that would have been available to pay down debt to vanish. It is known as a dissipated asset, one that may have been transferred, sold, gifted, or spent and is no longer available to pay towards your IRS tax debt. If the IRS determines that an asset has been dissipated, it will then examine whether the asset should be included in evaluating your case.

Generally, any assets that have been sold or transferred for five or more years will not be considered in evaluating your case. Any dissipated items of less than five years must meet one of the following exemptions in order to be excluded:

1. used for trade or business;
2. used to pay down tax liability;

3. used for a necessary expense recognized by the IRS; and

4. the dissipated asset is the reason why your IRS tax debt exists.

Dissipated Assets and Installment, Currently Not Collectible and Offer in Compromise Agreements

If you are currently negotiating or considering an Installment Agreement, Currently Not Collectible, or Offer in Compromise, having items identified as dissipated assets may exclude you from being eligible. If they are determined sufficient to pay off your tax debt, and were used for an expense or item that the IRS deems unnecessary, it will affect your eligibility.

In an Offer in Compromise case, if the dissipated asset does not qualify for an exemption, the item will be used to calculate your equity in assets. That means that the result may actually increase your settlement offer, or create a rejection if the dissipated asset would have paid off your tax liability in full.

Real Life Example: Oscar filed an Offer in Compromise offering $1,200 to settle his $75,000 tax debt. During Oscar's IRS examination, the examiner found that he had sold a car three years prior for $10,000, and used the funds to pay off outstanding credit card debt, a non-allowable expense. As a result, the examiner increased Oscar's Offer in compromise from $1,200 to $11,200. He still had an acceptable offer on the table because $11,200 is less than his tax debt of $75,000, but the dissipated asset caused a drastic increase of his offer.

Retired Debt

A Retired Debt occurs when an allowable expense is expected to expire prior to the months allotted for the Offer in Compromise or CSED, and will affect the ability to pay. When a debt is going to retire but will not affect a taxpayer's ability to pay, it does not create a retired debt issue.

The formula for determining a retired debt issue is:

Retired Debt = Net Income + expiring payment

If the result is a negative number, then there is no retired debt issue. If the result is a positive number, then a retired debt issue exists. This can affect your eligibility for a Currently Not Collectible, Installment Agreement, or Offer in Compromise.

Example 1: Maggie provided financials for a Currently Not Collectible and was eligible. Her car payment of $250 would end in 12 months. Currently, she has a negative income of $150 after her allowable expenses are deducted. In twelve months, her car payment expires, creating a positive income of $100 (**–$150 + $250 = $100**).

In this case, the IRS will allow Maggie to remain in a Currently Not Collectible status for 12 months and then request her to make monthly payments of $100 after the car payment terminates.

Note: IRS rules for the Offer in Compromise have changed to allow up to $400 of car payments even after the actual car payments have ended.

Example 2: Arnold provided financials for an Installment Agreement and was eligible for a monthly payment of $300. His child support obligation of $400 per month would end in 24 months when his son turned 18. As a result, after the 24 months, the IRS will increase Arnold's monthly payment from $300 to $700 (**$300 + 400 = $700**).

Example 3: Paula submitted a Lump Sum Cash Offer in Compromise of $500 in order to settle her tax debt of $25,000. Her financial statement indicated that she currently has a negative monthly income of $300 and a student loan payment of $200 that is set to expire in 36 months. When that happens, Paula's income would be reduced to a minus $100 (**−$300 + $200 = −$100**).

Paula is still negative. As a result, the IRS determined that there was not a retired debt issue—even without the student loan payment, she would still have a negative monthly income. No changes were therefore made to her offer and it was accepted by the IRS.

Steven's Tip: Creating a resolution takes work and can't be taken lightly. The IRS is in the business to collect all moneys due and owed it. If your circumstances prevent you from meeting your obligations when they occurred, the IRS will work with you … but up to a point. Throughout this chapter, the reference to deadlines and time frames has been stressed—don't ignore them. Throughout, you've been given the formulas that enable you to work with and understand how the IRS can be negotiated with.

It all starts with, and ends with, communication and follow-up.

Endnotes

[87] IRS.gov/pub/irs-pdf/f656b.pdf

Inside this chapter

CHAPTER 22

Special Cases: Meet the Revenue Officer, High Dollar Cases, and CAP Hearings

There are some cases that are so complex that I felt it appropriate to discuss them separately. If you have one of the cases that follow in the next two chapters, obtaining a resolution may not be easy, or you may have several hurdles to overcome prior to obtaining a resolution. Don't try this path alone, this is where you need a tax resolution specialist at your side.

Revenue Officers and Your Case

When an IRS Revenue Officer (RO) enters your life, the collection game is stepped up. He or she may show up at your door without warning. The quest: your assets ... whatever they are—to seek, collect, liquidate, and pay off your past debt. A RO is a serious manner. Not that dealing with the IRS isn't serious—Revenue Officers are usually assigned to cases in which individuals:

- have several delinquent tax returns;
- owe a substantial amount of back taxes, normally over $250,000;
- could not be located systematically;
- have a business that has several delinquent tax returns;
- have a business that owes payroll taxes over $10,000; or
- have a business that has a history of owing payroll taxes every quarter or year.

The goal of the Revenue Officer: to perform seizure of your assets by any means possible to pay your back tax obligations.

When a RO is assigned to your case, it is important that you understand their role: to collect the back taxes owed by any means reasonable and necessary to serve and protect the government's interest.

Don't be surprised to experience a much more aggressive posturing. Several collection actions may be taken simultaneously such as issuing a tax lien, bank levy, and wage garnishment at the same time. RO's may also make unexpected field visits to your residence or place of business. The goal: to perform seizure of your assets.

Dealing with a Revenue Officer

When a RO is assigned to your case, it can be a very stressful experience. To avoid undue stress, it is important that you respond to the RO's request within the time allotted. Cooperation is the key to having a successful resolution with a RO. Failure to cooperate can have dire consequences.

It is also important to understand that a RO is governed by the *Internal Revenue Manual*. Although more aggressive in taking collection action, there are policies and procedures that must be followed. A RO must notify you of any collection action that it intends to take or has taken. Expect the RO to pick up where the system left off.

For example, you are required to receive *two notices of intent to levy* and a *final notice of intent to levy* prior to a bank levy or wage garnishment being issued. If you have already received the first two notices, but not the final notice of intent to levy, when a RO is assigned to your case, he or she will resume collection action by filing the final notice of intent to levy prior to issuing a notice of bank levy, or notice of wage garnishment, or both.

A RO will request various information such as a completed financial statement on the Form 433-A or 433-B and any supporting documentation. Proof that you have taken measures to correct your past mistakes in order to demonstrate that you will not owe in the future may be requested by the RO. Once all information requested has been obtained and verified as accurate, the RO is required to adhere to your financial statement.

Once you and the RO have reached an agreement on the resolution, the proposal will be submitted to his or her manager for approval. What happens if you can't reach agreement? Are you stuck with an either/or situation? No—you can request help in resolving your dispute with the RO by:

1. asking for the RO's manager to call you back;

2. having an independent review;

3. appealing under the Collection Appeal Program (CAP) on Form 9423; or

4. seeking the assistance of the Taxpayer Advocate.

Demanding a Manager Call Back

Prior to requesting an Independent Reviewer or CAP Hearing, you should request to speak to the RO's manager to discuss your case. Your goal is to persuade the manager to accept your proposal, overriding whatever the RO proposed. If the manager does not agree with it, you may then request an Independent Reviewer as your next step.

You may also request a manager call back when the RO has:

- failed to return your call within a reasonable time;
- failed to adhere to IRS policies and procedures; or
- failed to discuss any unresolved issues you may have.

Alert: You should always request to speak to the RO's manager prior to escalating the matter to another department.

Requesting an Independent Reviewer

When an agreement cannot be reached with either the RO or the RO's manager, you may request an Independent Reviewer (IR) be assigned to your case. Still an employee of the IRS, an IR is required to make an impartial decision solely on the information provided. At this juncture, he or she may choose to accept your proposal, the RO's proposal, or make an independent determination which could be a variation of what's already on the table or even something that has not been proposed to date. You will then be given the opportunity to either accept the IR's determination, or file for a CAP—the Collections Appeals Program Hearing.

Involving the Taxpayer Advocate

Along the way, you may engage the Taxpayer Advocate Service (TAS). The office offers free assistance in helping you to resolve your IRS tax matter when you cannot resolve the tax debt on your own. The National Taxpayer Advocate, is an independent organization within the IRS and reports directly to the National Taxpayer Advocate office. To find a contact with your state, use this link: *IRS.gov/uac/Contact-a-Local-Taxpayer-Advocate*.

In select states, a free video conferencing has been created to work with you—you can find those locations within the site above.

TAS generally assists taxpayers and businesses under the following circumstances:

1. currently experiencing a financial hardship;

2. facing an immediate adverse action, and have tried to contact the IRS but no one has responded; or

3. the IRS has failed to respond within the allotted time promised.

Individuals or businesses meeting these criteria will have a TAS repesentative covering their area or location assigned to their case. The goal: to assist you or your business in resolving whatever the IRS tax problem is. In addition, the TAS also assists in audits, document processing, and refunds. To contact your local TAS, call: 877-777-4778.

Note: There are no guarantees in how quickly the TAS will respond. The office can take months to start taking action and can be just as ineffective as the department you are currently working with.

Requesting a Collections Appeals Program Hearing

When your proposal has been denied, and you have exhausted all of the previous measures, you can file under the Collections Appeal Program (CAP). You must complete the Form 9423 and submit the Form to the RO or department that denied your request. Typically, a CAP is a faster appeal process than one filed in Tax Court.

Note: The decision made by the CAP representative *cannot* be appealed in Tax Court. While your appeal is pending, the IRS generally will not take any further collection action until a decision has been made.

You may go through the CAP process if you've received any one of the following notices:

- Notice of Federal Tax Lien
- Notice of Levy
- Notice of Seizure
- Denial or Termination of Installment Agreement

Once you make the decision to go forward with a CAP procedure, it's important to understand the process/procedure you need to follow.

1. *If your only collection contact has been a notice or telephone call, start here:*

   - Call the IRS telephone number shown on your notice;
   - Explain why you disagree and that you want to appeal the decision; and
   - Be prepared to offer a solution.

Before you can start the appeals process with the Office of Appeals you will need to first discuss your case with a Collections manager.

2. If you have already been in contact with a Revenue Officer:

- Call the Revenue Office you've been dealing with;
- Explain why you disagree and that you want to appeal the decision;
- Be prepared to offer a solution; and
- Complete Form 9423, *Collection Appeals Request.*

Before you can start the appeals process with the Office of Appeals you will need to discuss your case with a Collections manager.

> **Alert:** You have *only two days* from your conference with the Collections manager to submit the Form 9423 to the Revenue Officer.

A CAP Hearing Officer will be assigned to your case upon receipt of the Form 9423. You will then be contacted by the CAP Hearing Officer to discuss your case and a determination will be made. He will send a copy of the final decision to both you and the RO. Both you and the RO will then be required to adhere to the decision made by the CAP Hearing Officer.

Think of a CAP Hearing as the last resort and the end of the road … what happens here is what happens.

High Dollar Debts in Excess of $250,000

In the past, cases in which individuals owed more than $100,000 in back taxes were called High Dollar cases, and would have their account assigned to the Large Dollar Unit (LDU) at the IRS. However, the IRS eliminated this unit, and will generally assign cases owing $250,000 or more to a

Revenue Officer. Cases in which individuals owe less than $250,000 would likely be resolved by the Collections Department at the IRS.

Cases with large sums owed are handled differently from those in which the balances are below $250,000. When you owe a large amount, think of your situation as the "tell all"— as in you need to substantiate your income, bank statements, and provide proof of any expenses that exceed the national standards if requested. The Collections representative or Revenue Officer may require that you mail in your documents that validate your information unless you have a current bank levy or wage garnishment already in process, in which case you would be allowed to fax your substantiation directly to the representative or Revenue Officer.

> If you choose to go through the Collections Appeals Program (CAP) process, you cannot go to Tax Court on the Appeals' decision.

Don't take chances with your mail delivery: always send correspondence to the IRS via certified mail, or any method that has verified tracking. Documents may get lost internally, you want proof you sent them.

Maintaining your standard of living

Individuals who owe significant funds to the IRS are likely to live and spend money above what would be considered "average" or outside the guidelines set by the national standards discussed in Chapter 20, *Expenses and Payments*. If that's you, you may have some surprises and changes in store that the IRS will set, and you won't like.

With all cases that are considered High Dollar cases, the national standards are strictly applied. In High Dollar cases, the IRS will generally not allow any expenses that exceed the national standards with the exception of health care expenses. As a result, if your current standard of living exceeds the national standards established by the IRS for your county or region, you may be advised by the representative or Revenue Officer to modify your current living situation so that you can conform to the national standards, and be able to pay back your tax debt.

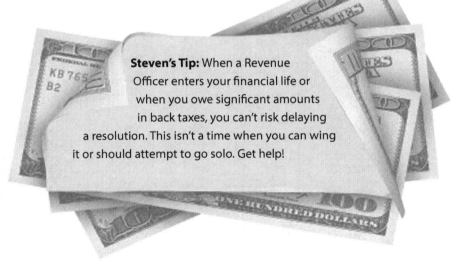

Steven's Tip: When a Revenue Officer enters your financial life or when you owe significant amounts in back taxes, you can't risk delaying a resolution. This isn't a time when you can wing it or should attempt to go solo. Get help!

Inside this chapter

Special Cases ...
Owing Payroll Taxes

One of your responsibilities as a business is to make sure you pay taxes that are withheld from your W-2 employee's payroll checks. As an employer, you are also liable for Social Security and Medicare payments/taxes withheld along with your portion of the Social Security tax.

The typical wages that are subject to federal employment taxes include salaries, vacation allowances, bonuses, commissions, and fringe benefits. Employers are required to make payroll tax deposits either monthly or quarterly. In general, you must deposit all federal income tax withheld from your employees' income, and both the employer and employee social security and Medicare taxes. You will then be required to file employment tax returns on the Form 941 for each quarter, and 940 at the end of the year.

As mentioned earlier, when it comes to businesses and IRS issues, it's often going to come from payroll taxes, as in not paying them in a timely manner. It's one of the most common ways that businesses keep going, along with avoiding paying taxes—payroll tax debt can stay invisible for a good year before the IRS will start hounding a business owner. Rarely does an employee think to verify whether his withholdings have been paid to the IRS on his behalf. The chaos that can be created for you and your business can be catastrophic as the thousands and thousands of dollars in missed payments build up.

Resolving Payroll Tax debt

If you as an employer owe $10,000 or less, you will be able to resolve your tax liability with the Business Account Customer Service Department (Business ACS) of the IRS. To seek help, you must first be compliant by filing all required tax returns. You then can choose to resolve your account through a Streamlined Installment Agreement or a Currently Not Collectible if you no longer have active payroll or W-2 employees. As indicated in Chapter 21, *Resolutions, Offers and Agreements*, Streamlined Installment Agreements don't require a financial statement; the Currently Not Collectible does. You can either print out Form 433-B online at the*IRS.gov* website or you can give your information to the IRS representative over the phone.

If you owe over $10,000 in payroll taxes, have unfiled employment tax returns, or a consistent pattern of noncompliance, the IRS will be far more aggressive. It may assign the case to a Revenue Officer (see Chapter 22, *Special Cases ... Meet the Revenue Officer, High Dollar Cases and CAP Hearings*). If a Revenue Officer is assigned, don't be surprised to find him or her on your business doorstep in what's known as a *field visit*.

A financial statement will be requested on the Form 433-B in order to determine your ability to pay any taxes owed. He or she will require that all payroll tax deposits be made, and employment tax returns are filed.

In most cases when a RO is assigned, you can expect to enter into either an Installment Agreement or a Streamlined Installment Agreement if applicable. The length of time of either will last no longer than 24 months. It is unusual for a RO to place an employer on Currently Not Collectible status when the business is still in operation. In rare cases, what is known as an *In-Business Currently Not Collectible* may be granted in order to allow the company to remain in operation.

If this is done, the RO may file a tax lien or initiate the Trust Fund Recovery Penalty (TFRP) against your business in order to protect the government's interest.

> In most cases when an RO is assigned, you can expect to enter into either an Installment Agreement or a Streamlined Installment Agreement if applicable. The length of time of either will last no longer than 24 months.

If your business is not profitable and has been unable to make its payroll tax deposits, the RO is likely to analyze the case to determine whether it is better to close the business and liquidate the assets to pay back some or all of the taxes due.

Employers intending to remain in operation must be able to demonstrate that the business is able to afford to make the required monthly payment, and remain current in making its payroll tax deposits and return filings.

The Trust Fund Recovery Penalty

Forget about what you normally think of as a Trust for your assets and asset accumulation. This type of trust has nothing to do with your future comfort. In fact, it's got a whopping penalty possibility attached to it.

In truth, it is a tax assessed against a taxpayer that said they were going to send money to the IRS on behalf of others (you as an individual or your company—that taxpayer could be you or someone acting on your behalf) but never did.

In order to encourage employers to make prompt payment of the taxes owed, the IRS may assess a Trust Fund Recovery Penalty (TFRP). Whoever within a business collects taxes on behalf of the IRS and fails to forward them to it, will find Internal Revenue Code Section 7501 comes into play. Revenue Officers go out and assess and collect those unpaid taxes against those who did not collect and forward those taxes to the IRS. The **Trust Fund Recovery Penalty** is equal to 100 percent of the unpaid taxes held in trust—that means what wasn't paid, and is owed, could be double.

> If your business is in a situation that payroll tax payments were ignored, count on the IRS Revenue officers to be overaggressive in imposing the penalty rather than allowing someone to get away with it.

Personal Liability for Business Debt

When it comes to collecting back payroll taxes, the IRS will go after anyone who it believes had a responsibility to make sure payments were made. To be liable for the Trust Fund Recovery Penalty, a person must have had a duty to collect and pay the taxes, and willfully failed to do so. At least, that's what the law says. If your business is in a situation that payroll tax payments were ignored, count on the IRS Revenue officers to be overaggressive in imposing the penalty rather than allowing someone to get away with it.

In all TFRP cases, the RO will require a financial statement in order to determine which individual or individuals were responsible for making the payroll tax deposits or payments. He will meet with those individuals and conduct a TFRP Interview in order to determine:

1. Whether the individual was responsible for collecting and making the required payroll tax deposits or payments; and

2. Whether the individual *willfully* failed to collect and/or make the required deposits or payments.

You are considered the person responsible for making the payroll tax deposits if you had the duty or power to perform the task of collecting and making the required payroll tax deposits or payments. In most cases, the person responsible will be the owner of the business, the Certified Public Accountant (CPA), an officer or Chief Financial Officer (CFO) of the business, or an employee charged with this responsibility. The IRS will also find willfulness when the person responsible was aware or should have been aware of the outstanding taxes, and intentionally disregarded the law, or was indifferent to its requirements.

Note: The IRS does not require that the person have an evil intent or bad motive to disregard the law in order for *willingness* to be found.

Once the RO makes a determination of who should be held responsible, a letter stating that a TFRP will be assessed and mailed. You will be given 60 days, or 75 days if you reside outside of the United States, in order to file an appeal. The letter will also explain your appeal rights—*IRS Publication 5* contains further details and instructions on how to prepare and file your appeal.

> The **Trust Fund Recovery Penalty** is equal to 100 percent of the unpaid taxes held in trust.

If you do not appeal or succeed with your appeal, a TFRP will be assessed personally against you, and cannot be removed until the debt is paid in full, or through the filing of and acceptance of an Offer in Compromise. Once the IRS has you in its sights and the TFRP is assessed against you, it may then take collection action against you personally. That means that it could issue levies, wage garnishments, liens, and/or initiate the seizure of assets.

Collection action is usually not undertaken while the business is still in operation. That will change quickly if the business closes—collection action will follow in order to collect any payroll taxes owed before all assets disappear.

Distancing Yourself from a TFRP

The best way to avoid having a TFRP personally assessed against you is to keep your business compliant and viable. Do this by:

- Making all payroll tax deposits in a timely manner;
- Filing any and all required employment tax returns promptly; and
- Paying any balances due immediately.

If an RO is assigned to your case, comply with all requests and provide any documentation requested by the required deadline. Your cooperation and willingness to change your past practices will be beneficial and may help to avoid having a TFRP assessed against you.

Liabilities if Your Business Closes

If taxes are owed, the IRS is on the hunt when a business closes. The most likely person to start with for payment is you—the owner or one of the owners of the business. Once the business closes, the IRS will then undertake collection action against the individual or individuals held responsible for the TFRP if the business is not able to pay off its tax debt in full. It will then require financial information from each person against whom the TFRP was assessed.

When a TFRP has been assessed against two or more individuals, the tax debt becomes joint and severely liable. This means that the IRS may collect all of the tax debt from one individual. This is typically done when one individual has little or no funds or assets while the other has the ability to pay the tax debt in full. The individual from whom the full tax debt was collected may then seek reimbursement from the other individual or individuals involved.

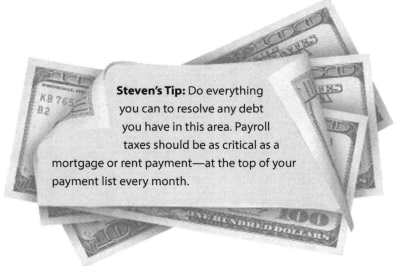

Steven's Tip: Do everything you can to resolve any debt you have in this area. Payroll taxes should be as critical as a mortgage or rent payment—at the top of your payment list every month.

Inside this chapter

CHAPTER 24

Bankruptcy, Separation, Divorce, and Debt

Let's face it—events happen that you can't control. Sometimes you've exhausted all means to get your financial life back in order—for you personally and/or your business. Bankruptcy now becomes an option, a legal process in which bad debts are either extinguished or a plan may be implemented for repayment depending on which chapter of bankruptcy you file your petition. On the personal side, a bankruptcy filing only discharges income tax debt—it does not discharge other types of taxes including payroll taxes, TRFP penalties, etc.

Filing for a bankruptcy places an automatic stay on collection action by the IRS, but extends the IRS CSED so that it has more time to collect on any remaining tax debt that was not discharged. Seldom is bankruptcy a better option than trying to negotiate directly with the IRS for moneys owed it. The exception would be if aggressive collection action is being taken against you, filing for bankruptcy will obtain a stay on the collection process. Depending on which chapter you file, you may force the IRS to accept a payment plan, which would include some or all of your income tax debt being reduced, or having it completely discharged.

Bankruptcy and Your Credit

The downside to filing a bankruptcy petition is that this action will last on your credit report for 10 years. This may prevent you from qualifying for various loans, as well as jobs. Prior to filing bankruptcy, you should weigh the pros and cons and determine whether it would cause more harm than good.

Differences Between Chapter 7 and Chapter 13 Bankruptcies

The two most common forms of bankruptcy that provides some assistance in resolving an IRS tax debt are Chapter 7 and Chapter 13 bankruptcy. It is important to understand that each form resolves IRS tax debt differently. Chapter 7 is the only bankruptcy option that may discharge some or all of your IRS tax debt, while Chapter 13 may either reduce a portion of your debt, and establish a payment plan to repay the remaining balance, or simply establish a repayment plan for paying off your IRS tax debt. In a bankruptcy proceeding, it is important to know that only income tax debt can be discharged. All other tax debts cannot be discharged by filing bankruptcy.

Chapter 7 Bankruptcy

In a Chapter 7 Bankruptcy, the court may either discharge all or a portion of your IRS income tax debt. However, in order for the income tax debt to be discharged, it must meet the following guidelines:

- The tax debt must have been due at least three years prior to your bankruptcy filing. This is called the Three-Year Rule.

- The tax return must be filed at least two years prior to your bankruptcy filing. This is called the Two-Year Rule.

- The taxes owed must have been assessed against you at least 240 days prior to your bankruptcy filing. This is called the 240-Day Rule.

- The tax debt cannot be the result of tax fraud or tax evasion.

- The tax debt must be income tax debt only.

If approved, a Chapter 7 discharge of income taxes will remove your obligation to pay back the taxes owed. However, if any tax liens were filed against you prior to bankruptcy, the tax lien will remain in effect up to the value of your equity in assets. For example, if a tax lien of $50,000 has been filed against you, but your remaining assets are valued at $10,000, the tax lien will remain in effect up to $10,000.

A Chapter 7 filing is not recommended for individuals who may have substantial assets, as some assets may be exempt while others are not. All assets not exempted will be included in the bankruptcy and may be used to satisfy outstanding debts.

Chapter 7 Bankruptcy can only be filed once every six years, but is the *only* bankruptcy option for discharging IRS income tax debt.

Chapter 13 Bankruptcy

The most common form of a bankruptcy filing is a Chapter 13. It is used for *resolving* IRS income tax debt within a repayment plan that will be determined by a court trustee. It *does not discharge* the income tax debt but will require that you make monthly payments for a specified amount and for a specified length of time which may be a minimum of three years to five years maximum.

The court trustee may also reduce the amount of the income tax debt if four conditions are met:

1. The debt must be income tax debt.
2. The Three-Year Rule must be met.
3. The 240-Day Rule must be met.
4. No liens were filed by the IRS, or if a lien was filed, there is no property upon which the lien may be applied.

If these conditions are not met, the tax debt must be paid in full, and the payment plan established in the bankruptcy proceeding will be adjusted in order for the tax debt to be paid in full within the allotted time. The Two-Year Rule requiring that all tax returns must be filed prior to filing a Chapter 7 is not applicable in Chapter 13.

The benefit of Chapter 13, *Foreign Financial Assets—When and How to Report* is that it will stop all penalties and interests from continuing to accrue from the date the bankruptcy is filed, unlike an IRS Installment Agreement or Streamlined Installment Agreement where the penalties and interests will continue to accrue. It may also reduce penalties and interests owed to the IRS. Chapter 13 also forces the IRS to accept the repayment plan proposed by the Bankruptcy Court and cannot collect more than the judge approves. This option may also be beneficial in cases where a RO is assigned that refuses to establish a reasonable Installment Agreement or resolution.

Divorced and Debt Aren't Always Separate

Individuals are considered divorced on the date that the divorce is made final in a court of law. Contrary to what many believe, divorce does not discharge a tax debt. The IRS holds that husband and wife are jointly and severally liable for the tax debts in which a joint return was filed. As a result, it may pursue one or both parties in order to collect the full amount of tax debt owed as both are held liable for the tax debt that was created during the marriage.

If the husband or the wife paid the tax debt in full and the other did not contribute anything to its creation, his or her only recourse is to pursue a civil action in a court of law to collect the portion that should have been paid by the former spouse.

Debt and Separation

Sometimes divorced couples still reside in the same household. When this occurs, the IRS may establish a resolution with one party that protects the other from collection activity. If they are separated or living apart, the spouse setting up the resolution with the IRS may choose to establish a resolution only for him or her and exclude the other spouse. When this happens, the IRS will perform a task called *Mirroring the Account* in which case, the spouse establishing the resolution will be protected from further collection action, but the IRS will pursue collection action against the former spouse.

In Offer in Compromise cases, if the offer is accepted for one party where the taxes were owed jointly, the IRS will reduce the total debt by the amount of the offer, and pursue the other party for the remaining tax debt.

In some cases where parties are divorced and living apart, they may still be able to resolve the account jointly. In Offer and Compromise cases, both parties may submit the offer jointly using separate Forms 433-A OIC, or Form 433-A and then one Form 656 if resolving joint liabilities only.

In the case of Currently Not Collectible, parties living separately cannot submit a Currently Not Collectible on behalf of the spouse (or former spouse), each person would need to submit a request for Currently Not Collectible separately. However, one spouse may set up an Installment Agreement and agree to pay back the full amount of the joint tax liability if he or she chooses to do so. This would prevent the IRS from pursuing collection action against the other spouse. Chapter 21, *Resolutions, Offers and Agreements* would be helpful to review so that you have a clear understanding of what each agreement is.

Assisting Your Ex

The decision to help or not to help an ex-spouse is completely within your discretion. It can provide simplicity as *Mirroring* cases may cause confusion when two taxpayers are making payments on the same tax liability. In some cases, such as Offer in Compromise, it may be easier to have the case resolved when both spouses are eligible for the status rather than trying to resolve the tax debt separately. You should weigh the pros and cons of your decision and make an informed choice.

Seeking Non-Liable Status

You may be considered a Non-Liable Party (NLP)—someone who lives with and shares living expenses with a taxpayer who owes back taxes to the IRS. You though, don't owe the IRS for the back taxes. NLPs can be a spouse, parent, or roommate. When you live with an NLP, a special calculation must be done and can affect your eligibility for the resolution you are seeking.

Pro-Rating Expenses

When an NLP resides in your household, you may be required to pro-rate your shared expenses based on the income of all parties residing in the household. A percentage will be determined for which you are responsible for the shared household expenses. This percentage is determined by adding the incomes of everyone in the household, then dividing your income by the total household income.

Pro-rationing is more likely to be demanded when a taxpayer shares expenses and co-mingles bank accounts, funds, etc. This is more common among married individuals and when negotiating an Offer in Compormise.

The Pro-Ration Formula is as Follows:

Taxpayer's share = taxpayer's monthly gross income ÷ (taxpayer's monthly gross income + NLP's monthly gross income) x 100.

Example: Stephan was married to Barbie. They lived in the same household with one minor child. Barbie was not liable for Stephan's IRS tax debt he had incurred. They shared expenses for food, clothing and miscellaneous items, housing and utilities, and out-of-pocket health care expenses. His monthly gross income was $4,000 and hers $2,000.

The national standard for food, clothing and miscellaneous items for a household of three individuals (H + W + child = 3) is $1,249. Total housing and utilities was $2,000 and was within the IRS standard for their county. The national standard for out-of-pocket health care was **$180 (60 x 3 = $180)**. With this information, Stephan's portion of the shared expenses is calculated as:

Income share: $4,000 (taxpayer's monthly gross income) ÷ ($4,000 (taxpayer's monthly gross income) + $2000 (NLP's income) x 100 = 67 percent. His portion of the shared expenses is 67 percent. Next, multiply the shared expenses by 0.67 or 67 percent.

Expense portion of food, clothing and miscellaneous items: **$1,249 x 0.67 = $836.83** or **$837**. Stephan is responsible to pay $827 for this shared expense and would report this figure on his Form 433-A or 433-F.

Housing and utilities portion: **$2,000 x 0.67 = $1,340**. He will claim $1,340 for this item on his Form 433-A or 433-F.

Note: If Stephan's housing and utilities exceeded the national standard for the housing and utilities for his household size based on his county, he would pro-rate his share based on the maximum allowed by the national standard if negotiating an Offer in Compromise. In Currently Not-Collectible or an Installment Agreement cases, he may be allowed to exceed the national standard if he provides proof of this expense.

Out-of-pocket health care portion: **$180 x 0.67 = $120.60 or $121**. As a result, he would claim $121 for this expense on his Form 433-A or 433-F.

Non-Disclosure of Income by a Non-Liable Individual

Some people are married; some are not. In a situation where one does not have a liability or responsibility for the debts of the other, the NLP may not want to include his or her income so that a proper pro-ration may be conducted. When that happens, the IRS may try to obtain what the income is internally if the NLP is a spouse. Previous joint tax returns would include income and the Social Security number. If information is obtained internally, the IRS will perform its own pro-rationing calculation. You should double check the representative's calculation based on the information they have obtained as the representative may pro-rate incorrectly. In cases where the information cannot be obtained, the IRS will then use the default pro-ration of 50 percent of all shared expenses. The most common shared expense is housing and utilities. All other allowable expenses will be based on what you submitted to the IRS.

> **Example:** Lars and Marisa were roommates but were not married. Lars owed the IRS but Marisa was not liable for his tax debt. She refused to provide her income to him so that he could pro-rate the shared expenses. When he informed the IRS representative of this, the representative tried to obtain her information internally, but was not successful. So the representative used the default pro-ration of 50 percent in order to determine his share of the housing and utilities expenses.
>
> Lars reported that his total housing and utilities expense for him and his roommate was $1,400. The representative then determined that his share was $700 (**$1,400 x 0.50 = $700**). All other expenses were based on what he reported.

Steven's Tip: If there was one word to sum up separation, divorce, bankruptcy, and debt, it would be: complicated. It's not just the financials, it's the emotional and the stress factors that accompany both taxes, the turmoil that relationships and financial issues can create. In all the situations and scenarios described within this chapter, my years advising and working with individuals has shown me that the most common mistake made is trying to handle it alone. Don't.

Inside this chapter

CHAPTER 25

Tax Resolutions Scams and Scandals

Tax scandals have plagued the United States in the last decade. Taxpayers and organizations have been victims of tax scams both by tax resolution firms as well as the IRS. In order to avoid being a victim of either, it is important that you understand your rights and what representatives and the IRS can and cannot do. Knowing your rights will help you to detect foul play and help you understand what options you have to resolve those types of problems. Knowing, and understanding them will set up safeguards to prevent you from being enveloped in a tax resolution scandal.

In the last decade, major tax resolution firms have been sued by taxpayers and state authorities for allegedly misrepresenting their ability to resolve IRS tax debt, and for some, this resulted in the company going out of business.

J.K. Harris & Co. was founded by CPA John K. Harris in 1997 and became the largest tax resolution firm in the United States. This firm has been sued several times by taxpayers. In fact, in 2007, it settled a class action suit that was filed in the South Carolina Circuit for approximately $6.2 million. Then in 2008, J.K. Harris also settled a suit with several Attorneys General of 18 different states for approximately $1.5 million.

Roni Lynn Deutch, a Professional Tax Corporation, was founded in 1991 by Tax Attorney Roni Lynn Deutch, LLM. In 2007, the New York City Department of Consumer Affairs brought suit against Deutch in which the firm settled by agreeing to pay $200,000 restitution to consumers and $100,000 in fines to the City of New York. Then in 2010, then California Attorney General Jerry Brown, and now Governor of California, filed suit against Deutch in California Superior Court in the County of Sacramento for $33.9 million in civil penalties and restitution to taxpayers, and a permanent injunction. Deutch then publicly announced that her firm would be closing in May of 2011. Now out of business, her case is still ongoing in the Superior Court of California, in the County of Sacramento.

TaxMasters Inc. was founded by CPA Patrick Cox in Houston, Texas. In 2010, it was sued by the Texas Attorney General on behalf of over 1,000 taxpayers. The Attorney General of Minnesota filed suit against TaxMasters for allegedly misleading Minnesota residents about its ability to reduce their tax debt and for making unrealistic promises.

Each of these firms had an "F" rating with the Better Business Bureau. Each were high-profiled within the media. Each did extensive promotional advertising. And each bamboozled many thousands of taxpayers.

Identifying and Selecting Competent Tax Resolution Professionals

It is important to remember that if something sounds too good to be true, it usually is. Do not be misled by companies who promise to reduce your tax debt prior to conducting an assessment of your financial profile. Prior to determining your eligibility for a settlement, the firm must ask you questions about your income, expenses, and assets. If these questions are not asked, your only eligibility would be for a Streamlined Installment Agreement assuming you owe $50,000 or less.

Do not believe the success rates reported by tax resolution professionals without conducting independent research.

Don't be fooled by their promises or television commercials. Selecting a reputable tax professional can save you from more than the stress of dealing with the IRS; it can save you time and money. Below are tips for selecting a reputable tax professional:

1. **Investigate the reputation of the tax resolution professional.** If the tax resolution professional/company has derogatory remarks about it or has been sued before by taxpayers like yourself and has lost, this is an indication that you could end up being the victim of a tax scam. A reputable tax resolution professional/company will have great rapport with clients as well as other tax resolution professionals/companies. A starting point in your research may be the Internet, or the Better Business Bureau. On the Internet, do a Google search with the company's name followed with: "complaint," "con," "lawsuit," "problems," "scam," "fraud." Read everything. It's consumer beware.

2. **Do not believe a tax resolution professional who makes promises or guarantees.** The only thing a tax

resolution professional/company can guarantee is that they will do their best or put forth the best effort on your case. Tax resolution professionals and companies cannot promise or guarantee an outcome on your case because the final determination is made by the IRS on your case. They cannot guarantee that you will qualify to settle your debt for less, or that they can stop IRS collections. If you encounter a tax resolution professional or company that makes you any such promise or guarantee, you should not hire that individual or firm.

3. **Do not believe the success rates reported by tax resolution professionals without conducting independent research.** You should be fully aware that the success of one case does not guarantee the success of another. Do not fall into this trap by thinking that your case is more likely to be successful if someone or a company has resolved many cases successfully. Reputable tax resolution professionals will not disclose their success rate or indicate that their success on another case guarantees the success of your case.

4. **Do not pay unreasonable fees.** Most tax resolution professionals will charge a flat fee for their services. Typically, the cost may vary with the service. All fees should be reasonable. One way to tell if the fees are, in fact, reasonable is by researching how much other tax professionals charge for the same service. You are allowed to discuss your case with other tax professionals

prior to choosing one to handle your case. Be prudent in your research so that you will not pay more than necessary to have your case resolved.

5. **Make sure that the tax resolution professional is responsive to your needs.** Never retain someone that you cannot get a hold of. A reputable tax resolution professional/company will understand that client communication is the most important responsibility in representing taxpayers, its clients. You have a right to know what is going on with your case, and you have the right to contact the tax professional to ask any questions that you may have concerning your case.

If you feel like you cannot get ahold of your tax resolution professional, the company that he or she works with, or they fail to respond to your calls within a reasonable time (usually 24 to 48 hours), you should consider hiring one who is able to meet your needs. You must ensure that you allow a reasonable response time. Do not expect a call back right away. Allow the tax resolution professional a reasonable time to respond to your request.

6. **Read the Retainer Agreement thoroughly.** All tax resolution professionals and companies should have a retainer agreement or contract that you are required to sign prior to retaining their services. The contract should explain what service/services are being provided, and what you are paying for. Do not sign an agreement without reading and understanding every clause. Ask

questions for any items that you do not understand or that raises a concern. If there isn't a retainer agreement or contract, this is a strong indication that it may be a scam.

IRS Tax Scandal of 2013

In general, the IRS handles cases professionally and follows the guidelines, policies and procedures of the *Internal Revenue Manual* (IRM). In 2013, however, a scandal erupted involving the IRS and its treatment of various 501(c)4 tax exempt organizations.

Donations given to 501(c)4 organizations are usually not tax deductible and donors are kept anonymous unless the donations are $5,000 or more. If they exceed $14,000, they may be subject to the gift tax.

While these organizations are prohibited from donating to the campaigns of political candidates, they are able to participate in lobbying and campaigning. The IRS experienced a rapid increase in applications for 501(c)4 status. Applications nearly doubled after the January 2010 Supreme Court decision that loosened campaign-finance rules.

It has been alleged that employees of the IRS inappropriately targeted conservative 501(c)4 organizations by applying more scrutiny than to those supporting liberal causes, and it deviated from the policies and procedures dictated by the IRM. Tea Party groups that were investigated by the IRS reported that the IRS made unusually extensive demands, such as asking them to provide social-media posts, books that members had read, and whether any members of the group planned to run for public office in the future.

In some cases, the questioning took almost three years, which prevented some groups from participating in the 2010 and 2012 elections. General Russell George, Treasury Inspector, is investigating the scandal in order to determine whether the IRS has correctly applied the law to these 501(c)4 groups, or whether political influence was a contributing factor of the inappropriate targeting of conservative 501(c)4 groups.

> Taxpayers/organizations cannot be discriminated against for their political party affiliation by the IRS.

The acting IRS Commissioner, Steven Miller, was fired by President Obama. Miller alleged that the targeting of conservative groups was the result of mismanagement, and not due to partisan politics. In the first hearing, Miller acknowledged that he was aware of the investigation for almost a year. He refused to release the names of the IRS employees that targeted the conservative groups, and Republicans learned that Deputy Treasury Secretary, Neal Wolin, was aware for almost a year that a government watchdog was looking into inappropriate targeting by the IRS.

If You Suspect Foul Play ... What Should You Do?

The recent IRS scandal of 2013 was not the first time that the IRS has been involved in a scandal. It has been accused of corruption ever since the institution of the income tax in order to raise funds for the Civil War. The IRS also faced similar scrutiny during the hearings of the 1990s that led to the Tax Reform and Restructuring Act of 1998, which changed the rules on how IRS employees identified themselves and conducted audits. It is important to understand the *Internal Revenue Manual*[89] so that you may be aware of what information the IRS employees are entitled to ask for and under what circumstances. It provides the procedures and guidelines for which IRS employees must act or conduct various tasks.

The IRS cannot arbitrarily select certain taxpayers or organizations for review. It must apply the same standard to all, a standard which would be outlined in the IRM.

Taxpayers have rights as outlined in the *Taxpayer Bill of Rights*.[90] In order to understand your rights; clearly you must learn what your rights are. So take some time to read the *Taxpayer Bill of Rights* so that you will know when those rights are violated by an IRS employee. Generally, the IRS may request any information that is related to the tax matter at hand. However, it must provide you with a reason for why the information is being requested and what it is to be used for.

Generally, the IRS cannot:

- Discriminate against taxpayers or organizations—you cannot be discriminated against because of your color, race, sex, religion, national origin, disability, or age, or political party affiliation.

- Disclose your information to unauthorized third parties—your information should be kept private and confidential by the IRS.

• Be unprofessional—IRS must provide professional and courteous service.

There may be times when you encounter an IRS agent that is overzealous in their collection efforts, goes beyond the scope of their authority, or does not follow the *Internal Revenue Manual.* When this occurs, you should first contact the manager of the IRS employee. If you are unable to resolve the issue with the manager, you may then contact the Taxpayer Advocate Service (TAS) for assistance. If the TAS is not able to assist in the matter, you may then consider writing a letter to the IRS director for your area or the center where you file your tax return. You also have the right to appeal the IRS decision, or file suit against the IRS in a court of law.

Steven's Tip: If you are uncertain of your rights during an audit or in negotiating with the IRS, it's wise to seek assistance. If you suspect that something is amiss or that you are being discriminated against, it's wise to seek assistance. Too many times, taxpayers go along with the IRS, not knowing or understanding that they could do better.

Endnotes

[89] IRS.gov/irm/index.html
[90] IRS.gov/pub/irs-pdf/p1.pdf

CHAPTER 26

Afterword ...
Tips for Staying
Out of Trouble

The school of hard knocks and hindsight are great teachers. Of course, it would be easier if you didn't have to take those routes in the first place. The tax guide, entitled

Tax Relief and Tax Resolution
The Ultimate Guide to Paying Less to the IRS Starting NOW

is comprehensive and designed to help guide you through IRS audits and resolving your IRS tax debt. It is recommended that you retain a tax professional to assist you when dealing with the IRS. If you choose to represent yourself, it still should assist you in dealing with the IRS. Remember that it is important that you file all tax returns for the past six years in order to be in compliance with IRS tax laws.

Filing complete and accurate returns is the best way to avoid being audited by the IRS. Be sure to select a reputable tax preparer to prepare your income tax returns. In the event of an IRS tax audit, be sure to respond to the IRS audit examination or request for information within the time frame allotted, and request more time if necessary. In the event you owe back taxes to the IRS, you should act quickly to obtain a resolution on your case. If you are unsure of your options or unsure about IRS procedures, you should consider hiring a tax professional that specializes in tax resolution. In the resource section on my website, you will find names and websites of those I recommend.

Throughout, I've stressed professional assistance in dealing with IRS matters, especially when there is significant debt owed to the IRS. My decades of experience have repeatedly shown that it is better to have professional assistance than to try to handle the matter by yourself.

If you choose to do deal with the IRS on your own, the details of the steps that you need to take along with the various policies and procedures of the IRS will be found within this guide and will be of great assistance.

Below are a series of Tips for W-2/1099 Taxpayers and Businesses and Business Owners to ease the pain of filings and dealings with the IRS as you go forward.

Tips for W-2/1099 Taxpayers

In order to avoid owing the IRS in the future, it is important that you do the following:

1. **File all required tax returns on time,** and pay any taxes due in full. If you are not able to prepare the returns on your own, be sure to select a reputable tax professional

to assist you in preparing and filing your tax returns on time.

2. **Correct the mistakes that caused you to owe your previous tax debt.** Never make the same mistake twice as it may have dire consequences with the IRS—its memory is long and you are in the system.

3. **Ensure that you are claiming the correct amount** of exemptions on your W-4 so that you can have sufficient taxes withheld from your W-2 income. **Note:** You should never claim more exemptions than you have reported when you file your 1040 Income Tax Return.

4. **If you are a 1099 Independent Contractor or self-employed,** be sure to make all required Estimated Tax Payments either on a monthly or quarterly basis (every three months).

5. **Do not take a distribution from your 401K or retirement** without having federal taxes deducted. If you are under 59½ years old, you should also request that an additional 10 percent or 20 percent be withheld as you will likely be subject to the early withdrawal penalty.

6. **Respond to all IRS notices or inquiries** within the time specified on the notice. Do not ignore any mail you receive from the IRS as it may backfire and lead to a horrific outcome. If you are unsure about how to respond, get help. Consult a reputable tax professional for assistance.

7. The key to staying out of trouble in the future is to ensure that you do not owe the IRS ever again.

Tips for Businesses and Business Owners

In order to avoid owing the IRS in the future, it is important that you do the following:

1. **File all required business tax returns on time.** Tax returns must be filed, beginning with the first tax year that the business began operating. If you have employees, you are required to file Form 941 Employer's Quarterly Tax Return for each quarter (every three months) for each year in which the business is in operation and has employees; and the Form 940 Employers Annual Federal Unemployment Tax Return (FUTA) at the end of every tax year.

   If you owe a balance on your returns, pay off the balance in full when you file the return. Be sure to choose a reputable tax professional to prepare your tax returns.

2. **Be sure to make your payroll tax deposits on time** either monthly or quarterly. Generally, payroll tax deposits are due by the 15th of every month if you are making monthly tax deposits, or by the 15th of the first month following the end of a quarter, if you are making quarterly tax deposits. This practice will ensure that you do not owe payroll taxes to the IRS.

3. **Do not misclassify employees** as 1099 Independent Contractors when they are actually W-2 employees in

order to avoid paying payroll taxes. If discovered by the IRS, you may incur a large tax debt as a result.

4. **Keep your Business Income and Expenditures separate** from your personal expenditures. Have separate accounts for your business and do not use your business account to pay for personal expenditures. If you are unsure of how to do this, it is highly recommended that you hire a reputable Certified Public Accountant (CPA) to assist you in the accounting of your business transactions and affairs.

   A CPA can assist you in the financial planning, spending, and reporting required for your business, and can save you from incurring tax problems with the IRS.

5. **Always respond to any IRS notices or inquiries** that you receive in a timely manner. Do not ignore any mail you receive from the IRS. If you are unsure about how to respond, be sure to consult a reputable tax professional for assistance.

6. **Hire a reputable legal professional** such as an attorney to assist you in making sound business decisions and practices. It is important that you understand what is required of you by law when opening and operating a business. Hiring an attorney prior to opening and operating a business can help to prevent you from making futile mistakes that may cost you your livelihood and investment.

7. **The key to staying out of trouble** in the future is to ensure that you do not owe the IRS ever again.

How to Invest in Real Estate Tax-Free Using a 401(k)/IRA

Many look at real estate as a way to secure their financial well being for retirement. The benefits range from increased value generated from the anticipated appreciation in real estate properties to the actual rental income these properties can generate. However, some have used their retirement income saved in an IRA/401(k) in order to purchase real estate only to find that they are subject to early withdrawal penalties and a large tax bill.

FEDERAL RESERVE

KB 46279860
B2

THIS NOTE IS LEGAL TENDER
FOR ALL DEBTS, PUBLIC AND PRIVATE

Anna Escobedo Cabral

Treasurer of the United States.

G 2

100

Using Your 401(k)/IRA to Invest in Real Estate

There is a way to use your 401(k)/IRA to invest in real estate without incurring the tax obligations and early withdrawal penalties few know about. It's a major tax planning opportunity.

- If you have a current IRA/401(k) with your employer, first contact your plan administrator in order to determine whether investing in real estate is an option provided under your existing retirement plan. If it is not an option, ask your plan advisor whether it can be added.

- If you have a current IRA/401(k) and investment in real estate is not an option, you need to set up a Solo 401(k) or Self-Directed IRA, and then roll over your current IRA/401(k) into that solo 401(k)/Self-Directed IRA. It is generally easier to invest in real estate using a solo retirement plan than it is to invest into a full-time employer 401(k) plan.

In order to invest into a full-time employer 401(k) in real estate, the employer sponsoring the plan must allow for real-estate investing. Unfortunately, most employers choose not to offer it as an investment option.

Having a Solo 401(k) for the self-employed with no full-time employees (other than the business owners and their spouses) means that you are the business owner/individual serving as the employer. You can elect to include real estate investing as an available option.

To set up a Solo 401(k) or Self-Directed IRA, contact an investment firm/brokerage that allows investment in real-estate. The IRS allows this type of investment to remain tax free under your retirement plan, and revenue earned from the investment remains in the retirement plan. If your 401(k) administrator does not allow real estate investments in the plan, you cannot buy real estate using that plan, regardless of IRS allowance.

Limitations in Using 401(k)/IRA to Invest in Real Estate

Although IRS rules permit you to engage in almost any type of real estate investment—there is no list of approved investments for retirement plans—there are special rules contained in the Employee Retirement Income Security Act of 1974 (ERISA) that apply to retirement plan investments. There are three main restrictions on investments into 401(k)/Self-Directed IRA plans:

- Participant-directed accounts and IRAs cannot invest in collectibles, such as art, antiques, gems, coins, or alcoholic beverages, but they can invest in certain precious metals only if they meet specific requirements (Code §408(m)).

- Individual retirement accounts also are not permitted to invest in life insurance (Code §408(a)(3)).

- Certain transactions involving a disqualified person are also prohibited. Who is a disqualified person? A disqualified person is any of the following:

  1. The plan's fiduciary;

  2. A person providing services to the plan;

  3. An employer who has employees covered by the plan;

  4. An employee organization whose members are covered by the plan;

  5. Any direct or indirect owner of 50 percent or more of the following:

     - The combined voting power of all voting classes of stock, or the total value of shares of all classes of stock of a corporation that is an employer or employee organization described in (3) or (4) above;

     - The capital interest or profits interest of a partnership that is an employer or employee organization described in (3) or (4); or

     - the beneficial interest of a trust or unincorporated enterprise that is an employer or an employee organization described in (3) or (4);

6. A member of the family of any individual described in (1), (2), (3), or (i.e., the individual's spouse, ancestor, lineal descendant, or any spouse of a lineal descendant);

7. A corporation, partnership, trust, or estate of which (or in which) any direct or indirect owner described in (1) through (5) holds 50 percent or more of any of the following:

   - the combined voting power of all classes of stock entitled to vote or the total value of shares of all classes of stock of a corporation;
   - the capital interest or profits interest of a partnership; or
   - the beneficial interest of a trust or estate.

8. An officer, director (or an individual having powers or responsibilities similar to those of officers or directors), a 10 percent or more shareholder or highly compensated employee (earning 10 per cent or more of the yearly wages of an employer) of a person described in (3), (4), (5), or (7);

9. A 10 percent or more (in capital or profits) partner or joint venture of a person described in (3), (4), (5), or (7); or

10. Any disqualified person, as described in (1) through (9) above, who disqualified with respect to any plan to which a multi-employer plan trust is permitted to make payments under section 4223 of ERISA.[91]

Types of Real Estate Transactions that Can Be Invested In

Below is a partial list of real estate-related investments that you can make with a Solo 401(k) both locally, nationally or in foreign areas:

- Undeveloped land
- Residential homes
- Commercial property
- Apartments
- Duplexes
- Condominiums
- Townhomes
- Mobile homes
- Real estate notes
- Real estate purchase options
- Tax liens certificates
- Tax deeds

In order to avoid taxation when using your 401(k)/IRA to invest in real estate, the following steps should be followed:

- Set-up a Solo 401(k) Plan with a 401(k) plan administrator/ IRA Financial Group. Remember to choose a plan administrator that allows investment in real estate as an option.

- Identify the property that you would like to invest in.

- Purchase the property directly with the Solo 401(k)/IRA Plan and ensure that title to the property as well as all transaction documents are in the name of the Solo 401(k)/IRA Plan. Documents pertaining to the property investment must be signed by you as the trustee of the plan.

- Ensure that all expenses paid for the property and revenue derived from rental or sale of the property go directly to the Solo 401(k)/IRA. No 401(k)/IRA related revenue should be deposited into your personal accounts.

- Repairs or improvements to the property must be performed by outside parties, not by you or family members (e.g., spouse, parents, and children). Remember to pay all ongoing expenses with funds from the Solo 401(k)/IRA's checking account. Never pay these expenses with your personal funds. For this reason, it's important that the self-directed 401(k)/IRA maintains enough liquid cash in order to cover expenses such as home owners association dues, property taxes, etc.

- Neither you nor certain family members may occupy the solo 401(k) own real-estate property.

- If you choose to manage the real-estate property, you should not compensate yourself for doing so. Management of the property includes functions such as, seeking renters, showing the property, arranging for repairs (but not performing the repairs) and collecting rental payments.

- Neither you, nor any other disqualified person may use the 401(k)/IRA owned real estate as security for a personal loan as this would be considered a prohibited transaction (IRC 4975).

How the Transaction Should Be Structured

When using a Solo 401(k) to make a real estate investment there are a number of ways you can structure the transaction.

- You can use your Solo 401(k) funds to make 100 percent of the investment. (You should make the entire real estate purchase, including closing costs, taxes, fees, and insurance, using the funds in your Solo 401(k)/IRA.)

- You can borrow money for your Solo 401(k). You may obtain financing through a loan or mortgage to finance a real estate purchase using a Solo 401(k)/IRA. Solo 401(k)/IRA participants may also borrow up to either $50,000 or 50 percent of their account value, whichever is less to help finance the real estate investment.

- If using financing through a third-party loan to purchase real estate (other than a loan from the 401(k)/IRA Plan), the loan must be a non-recourse loan otherwise it would be considered a prohibited transaction. A non-recourse loan is one in which the property is used for collateral. This means that in the event of a default, the lender may only collect the property, but cannot collect from the 401(k)/IRA plan itself. Remember that loans directly or indirectly involves a disqualified person is prohibited. This means that you cannot loan or borrow the money from a disqualified person.

Note: Using a Solo 401(k) to finance a real estate investment will not trigger Unrelated Business Income Tax (UBTI)—which imposes a tax in the range of 35 percent on all income/gains relating to the debt financed portion of the investment.

In Summary:

Income or gains generated by a 401(k)/IRA Plan generates tax-deferred/tax-free revenue. This means that you will not be required to pay taxes on the income earned from the real estate so long as the funds remain in the 401(k)/IRA account. By doing this, the 401(k)/IRA earns tax-deferred income and gains. Taxes will be paid on a future date, rather than in the year that the income is produced.

If you secure a loan/mortgage using the Solo 401(k)/IRA account, you cannot lose more than the property, and cannot be pursued personally. The lender may only seize the invested property, and cannot claim other funds in your 401(k).

Endnotes

[91] IRS.gov/Retirement-Plans/Retirement-Plans-FAQs-regarding-Plan-Investments.

Appendix

APPENDIX A

How Do I Complete the Form 433-A?

Please visit the following link for a copy of the Form 433-A Collection Information Statement:

IRS.gov/pub/irs-pdf/f433a.pdf

- **Wage Earners** (W-2 Employees): Complete sections 1, 2, 3, 4, and 5.

- **Self-Employed** (1099 or Business owners): Complete sections 1, 3, 4, 5, 6 and 7.

Note: If you cannot fit your responses in the spaces provided, you can attach a separate sheet of paper and provide the remainder of the information.

Instructions

Line Item on Form	Instructions on How to Complete Line Item
Name on Internal Revenue Service (IRS) Account	Enter your name as it appears on your tax return if you are single or file tax returns as married filing separately. If you are married and file taxes jointly or owe joint taxes, enter the name of the person listed first on the tax return (usually the husband).

Line Item on Form	Instructions on How to Complete Line Item
Social Security Number *SSN* on IRS Account	Enter your social security number if you are single or file tax returns as married filing separately. If you are married or owe taxes jointly, enter the SSN of the individual listed first on the tax return (usually the husband).
Employer Identification Number (EIN)	If being completed for a business owner or self-employed individual with an EIN, enter the EIN.
Section 1: Personal Information	This is the section for entering your personal Information.
1a: Full Name of Tax-payer and Spouse (if applicable)	Enter your name if single, if married and owe taxes jointly, enter your name and your spouse's name.
1b: Address	Enter the address of your primary residence and county. If you receive your mail at a different location, enter your mailing address directly below your primary residence and indicate that it is your mailing address.
1c: Home Phone	Enter your home phone number (if applicable).
1d: Cell Phone	Enter your cell phone number (if applicable).
1e: Business Phone	Enter your business cell phone number (if applicable).
1f: Business Cell Phone	Enter your business cell phone number (if applicable).
2a: Marital Status	Check the box that applies to your current marital status. Check married if you are currently legally married (does not apply to domestic partnerships), or check unmarried if you are single, divorced or widowed.
2b: Dependents	Enter the name, age, and relationship of your dependents. They must be claimed on your most recent tax return to be considered dependents, unless it is a new born baby.
3a: Taxpayer	Enter your SSN, Date of Birth, and driver's license number and the state in which you were licensed to drive.
3b: Spouse	Enter your spouse's SSN, Date of Birth and driver's license number and state in which they were licensed to drive.

Line Item on Form	Instructions on How to Complete Line Item
Section 2: Employment for Wage Earners	This is the section for entering your employment information if you are a W-2 employee. If you are a 1099 or self-employed individual, you may skip this section.
4a: Taxpayer	Enter the name of your employer if you are single. If married, enter the name of the person's name appears first on the tax return.
4b: Address	Enter your employer's address. If married enter the address of the person's employer whose name is listed in 4a.
4c: Work Telephone Number	Enter your employer's telephone number. If married, enter the employer's address of the person listed in 4a.
4d: Does employer allow contact at work?	Check yes if you/spouse may receive calls at work, or no if you are not allowed to receive calls at work.
4e: How long with this employer?	Enter the years you/spouse have been with the current employer in the box labeled years. If less than one year, enter zero "0". Then enter the number of months you/spouse have been with the current employer
4f: Occupation	List your occupation/job title.
4g: Number of Withholding Allowances claimed on Form W-4	Enter the number of exemptions you claim on your Form W-4 you provided to your employer. (*Note:* you should never claim more exemptions on your W-4 than what is claimed on your tax return.)
4h: Pay Period: weekly, monthly, bi- weekly, other	Select the box for your appropriate pay period. If your pay period is not listed here, select other.
5a: Spouse's Employer Name	Enter the name of your spouse's employer, or the person's whose name appears second on the tax return.
5b: Employer Address	Enter your spouse's employer's address or the employer address of the person listed in 5a.
5c: Work Telephone Number	Enter your spouse's employer telephone number, or the telephone number of the person's employer listed in 5a.

Line Item on Form	Instructions on How to Complete Line Item
5d: Does employer allow contact at work?	Check yes if your spouse may receive calls at work, or no if he or she is not allowed to receive calls at work.
5e: How long with this employer?	Enter the years you/spouse have been with the current employer in the box labeled years. If less than one year, enter zero "0". Then enter the number of months you/spouse have been with the current employer.
5f: Occupation	List you/your spouse's occupation/job title.
5g: Number of Withholding Allowances claimed on Form W-4	Enter the number of exemptions you/your spouse claim on your Form W-4 you provided to your employer. (Note: you should never claim more exemptions on your W-4 than what is claimed on your tax return.)
5h: Pay Period: weekly, monthly, bi- weekly, other	Select the box for your spouse's appropriate pay period. If their pay period is not listed here, select other.
Section 3: Other Financial Information (Attach copies of applicable documentation)	This section asks for other financial information. If applicable to your case, you will need to provide documentation of the status.
6: Are you a party to a lawsuit? (applies to you or spouse when applicable)	If the answer is no, check no and move on to question 7. If yes, check yes, and proceed to provide the following: **I. Plaintiff**: person filing the law suit, or Defendant –person being sued. **II. Location of filing**: where was the lawsuit filed (city and state). **III. Represented by**: Name of attorney is applicable or write "self" if you are representing yourself. **IV. Docket/Case No.**: Docket or Case Number provided by the court. **V. Amount of Suit:** How much are suing for or being sued for? **VI. Possible Completion Date**: List the month, day and year that you expect the case to end. **VII. Subject of Suit**: Why are you being sued, or on what grounds are you being sued?

Line Item on Form	Instructions on How to Complete Line Item
7: Have you ever filed bankruptcy?	If no, check no, and move on to question 8. If yes, check yes, then proceed to provide the following:
	I. Enter the month, day, and year you filed for bankruptcy.
	II. Enter the month, day, and year your case was dismissed.
	III. Enter the month, day, and year your case was discharged. (Note: If your case in Bankruptcy is still active, the IRS will not negotiate a resolution. You must wait until your bankruptcy case is over before negotiating with the IRS).
	IV. Enter the Petition Number for your case (Number provided by the Bankruptcy Court when you filed your petition).
	V. Location Filed: enter the location of the court where you filed your petition for bankruptcy.
8: In the past 10 years, have you lived outside of the U.S for 6 months or longer?	If no, check no, and move on to question 9a. If yes, check yes, then proceed to provide the following:
	I. Dates lived abroad: From: Enter the month, day, and year you left the US.
	II. To: Enter the month, day, and year you reentered the US.

Line Item on Form	Instructions on How to Complete Line Item
9a: Are you the beneficiary of a trust, estate, or life insurance policy?	If no, check no, and move on to question 9b. If yes, check yes, then proceed to provide the following: **I. Place** where the trust is recorded: provide the address. **II. EIN:** Provide the EIN number of the trust. **III. Name of trust, estate or policy**: provide the name of the trust, estate, or life insurance policy. **IV. Anticipated amount to be received**: List the amount you expect to receive from the trust or life insurance. **V. When will the amount be received**: List the date you expect to receive the funds, if not until death or the happening of some event, list upon death, or unknown, then provide a copy of the policy or trust document.
9b: Are you a trustee, fiduciary, or contributor of a trust? • **Trustee:** manages the operation of the trust. • **Fiduciary**: may manage the operation of the trust or have a responsibility to maintain the trust or act on behalf of the beneficiaries. • **Contributor**: finances or contributes to the trust.	If no, check no, and then proceed to question 10. If yes, check yes, then proceed to provide the following: **I. Name of trust**: provide the name of the trust. **II EIN:** provide the EIN number for the trust.
10: Do you have a safe deposit box (business or personal)?	If no, check no and proceed to question 11. If yes, check yes, then proceed to provide the following: **I. Location**: Provide the name, address and box number(s) for your safe deposit box. **II. Contents**: What does your safe deposit box contain. **III. Value**: How much are the contents worth combined?

Line Item on Form	Instructions on How to Complete Line Item
11: In the past 10 years, have you transferred any assets for less than their full value?	If no, check no, then proceed to question 12. If yes, check yes, then proceed to provide the following: **I. List Assets:** Provide a list of assets that you transferred for less than full value within the last 10 years. **II. Value at Time of Transfer:** List the "full value" of each asset at the time of the transfer. **III. Date Transferred:** Provide the month, day, and year of the transfer(s). **IV. To Whom or Where was it Transferred:** Provide the name(s) of the recipients of the asset.
12: Cash On Hand: cash that you do not keep in a bank account.	Provide the average amount of cash you have in your wallet, or on hand every month. Usually $20 for an OIC.
13 a, b, and **c:** Personal Bank Accounts – Includes checking, money market, savings, and stored value cards.	**I. Provide the type of account** in the first column (checking, savings, money market, etc.). **II. Provide the full name and address** of the bank, savings & loan, credit union, or financial institution in the second column. **III. Provide the account number** of your account(s) in the third column. **IV. Provide the date** in which you obtained the account balances, and then list the account balance (you may list the average amount left in these accounts every month for more accurate accounting).
13 d: Total Cash	Add lines 13a through 13 c, and any attachments, and provide the total on this line.
Investments	Includes stocks, bonds, mutual funds, stock options, certificates of deposit, and retirement assets such as IRAs, Keogh, and 401K plans. Also includes companies or businesses in which you are an officer, director, owner, member, or have a financial interest.

Line Item on Form	Instructions on How to Complete Line Item
14a through 14c: Investment Accounts	**I. Provide the type of Investment or Financial Interest** in the first column. **II. Provide the full name and address** of the financial institution or company, and telephone number in the second column. **III. Provide the current value** of the account in the third column. **IV. Provide date the valuation** is being determined by, and the loan balances if any in the fourth column. **V. Provide the equity** in these accounts by performing the following calculation (Current Value x 50% or 70% - loan balance = Equity). Do not follow the calculation provided by the IRS for this section as it does not take into account the taxes or early withdrawal penalties.
14d: Total Equity	Add lines 14a through 14c and any attachments, and place the total on the line provided.
Available Credit	Includes all lines of credit and bank issued credit cards.
15a and **15b** **Note:** You may skip this section because the IRS will not grant credit card payments as an expense, but may use available credit to suggest paying off tax debt.	**I. In column one,** provide the credit limit for each card. **II. In column two,** provide the date the value was determined, and the amounts owed on each card. **III. In column three,** provide the date the value was determined, and the available credit for each card (Available Credit = Credit Limit – Amount owed).
15c: Total Available Credit	Add lines 15a, 15b, and any attachments and provide the total on the line provided.
16a: Life Insurance	Do you own or have any interest in any life insurance policies with cash value? (Must be Whole Life, not Term Life). If no, check no, then proceed to question 17. If yes, check yes and proceed to 16b.
16b: Name and Address of Insurance Company	Provide the name and address of the whole life insurance company or companies in each column.

Line Item on Form	Instructions on How to Complete Line Item
16c: Policy Number(s)	Provide the policy numbers for each whole life insurance policy.
16d: Owner of Policy	Provide the owner of the policy. If owned by you or spouse, write your name or your spouse's name. If you or your spouse are a beneficiary of a whole life policy, the write the name of the owner.
16e: Current Cash Value	Provide the current cash value of each whole life policy. (**Note**: Term Life Insurance has no cash value, so do not include it in this section.)
16f: Outstanding Loan Balance	Provide the balances of any loans you currently have outstanding on each policy.
16g: Total Available Cash	Subtract amounts from 16f through 16e and any attachments and provide the total on the line provided.
Real Property	Include all real property owned or being purchased. Do not include rental property.
17a and **17b**	**I. Property Description**: Provide a description of the property (single family dwelling, condo, duplex, land, etc.) **II. Purchase Date**: Provide the month, day, and year that you purchase the property. **III. Current Fair Market Value (FMV)**: Provide the current value of the property. **IV. Current Loan Balance**: Provide the current balance of any outstanding loans on the property. **V. Amount of Monthly Payment**: Provide your monthly loan payment. **VI. Date of Final Payment**: Provide the month, day, and year the loan will be paid in full (you may estimate based on loan terms). **VII. Equity**: Provide the equity of the property (Equity = FMV x 80% - Loan Balance). Do not use the equity calculation provided by this form.
17c: Total Equity	Add lines 17a, 17b, and any attachments and provide total on the line provided.
Personal Vehicles Leased and Purchased	Includes boats, RVs, motorcycles, all-terrain and off-road vehicles, trailers, etc.

Line Item on Form	Instructions on How to Complete Line Item
18a and **18b**	**I. Provide the year, make, and model** of the vehicle. **II. Provide the Purchase/Lease Date** of the Vehicle: provide the month, day, and year you purchased the vehicle. **III. Provide the Current Fair Market Value (FMV)** of the vehicle. **IV. Current Loan Balance**: Provide the current loan balance of the vehicle. **V. Amount of Monthly Payment:** Provide your monthly payment amount. **VI. Date of Final Payment:** Provide the month, day, and year of your final payment (you may estimate based on loan terms). **VII. Equity:** Provide the equity in the vehicle (Equity = FMV x 80% – loan balance). You can deduct an allowance of $3,450 per vehicle for up to two vehicles if married filing jointly and the vehicles are used for work.
18c: Total Equity	Add lines 18a through 18b and any attachments and provide the total on the line provided.
Personal Assets (Skip this section if your personal assets total is $10,000 or less for IA or CNC cases. In OIC cases, exclude if less than the levy exemption of $7,900.)	Include all furniture, personal effects, artwork, jewelry, collections, antiques, or other assets. Include intangible assets such as licenses, domain names, patents, copyrights, mining claims, etc.
19a and **19b**	**I. Provide the Property Description** (couch, painting, etc.) **II. Provide the Purchase/Lease Date**: Provide the month, day, and year you purchased the asset. **III. Provide the Current Fair Market Value (FMV)** of the asset. **IV. Provide the Current Loan Balance** if any. **V. Amount of Monthly Payment**: Provide the monthly payment. **VI. Date of Final Payment**: Provide the month, day, and year the loan will be paid in full. **VII. Equity**: Provide the equity in the asset (Equity = FMV x 80% - loan balance).

Line Item on Form	Instructions on How to Complete Line Item
19c: Total Equity	Add lines 19a, 19b, and any attachments and provide the value on this line. If equity is less than $10,000 exclude from financial for IA and CNC. If Equity is less than $7,900, exclude from OIC.
Section 5: Monthly Income and Expenses (**Note**: If you are self-employed, skip to section 6 and 7, then come back to section 5).	This is the section for entering your monthly income and expenses.
Source	Provide list of income sources. Fill in all that apply with your gross monthly income.
20: Wages (Taxpayer)	Fill in your monthly gross wages if you are a W-2 wage earner.
21: Wages (Spouse)	Fill in your spouse's gross monthly wages if they are a W-2 wage earner.
22: Interest: Dividends	Fill in your Interest/Dividends income. If married, combine both incomes.
23: Net Business Income	If self-employed/1099 Independent Contractor, fill in your net business income determined from section 7.
24: Net Rental Income	If you own rental property, fill in your monthly net rental income.
25: Distributions (K-1, IRA, etc)	Fill in your monthly distribution income. If married, combine both incomes.
26: Pension (Taxpayer)	Fill in your monthly pension income.
27: Pension (Spouse)	Fill in your spouse's monthly pension income.
28: Social Security (Taxpayer)	Fill in your monthly Social Security Income.
29: Social Security Income (Spouse)	Fill in your spouse's monthly Social Security Income.
30: Child Support	Fill in your or your spouse's monthly Child Support Income.
31: Alimony	Fill in your or your spouse's monthly Alimony payments.
32 - 33: Other Income	Fill in any other sources of income not listed.
34: Total Income	Add lines 20 – 33.

Line Item on Form	Instructions on How to Complete Line Item
Total Living Expenses	This is the section where you will provide your monthly expenses.
Expense Items	Provide a list of IRS allowable expenses.
35: Food, Clothing and Misc.	Always put the full amount of the IRS National Standard in this section even if you pay less. If you pay more than the National Standard, you must be able to provide proof of this expense. For OIC cases, you are not likely to be granted the higher amount absent a valid medical reason.
36: Housing and Utilities	Provide the total monthly cost of your housing expenses (rent, mortgage, electricity, gas, heat, trash, water, sewer, telephone, lawn and pool care, etc.). Always put the actual amount spent. If it exceeds the national standard, you will need to provide proof of your expenses. In OIC cases, you will never be allowed to exceed the national standard.
37: Vehicle Ownership Costs	Provide the monthly payment for your vehicle. If it exceeds the National Standard of $517, you will need to provide proof. In IA or CNC cases, the full amount may be allowed if reasonable, but in OIC cases, you will only be granted the maximum of $517 if you exceed this amount. If married and have two vehicles, add the two ownership costs together and place the total on this line.
38: Vehicle Operating Costs	Provide the monthly operating costs for your vehicle (insurance, gas, parking, tolls, maintenance, etc.). If married and have two vehicles, combine the two operating costs together. In IA and CNC cases, if the actual amount exceeds the National Standard for your region, you will need to provide proof. In OIC cases, you will only be granted the National Standard Maximum. Be sure to include the Additional Operational cost of $200 for older vehicles of 6 years or more old, and has 75,000 or more in mileage for OIC cases. The IRS usually accepts the maximum allowable.

Line Item on Form	Instructions on How to Complete Line Item
39: Public Transportation	If you do not own a vehicle, you can claim the maximum of $182. In IA and CNC, you may claim a higher amount if you pay more and can show proof, but in OIC, the maximum allowed per household is $182.
40: Health Insurance	Provide the monthly cost of your health insurance payment. If married, combine both payments.
41: Out of Pocket Health Care Costs	Provide your monthly cost of prescription, co-pays, medical supplies, etc. If you pay less than the National Standard, always claim the National Standard. If you pay more than the National Standard, you will need to provide proof in IA, CNC, and OIC cases. If married, combine both expenses.
42: Court Ordered Payments	Provide your monthly court ordered payment (Child Support, Alimony, Restitution, etc.). If married, combine both payments.
43: Child/Dependent Care	Provide your monthly cost for child care (babysitter, day care, etc.). If you do not claim the child/dependent on your tax return, absent a court order, or proof that the child/dependent lives with you, you may not be allowed to claim this expense. If married, both spouses must be employed in order to claim this expense.
44: Life Insurance	Provide your monthly term life insurance payment. Whole life insurance payments are not allowed. If married, combine both payments.
45: Current Year Taxes (Income/FICA).	Provide your monthly tax payments (includes Federal, Medicare, Social Security, State, Local, and Estimated Tax Payments for self-employed individuals). If married, combine both expenses.
46: Secured Debts	Provide the total of you and/or your spouse's monthly secured debt payments (Student Loans, other loans with collateral, work related expenses, etc.), then provide an attachment listing each secured debt expense. You will need to provide proof of these expenses.

Line Item on Form	Instructions on How to Complete Line Item
47: Delinquent State or Local Taxes	Provide your monthly state installment agreement payment. This is allowed in OIC cases in proportion to the amount owed the IRS.
48: Other Expenses	Provide the total of other expenses not listed on this form, then provide an attachment listing each expense. You will need to provide proof of these expenses.
49: Total Living Expenses	Add lines 35-48 and provide the total on this line.
50: Net Difference	Subtract Line 49 from Line 34. If positive, you are eligible for an IA of this amount and will not be eligible for a CNC. OIC will vary based on the type you wish to file (see Offer in Compromise section for details).
IRS Use Only	This column will be completed by the IRS. Do not complete this column.
Certification	By signing this form, you certify: "Under penalties of perjury, I declare that to the best of my knowledge and belief this statement of assets, liabilities, and other Information is true, correct, and complete.
Taxpayer's Signature	Sign on this line if you are single, or the spouse whose name appears first on the tax return for married couples.
Spouse's Signature	Your spouse or person whose name appears second on the tax return signs on this line.
Date	Provide the date in which you signed this document.
Sections 6 and 7	**To be completed by Self-Employed only.** If you are W-2 wage earner, skip these sections. You are done, but be sure to submit all pages of this form including sections 6 and 7.
Section 6: Business Information	In this section, you will provide your business information.
51: Is the business a Sole Proprietorship (filing Schedule C)	This must be a business owned by one individual and operated as a Sole Proprietorship. If no, check no, and you will need to complete a Form 433-B. If yes, check yes, and continue to question 52.

Line Item on Form	Instructions on How to Complete Line Item
52: Business Name & Address	If the business has a different address from what was entered in 1b, enter the Name and Business Address on this line.
53: Employer Identification Number (EIN)	Provide the EIN number for your business. You may use your Social Security Number if you do not have one. However, if you have employees, please obtain one immediately by visiting IRS.gov.
54: Type of Business	Provide a description of the business (what does it do, or what service does it provide?).
55: Is the business a Federal Contractor?	Check yes if you perform contract work for the Federal Government. Check no if you do not.
56: Business Website	Provide the web address for the business if you have one.
57: Total Number of Employees	Enter the number of employees that you have. If you do not pay yourself wages, exclude yourself. Enter zero (0) if you do not have any employees.
58: Average Gross Monthly Payroll	Enter the average gross monthly payroll before tax deductions (total of all employee income/salaries for the month).
59: Frequency of Tax Deposits	How often do you deposit Payroll taxes or Estimated Tax Payments (weekly, monthly, quarterly, annually, etc.).
60: Does the business engage in E- Commerce	Do you conduct business over the internet? If no, check no, then move on to question 62. If yes, check yes, then complete 61a and 61b.
61a–b: Payment Processor	**I. In column one,** provide the Name & Address of your payment processor (PayPal, Authorize. net, Google Checkout, etc.). **II. In column two,** provide the payment processor account number for each company.
Credit Cards Accepted by the Business	In this section, you will list whether you accept credit card payments from customers and provide the information for the types of card you accept.

Line Item on Form	Instructions on How to Complete Line Item
62a–c:	**I. In column one,** list the type(s) of credit cards your business accepts. **II. In column two,** list your merchant account number with each company. (If you only have one merchant number used for all, provide the same number for each card). **III. In column three,** provide the Name & Address of the Issuing Bank (bank that processes the payments).
63: Business Cash on Hand	Does your business keep cash on hand (cash that would not be kept in a bank account)? If so, provide the amount of cash the business keeps on hand on a monthly basis.
Business Bank Accounts	In this section you will list all business checking accounts, online and mobile accounts (PayPal, etc.), money market accounts, savings accounts, and stored value cards (payroll cards, government benefit cards, etc.). Do not include your personal accounts. Those should be listed in section 4.
64a – b: Bank Accounts	**I. In column one,** provide the type of account (checking, savings, etc.) **II. In column two,** provide the Full name and address of the banking institution, savings and loan, credit union, or financial institution. **III. In column three,** provide the account number for each account listed. **IV. In column four,** provide the date in which the balances were determined, then provide the available balances for each account (you may list the average monthly balances for these accounts).
64c: Total Cash in Banks	Provide the total of 64a, 64b, and any attachments on the line provided.

Line Item on Form	Instructions on How to Complete Line Item
Accounts/Notes Receivable	In this section, you will list outstanding payments you are waiting to receive from clients or vendors (includes e-payment accounts receivable, factoring companies, bartering, online auctions, etc.). If you have contracts awarded but not started (federal, state, local government grants or contracts, etc.) list them on an attachment separately from this section.
65a – 65e: Accounts/Notes Receivable	**I. In column one,** list the Account/Notes Receivable and the Address of the payor (person/vendor). **II. In column two,** list the status of the account (age, factored, other). **III. In column three,** list the date that the payment is due. **IV. In column four,** list the Invoice number or Government Grant/Contract Number. **V. In column five,** list the Amount Due (amount owed to you).
65f: Total Outstanding Balance	Add lines 65a through 65e, and any attachments, and provide the total on this line.
Business Assets	In this section you will list all assets owned by the business such as tools, books, machinery, equipment, inventory, or other assets used in trade or business. It also includes intangible assets such as licenses, patents, domain names, copyrights, trademarks, mining claims, etc.

Line Item on Form	Instructions on How to Complete Line Item
66a – b:	**I. Property Description** – Provide a description of the asset. **II. Purchase/Lease Date** – Provide the month, day, and year the asset was purchased. **III. Current Fair Market Value (FMV)** – Provide the FMV of the asset. **IV. Current Loan Balance** – Provide the amount of any loans outstanding for the asset. **V. Amount of Monthly Payment** – Provide the monthly payment amount for this account. **VI. Date of Final Payment** – Provide the month, day, and year the loan will be paid in full. **VII. Equity** – Provide the Equity for this asset (Equity = FMV x 80% - Loan Balance). **VIII. Location** – Provide the Address and County where the asset is located. **IX. Lendor/Lessor/Landlord** – Provide the name and address of the financing company and their phone number.
66c: Total Equity	Add lines 66a and 66b, and any attachments, and provide the total on this line.
Section 7: Sole Proprietorship Information	Complete this section only if you are Self-Employed (file a Schedule C or receive a 1099). The information provided here should match your Profit/Loss Statement.
Accounting Method Used	Check cash if you count your income and expenses as they are received or made. Check Accrual if you count your income and expenses once they are due regardless of whether they are received or not.
Income and Expenses during the Period	Provide the month, day, and year for the start date. Then provide the month, day and year for the end date. (Note: Your calculations should be determined by the prior 3, 6, 9, or 12 month period in order to determine your typical business income and expenses).
Total Monthly Business Income	In this section, for each item listed, provide the Gross Monthly Income received.
67: Gross Receipts	Include the gross monthly sales, or income received before expenses are deducted.

Line Item on Form	Instructions on How to Complete Line Item
68: Gross Rental Income	If you rent a property, include the gross monthly rental income before expenses are deducted.
69: Interest	Provide the gross monthly interest received.
70: Dividends	Provide the gross monthly dividends received.
71: Cash Receipts not included in lines 67 – 70	Provide the total of monthly cash receipts not reported on lines 67 – 70.
72 – 75: Other Income	Provide the monthly income for any other income received by the business.
76: Total Income	Add lines 67 through 75, then provide the total on this line.
77: Materials Purchased (items directly related to the production of a product or service).	Provide the monthly expense for materials purchased.
78: Inventory Purchased (goods bought for resale)	Provide the monthly expense for inventory purchased.
79: Gross Wages & Salaries	Provide the total monthly gross wages and salaries for all employees of the business.
80: Rent	Provide the monthly rent for your business office or location.
81: Supplies (items used in the business that are consumed or used up within one year such as books, office supplies, professional equipment, etc.)	Provide the monthly cost of business supplies.
82: Utilities/Telephone (includes gas, electricity, water, oil, trash collection, telephone, cell phone, business, internet, etc.)	Provide the monthly cost of business supplies.
83: Vehicle Gasoline/Oil	Provide the monthly cost of gas or oil used by company vehicles (do not include your personal vehicle, this is called Double Dipping, and is not allowed).
84: Repairs & Maintenance	Provide the monthly cost of repairs and maintenance for your business vehicles, office, or equipment.

Line Item on Form	Instructions on How to Complete Line Item
85: Insurance	Provide the monthly insurance costs for business vehicles, liability, etc.
86: Current Taxes (includes real estate, excise, franchise, occupational, personal property, sales, and employment taxes)	Provide your total monthly payments for current taxes.
87: Other Expenses	Include a list of other expenses not listed on lines 77 through 86 and place the total on the line provided.
88: Total Expenses	Add lines 77 through 87 and provide the total on this line.
89: Net Business Income	Subtract line 88 from line 76 and place the value on this line. If it is a positive number, then your business is viable, if negative, you are operating at a loss.
If Self-Employed, Return back to section 5 on page 4, and be sure to sign page 4.	
Note: Be sure to submit all pages (page 1 – 6) and attachments if applicable to the IRS.	

APPENDIX B

How Do I Complete the Form 433-B?

Please visit the following link for a copy of the Form 433-B Collection Information Statement for Businesses:

IRS.gov/pub/irs-pdf/f433b.pdf

This Form is to be completed by Businesses other than Sole Proprietorships (C-Corporation, S- Corporation, LLC, Partnership, etc.).

Note: If you cannot fit your responses in the spaces provided, you can attach a separate sheet of paper and provide the remainder of the information.

Instructions

Line Item on Form	Instructions on How to Complete Line Item
Section 1: Business Information	In this section, you will provide the business information.
1a: Business Name	Provide the name of the business.
1b: Business Street Address, Mailing Address, City, State, and Zip	Provide the street address, and mailing address of the business.
1c: County	Provide the county in which the building is located.

Line Item on Form	Instructions on How to Complete Line Item
1d: Business Telephone	Provide the telephone number for the business.
1e: Type of Business	Provide the type of business activity conducted (wholesaler, consultant, manufacturing, etc.).
1f: Business Website	Provide the web address for the business.
2a: Employer Identification No. (EIN)	Provide the EIN for the business.
2b: Type of entity	Check the appropriate box for the type of business entity: Partnership, Corporation, LLC, Other LLC – include number of members).
2c: Date Incorporated/Established	Date you filed Articles of Incorporation with the State, or formed the business.
3a: Number of Employees	Provide the number of employees (exclude yourself if you are not paid wages).
3b: Monthly Gross Payroll	Provide the gross monthly payroll (add all employee income before taxes and expenses are deducted).
3c: Frequency of Tax Deposits	How often do you deposit payroll taxes (monthly, weekly, quarterly, annually, etc.).
3d: Is the business enrolled in Electronic Federal Tax Payment System (EFTPS – online system for making tax deposits)?	Check yes, if you are enrolled, and no, if you are not.
4: Does the business engage in e-commerce (internet sales)?	If yes, check box yes and complete questions 5a and 5b. If no, check no, and proceed to question 6a.
Payment Processor	Includes PayPal, Authorize.net, Google Checkout, etc.
5a – 5b:	**I. In column one,** provide the name and address of the payment processor. **II. In column two,** provide your account number with the payment processor.
Credit Cards Accepted by the Business	In this section you will provide information on credit cards accepted by your business.

Line Item on Form	Instructions on How to Complete Line Item
6a – 6c:	**I. In column one,** provide the type of credit card (Visa, MasterCard, etc.). **II. In column two,** provide the Merchant Account Number for each card. **III. In column 3,** provide the name and address of the issuing bank that processes your credit cards.
7a – 7d:	Provide the following for each partner, officer, LLC Members, Major Shareholders, etc. **I. Full Name** – Provide the full name of the individual(s). **II. Title** – Provide the full name of the individual(s). **III. Home Address** – Provide the home address of the individual(s). **IV. Responsible for Depositing Payroll Taxes?** Check yes if they are responsible, or no, if they are not responsible. **V. Social Security Number** – Provide the social security of the individual(s). **VI. Home Telephone** – Provide the home telephone number of the individual(s). **VII. Work/Cell Phone** – Provide the work/cell phone number of the individual(s). **VIII. Ownership Percentage & Shares or Interest** – Provide their percentage of ownership and/or shares or interest in the company. **IX. Annual Salary/Draw** – Provide the annual salary/draw of the individual(s).
Section 3: Other Financial Information	In this section you will provide other financial information for the business and will be required to provide all applicable documentation.

Line Item on Form	Instructions on How to Complete Line Item
8: Does the business use a Payroll Service Provider or Reporting Agent	If no, check no, and proceed to question 9. If yes, check yes, and proceed to provide the following: **I. Name and Address** of the Payroll Service Provider or Reporting Agent. **II. Effective Dates** – provide the month, day, and year you hired the Payroll Service Provider or Reporting Agent.
9: Is the business a party to a lawsuit?	If no, check no and move on to question 10. If yes, check yes and provide the following: **I. Check** whether you are the plaintiff (person who filed the lawsuit) or defendant (person being sued). **II. Location Filing** – location where lawsuit was filed. **III. Represented by** – Name of person representing business in law suit if applicable. **IV. Docket/Case No.** – Court docket/case number. **V. Amount of Suit** – Amount you are suing or being sued for. **VI. Possible Completion Date** – Provide the month, day, and year the case is likely to be completed. **VII. Subject of Suit** – Reason you are suing or being sued.
10: Has the business ever filed bankruptcy? **Note**: If your business is still undergoing bankruptcy, you must wait until the case has been discharged before negotiating a settlement with the IRS.	If no, check no and move on to question 11. If yes, check yes and provide the following: **I. Date Field** – provide the month, day, and year you filed bankruptcy. **II. Date Dismissed** – provide the month, day, and year the case was dismissed. **III. Date Discharged** – provide the month, day, and year the case was discharged. **IV. Petition No.** – provide the petition number provided by the court when you filed for bankruptcy. **V. District of Filing** – Court location where bankruptcy was filed.

Line Item on Form	Instructions on How to Complete Line Item
11: Do any related parties (officers, partners, employees, etc.) have outstanding amounts owed to the business?	If no, check no and move on to question 12. If yes, check yes and provide the following: **I. Name and Address** – provide the name and address of the individual(s). **II. Date of Loan** – date loan was made to individual. **III. Current Balance** – provide date and value of balance owed. **IV. Payment Date** – date payment is due or was made. **V. Payment Amount** – amount of payment.
12: Have any assets been transferred in the last 10 years, from this business for less than full value?	If no, check no, then proceed to question 13. If yes, check yes, then provide the following: **I. List Asset** – Provide a list of asset or assets. **II. Value at Time of Transfer** – provide the FMV of the asset at the time of transfer. **III. Date transferred** – provide the month, day, and year the asset was transferred. **IV. To Whom or Where Transferred** – provide the name of the individual or location where asset was transferred.
13: Does the business have other business affiliations (subsidiary or parent companies)?	If no, check no, then proceed to question 14. If yes, check yes, then provide the following: **I. Related Business Name and Address** – provide the name and address of the affiliated business. **II. Related Business EIN** – provide the EIN of the business.
14: Any Increase/decrease in Income Anticipated?	If no, check no, then proceed to question 15. If yes, check yes, then provide the following: **I. Explain** - provide an explanation for anticipated change in income. **II. How much will it increase/decrease** – provide amount of increase/decrease. **III. When will it increase/decrease** – provide the date you anticipate the increase/decrease.

Line Item on Form	Instructions on How to Complete Line Item
15: Is the business a Federal Government Contractor	If no, check no and proceed to question 16 a. If yes, check yes and be sure to include the federal contracts in question 18.
Section 4: Business Asset and Liability Information	In this section you will provide information on business assets and liabilities.
16a: Cash on Hand (cash not in bank)	Provide the total cash on hand for the business on the line provided.
16b: Is there a safe on the business premises?	Provide the total cash on hand for the business on the line provided.
Business Bank Accounts	Includes online and mobile accounts such as PayPal, money market accounts, saving accounts, checking accounts, and stored value cards (payroll cards, government benefit cards, etc.). Also include safe deposit boxes including location, box number and value of contents, and attach a list of its contents.
17a – 17c:	**I. In column one,** provide the type of account – checking, savings, etc. **II. In column two,** provide the full name and address of the bank, savings & loan, credit union, or financial institution. **III. In column three,** provide the account number of each account. **IV. In column four,** provide the date the balances are determined from and then provide the account balances.
17d: Total Cash in Banks	Add lines 17a through 17c and provide the total on the line provided in column four.
Accounts / Notes Receivable	Includes e-payment accounts receivable and factoring companies, and any bartering or online action accounts. Also list all contracts separately including contracts awarded, but have not started. Also include Federal, State, and Local government grants and contracts.

Line Item on Form	Instructions on How to Complete Line Item
18a – 18e:	**I. In column one,** provide the name, address and telephone number of the account. **II. In column two,** provide the status of the account (age, factored, other). **III. In column three,** provide the date in which the payment is due. **IV. In column four,** provide the Invoice Number or Government Grant or Contract Number for the account. **V. In column five,** provide the amount due.
18f: Outstanding Balance	Add lines 18a through 18e and any attachments and place the total on the line in column five.
Investments	Includes stocks, bonds, mutual funds, stock options, certificates of deposit and commodities (gold, silver, copper, etc.).
19a – 19b:	**I. In column one,** provide the name of the company, address, and telephone number. **II. In column two,** check whether the investment was used as collateral on a loan. **III. In column three,** provide the current value of the investment. **IV. In column four,** provide the loan balance for any outstanding loans on the investment. **V. In column five,** provide the equity in the investment (Equity = Current Value – Loan Balance).
19c: Total Investments	Add lines 19a, 19b, and any amounts from attachments and place the total on the line provided in column five.
Available Credit	Includes all lines of credit and credit cards.

Line Item on Form	Instructions on How to Complete Line Item
20a – 20b:	**I. In column one,** provide the full name, address, and account number for the business line of credit and/or credit card. **II. In column two,** provide the credit limit. **III. In column three,** provide the date the balance is determined from, then provide the amount owed. **IV. In column four,** provide the date the available credit is determined from, then provide the amount of available credit.
20c: Total Credit Available	Add lines 20a, 20b, and any attachments, and provide the total on the line provided in column four.
Real Property	Includes all real property and land contracts the business owns, leases, or rents.
21a – 21d:	**I. Property Description** – provide a description of the property (land, commercial building, etc.). **II. Purchase/Lease Date** – provide the month, day, and year the property was purchased or leased. **III. Current Fair Market Value (FMV)** – provide the FMV of the property. **IV. Current Loan Balance** – provide the balance on any loans outstanding against the property. **V. Amount of Monthly Payment** – provide the monthly loan payment amount. **VI. Date of Final Payment** – provide the month, day, and year that your loan will be paid in full. **VII. Equity** – provide the equity of the property (Equity = FMV x 80% - current loan) **VIII. Location** – provide the address of the property. **IX. Lender/Lessor/Landlord** – Provide the name, address, and telephone number of the lender, lessor, or landlord.

Line Item on Form	Instructions on How to Complete Line Item
21e: Total Equity	Add lines 21a through 21d and any attachments, and place the total on the line provided.
Vehicles, Leased and Purchased	Includes boats, RVs, motorcycles, all-terrain and off-road vehicles, trailers, mobile homes, etc.
22a – 22d:	**I. Provide the year, make, and model** of the vehicle(s). **II. Purchase/Lease Date** – provide the month, day, and year the vehicle was purchased. **III. Current Fair Market Value** – provide the FMV of the vehicle. **IV. Current Loan Balance** – provide the current loan balance outstanding if applicable. **V. Amount of Monthly Payment** – provide the monthly payment on any outstanding loans. **VI. Date of Final Payment** – provide the month, day, and year the loan will be paid in full. **VII. Equity** – provide the equity in the vehicle (Equity = FMV x 80% – current loan). **VIII. Mileage** – provide the mileage on the vehicle. **IX. License/Tag Number** – provide the license and/or tag number for the vehicle. **X. Vehicle Identification Number (VIN)** – provide the VIN for the vehicle.
22e: Total Equity	Add lines 22a through 22d and any attachments then provide the total on the line provided.
Business Equipment and Intangible Assets	Include all machinery, equipment, merchandise inventory, and other assets. Also list intangible assets such as licenses, patents, logos, domain names, trademarks, copyrights, software, mining claims, goodwill, and other trade secrets.

Line Item on Form	Instructions on How to Complete Line Item
23a – 23d: List tangible Assets	**I. Asset Description** – provide a description of the asset (equipment, machinery, etc.). **II. Purchase/Lease Date** – provide the month, day, and year the asset was purchased or leased. **III. Current Fair Market Value (FMV)** – provide the FMV of the asset. **IV. Current Loan Balance** – provide the balance on any loans outstanding against the asset. **V. Amount of Monthly Payment** – provide the monthly loan payment amount. **VI. Date of Final Payment** – provide the month, day, and year that your loan will be paid in full. **VII. Equity** – provide the equity of the asset (Equity = FMV x 80% - current loan) **VIII. Location** – provide the address of the property. **IX. Lender/Lessor/Landlord** – Provide the name, address, and telephone number of the lender, lessor, or landlord.
23e – 23g: List Intangible Assets	**I. In column one,** provide a description of the intangible asset. **II. In column two,** provide the equity of the asset (Equity = FMV x 80% - current loan).
23h: Total Equity	Add lines 23a though 23g and any attachments and provide the total on the line provided.
Business Liabilities	Includes notes and judgments not listed previously on this form.

Line Item on Form	Instructions on How to Complete Line Item
24a–24b:	**I. Description** – provide a description of the business liability (accounts payable, judgment, etc.). **II. Secured/Unsecured** – check the box indicating whether the debt is a secured (property used as collateral) or unsecured debt (no collateral used). **III. Date Pledged** – date you incurred the debt. **IV. Balance Owed** – amount owed on the debt. **V. Date of Final Payment** – provide the month, day, and year the debt will paid in full. **VI. Payment Amount** – provide the monthly payment amount, or amount remaining to be paid. **VII. Name and address** – provide the name and address of the person or institution to which the debt is owed.
24c: Total Payments	Add lines 24a, 24b, and any attachments and provide the total on the line provided.
Section 5: Monthly Income/ Expense Statement for Business	In this section, you will list your monthly business and expenses.
Accounting Method Used:	Check cash if you count your income and expenses as they are received or made. Check Accrual if you count your income and expenses once they are due regardless of whether they are received or not.
Income and Expenses during the Period:	Provide the month, day, and year for the start date. Then provide the month, day and year for the end date. (**Note**: Your calculations should be determined by the prior 3, 6, 9, or 12 month period in order to determine your typical business income and expenses). The values provided will be based on the periods listed in this section.
Total Monthly Business Income	In this section, for each item listed, provide the Gross Monthly Income received.

Line Item on Form	Instructions on How to Complete Line Item
25: Gross Receipts from Sales/Services	Include the gross monthly sales, or income received from sales and services before expenses are deducted.
26: Gross Rental Income	If you rent property or equipment, include the gross monthly rental income before expenses are deducted.
27: Interest Income	Provide the gross monthly interest received.
28: Dividends	Provide the gross monthly dividends received.
29: Cash Receipts not included in lines 25 – 28	Provide the total of monthly cash receipts not reported on lines 25 – 28.
29 – 34: Other Income	Provide the monthly income for any other income received by the business.
35: Total Income	Add lines 67 through 75, then provide the total on this line.
Total Monthly Business Expenses	In this section you will provide your monthly business expenses.
36: Materials Purchased (items directly related to the production of a product or service).	Provide the monthly expense for materials purchased.
37: Inventory Purchased (goods bought for resale)	Provide the monthly expense for inventory purchased.
38: Gross Wages & Salaries	Provide the total monthly gross wages and salaries for all employees of the business.
39: Rent	Provide the monthly rent for your business office or location.
40: Supplies (items used in the business that are consumed or used up within one year such as books, office supplies, professional equipment, etc.)	Provide the monthly cost of business supplies.
41: Utilities/Telephone (includes gas, electricity, water, oil, trash collection, telephone, cell phone, business, internet, etc.)	Provide the monthly cost of utilities/ telephone used by the business.
42: Vehicle Gasoline/Oil	Provide the monthly cost of gas or oil used by company vehicles (do not include your personal vehicle, this is called Double Dipping, and is not allowed).

Line Item on Form	Instructions on How to Complete Line Item
43: Repairs & Maintenance	Provide the monthly cost of repairs and maintenance for your business vehicles, office, or equipment.
44: Insurance	Provide the monthly insurance costs for business vehicles, liability, etc.
45: Current Taxes (includes real estate, excise, franchise, occupational, personal property, sales, and employment taxes)	Provide your total monthly payments for current taxes.
46: Other Expenses	Include a list of other expenses not listed on lines 36 through 45 and place the total on the line provided.
47: IRS Use Only – Allowable Installment payments	Do not fill in this section. The IRS will determine whether you have allowable installment payments as business expenses.
48: Total Expenses	Add lines 36 though 47 and provide the total on this line.
49: Net Income	Subtract line 48 from line 35 and place the total on this line. If the number is positive, the business is viable. If negative, the business is operating at a loss.
Certification	By signing this section, you certify the following: "Under penalties of perjury, I declare that to the best of my knowledge and belief this statement of assets, liabilities, and other information is true, correct, and complete."
Signature	Should be signed by owner or officer of the business.
Title	Provide the title the individual signing this form has with the business.
Date	Provide the date the form was signed.
Print Name of Officer, Partner, or LLC Member	Print the name of the individual who signed this form.

APPENDIX C

How Do I Complete the Form 433-F?

Please visit the following link for a copy of the Form 433-F Collection Information Statement:

IRS.gov/pub/irs-pdf/f433f.pdf

This form must be completed by Wage Earners (W-2 Employees) and Self-Employed (1099 or Business owners)

Note: If you cannot fit your responses in the spaces provided, you can attach a separate sheet of paper and provide the remainder of the information.

Instructions

Line Item on Form	Instructions on How to Complete Line Item
Name(s) and Address	Enter your name if single. If married, enter your name and spouse's name (list in order names appear on tax return). • **Use the address of your primary residence.** If you have a different mailing address, list it below your primary residence and be sure to indicate that it is your mailing address. • **If the address you provided is different** from the address provided on your last return, check the box.

Line Item on Form	Instructions on How to Complete Line Item
Your Social Security Number (SSN) or Individual Taxpayer Identification Number (ITIN)	List your SSN or ITIN. If married, list in the order of how they appear on your tax return.
Your Spouse's Social Security Number (SSN) or Individual Taxpayer Identification Number (ITIN)	List your spouse's SSN or ITIN.
Your Telephone Numbers	List your Home, Work, and Cell Phone numbers if applicable.
Spouse's Telephone Numbers	List your Spouse's Home, Work, and Cell Phone numbers if applicable.
Enter the number of people in the household who can be claimed on this year's tax return including you and your spouse.	Provide the number of household members under 65. Then provide the number of household members over the age of 65.
If you or your spouse are self-employed or have self-employment income, provide the following information:	**I. Name of Business** **II. Business EIN** (Employer Identification Number) **III. Type of Business** **IV. Number of Employees** (do not include the owner).
Section A: Accounts / lines of Credit	Includes personal and business checking, online, mobile (PayPal, etc.), savings accounts, Certificate of Deposit (CD), Trusts, IRA, Keogh Plans, Simplified Employee Pensions (SEP), 401K, Profit Sharing Plans, Mutual Funds, Stocks, Bonds, etc. (Note: you may attach an extra sheet of paper listing other accounts if insufficient space is provided.)
Name and Address of Institution	Provide the Name(s) and Address of the Institution(s) for each account.
Account Number	Provide the account number for each Institution listed.
Type of Account	Provide the type of account (checking, savings, IRA, 401K, etc.).
Current Balance/Value	Provide the Current Balance/Value of the account.

Line Item on Form	Instructions on How to Complete Line Item
Check if Business Account	If any of the accounts you listed are for your business, check the box next to the account.
Section B: Real Estate	Includes your home, vacation property, time-shares, vacant land, and other real estate.
Description/Location/County	**I. Provide a description of the property** (single family dwelling, condo, land, etc.) **II. Provide the address of the property.** **III. Provide the county** in which the property is located.
Primary Residence/Other	If it is your primary residence, check the corresponding box. If it is property other than your primary residence, check other.
Monthly Payment(s)	Provide the monthly loan payments for each Property listed if applicable.
Financing	Provide the year purchased and the purchase price for each property.
Current Value	Provide the Current Fair Market Value(FMV) of the Property.
Balance Owed	Provide the loan balance on the property if any.
Equity	Provide the Equity for the property (Equity = FMV x 80% – Balance Owed).
Section C: Other Assets	Include personal and business cars, boats, recreational vehicles, whole life policies, tools, equipment, inventory, etc. **I. For Vehicles,** list the year, make, and model. **II. For Life Insurance Policies,** list the name of the insurance company.
Description	Provide a description of the asset.
Monthly Payment	Provide the monthly payment amount if applicable.
Year Purchased	Provide the year the asset was purchased.
Final Payment	Provide the month, day, and year of your final payment.
Current Value	Provide the Fair Market Value (FMV) of the asset.
Balance Owed	Provide the loan balance if applicable.
Equity	Provide the equity of the asset (Equity = FMV x 80% - Balance Owed). Subtract $3,450 per vehicle for primary and secondary for an OIC.

Line Item on Form	Instructions on How to Complete Line Item
Notes	This section is for IRS Use Only. Do not write in this section.
Section D: Credit Cards	Includes Visa, MasterCard, American Express, Department Stores, etc.
Type	List the type of card (Visa, MasterCard, etc.)
Credit Limit	Provide the full credit limit of the card.
Balance Owed	Provide the balance owed on the card.
Minimum Monthly Payment	Provide the minimum monthly payment for the card.
Section E: Business Information	In this section you will provide information on your Accounts Receivable and Credit Card Payments Accepted by your Business.
Section E1: Accounts Receivable owed to you or your business	Accounts Receivables are outstanding payments owed to you or your business.
Name	Provide the name(s) of individual or vendors owing money to you or your business.
Address	Provide the address of individuals or vendors owing money to you or your business.
Amount Owed	Provide the amount owed to you or your business.
List total amount owed from additional sheets	If you listed other accounts on a separate sheet, provide the total on this line. Be sure to attach the sheet to the completed Form 433-F.
Total amount of accounts receivable available to pay IRS NOW	Enter only the total amount of all accounts receivables listed.
Section E2: Name of Individual or Business on Account	Provide the name of the individual or business on your account for processing your credit card payments.
Credit Card	List the type of credit card(s) the business accepts (Visa, MasterCard, etc.).
Issuing Bank Name and Address	Provide the name and address of the bank that processes your credit card payments.
Merchant Account Number	Provide your Merchant Account Number for the company processing your credit card payment.

Line Item on Form	Instructions on How to Complete Line Item
Section F: Employment Information (**Note**: If you attach a paystub for each employer, you do not need to complete this section)	In this section you will provide your and/or spouse's employment information.
Your Current Employer	Provide the name and address of your employer.
How often are you paid?	Check the one that applies: Weekly, Bi-weekly, Semi-monthly, or Monthly.
Gross per pay period	Provide your gross monthly wage per pay period.
Taxes per pay period	Provide the Federal, State, and Local Taxes deducted from your paycheck per pay period.
How long at current employer?	How long have you been working for your current employer?
Spouse's Current Employer	Provide the name and address of your spouse's current employer.
How often are you paid paid?	Check the one that applies: Weekly, Bi-weekly, Semi-Monthly, or Monthly.
Gross per pay period	Provide your spouse's gross income per pay period.
How long at current employer?	How long has your spouse been employed with their current employer?
Section G: Non-Wage Household Income	Provide the monthly amounts for the items listed if applicable.
Alimony	List your and/or spouse's monthly Alimony Income.
Child Support Income	List your and/or spouse's monthly Child Support Income.
Net Self-Employment Income	List your monthly Self-Employment Income after deducting monthly expenses and taxes (attach Profit/Loss Statement).
Net Rental Income	List your monthly Rental Income after deducting monthly expenses and taxes (attach Profit/Loss Statement).
Unemployment Income	Provide your and/or spouse's Unemployment Income.
Pension Income	Provide your and/or spouse's Pension Income.
Interest/Dividends Income	Provide your and/or spouse's Interest/Dividend Income.

Line Item on Form	Instructions on How to Complete Line Item
Social Security Income	Provide your and/your spouse's Social Security Income.
Other	Provide the type of other income that you and/or spouse receives and the monthly amount.
Section H: Monthly Necessary Living Expenses	In this section you will provide the monthly expenses for the items listed.
1. Food / Personal Care	In this section you will provide your expenses for food and personal care items.
Food	In this section fill in the National Standard based on your household size, unless you pay more than the National Standard and have valid medical reason. For OIC cases, deviations are not likely to be allowed.
Housekeeping Supplies	In this section fill in the National Standard based on your household size.
Clothing and Clothing Services	In this section fill in the National Standard based on your household size.
Personal Care Products & Services	In this section fill in the National Standard based on your household size.
Miscellaneous	In this section fill in the National Standard based on your household size.
Total	Provide the total by adding food, housekeeping supplies, clothing and clothing services, personal care products and services, and miscellaneous.
2. Transportation	In this section you will provide your transportation costs.
Gas/Insurance/ Licenses/Parking/ Maintenance, etc.	Provide the monthly amount for these expenses combined. If less than the National Standard, use the National Standard. If you spend more than the National Standard, you will need to provide proof in IA and CNC cases. In OIC cases, you will not be allowed to exceed the National Standard.
Public Transportation	Use the National Standard of $182 if you do not own a vehicle. If you pay more than this amount, you will need to provide proof in IA and CNC cases. You will only be allowed the National Standard in OIC cases.

Line Item on Form	Instructions on How to Complete Line Item
3. Housing & Utilities	In this section you will provide your housing and utilities expenses.
Rent/Mortgage	Provide your monthly rent payment.
Electric, Oil/Gs, Water/Trash	Provide the monthly total for these expenses.
Real Estate Taxes and Insurance	Provide the Real Estate Taxes and Insurance if not included in the mortgage.
Maintenance and Repairs	Provide your monthly maintenance and repairs for your primary residence.
Total	Provide the total of these expenses.
4. Medical	In this section you will provide your monthly medical expenses.
Health Insurance	Provide you and/or your spouse's monthly Health Insurance Expense.
Out of Pocket Health Care Expenses	Provide you and/or your spouse's monthly out of pocket health insurance expenses (prescription, co-pay, medical supplies, etc.). Use the National Standard based on your household size if you spend less than that amount.
5. Other	In this section you will provide your other monthly expenses.
Child / Dependent Care	Provide your monthly child/dependent care expense (child/dependent must be claimed on your tax return. This expense cannot be claimed by married couples unless both spouses are employed absent a valid medical reason.
Estimated Tax Payments	Provide you and your spouse's monthly Estimated Tax Payment if self-employed or 1099 employee.
Term Life Insurance	Provide your and/or your spouse's monthly term life insurance payment.
Retirement	Provide your and/or your spouse's monthly retirement expense. It must be employer required in order to be allowed.
Retirement	Provide your and/or your spouse's voluntary monthly retirement expense.
Union Dues	Provide your and/or your spouse's monthly union dues expense.

Line Item on Form	Instructions on How to Complete Line Item
Delinquent State & Local Taxes	Provide your and/or your spouse's minimum monthly payment on State or Local Installment Agreement. The IRS will require proof of this expense.
Student Loans	Provide your and/or your spouse's minimum monthly student loan payment. The IRS will require proof of this expense.
Court Ordered Child Support	Provide your and/or your spouse's monthly child support payment (must be court ordered to be allowed). The IRS will require proof of this expense.
Court Ordered Alimony	Provide your and/or your spouse's monthly alimony payment (must be court ordered to be allowed). The IRS will require proof of this expense.
Other Court Ordered Payments	Provide your and/or your spouse's monthly court ordered payments not listed on this form. The IRS will require proof of this expense.
Other Expenses	List any other expenses you and/or spouse pay on a monthly basis that are not listed on this form. The IRS will likely require proof of these expenses.
Certification	You and/or spouse certify by signing this form: "Under penalty of perjury, I declare to the best of my knowledge and belief this statement of assets, liabilities and other information is true, correct and complete.
Your Signature	Sign on the line provided.
Spouse's Signature	Spouse should sign on the line provided.
Date	Place the date in which you signed the form.

APPENDIX D

How Do I Complete the Form 656?

Please visit the following link for a copy of the Form 656 Offer in Compromise:

IRS.gov/pub/irs-pdf/f656.pdf

This Form is to be completed by Individuals and Businesses submitting an Offer in Compromise. **Note**: For Individuals—complete this Form and the Form 433-A or 433-A OIC when submitting an Offer in Compromise. For Businesses, complete this Form and the Form 433-B and 433-B OIC for the business, and the Form 433-A or 433-F for each officer of the business when submitting an Offer in Compromise.

Instructions

Line Item on Form	Instructions on How to Complete Line Item
Attach Application Fee and payment	Attach check or money order for the $186 processing fee, and required deposit based on the type of offer you are submitting (*see* Offer in Compromise Section for details).

Line Item on Form	Instructions on How to Complete Line Item
Section 1: Your Contact Information	In this section you will provide contact information for you and/or your spouse if applicable.
Your First Name, Middle Initial, Last Name	Provide your First, Middle Initial, and Last Name.
If a Joint Offer, Spouse's First Name, Middle Initial, Last Name	If you are filing a joint offer with your spouse, provide their First, Middle Initial, and Last Name.
Your Physical Home Address	Provide the physical address for your primary residence.
Mailing Address	Provide your mailing address if different from your physical address.
Business Name	Provide the name of your business if you are filing an offer on behalf of a business.
Your Business Address	Provide your business address if you are filing on behalf of a business.
Social Security Number (SSN) (Primary)	Provide your SSN/ TIN. If filing a joint offer, provide the SSN/TIN of the person whose name appears first on the tax return.
Secondary	Provide the SSN/TIN of your spouse, or person whose name appears second on the tax return.
Employer Identification Number (EIN)	Provide the EIN for the business if filing on behalf of a business.
EIN not Included in Offer	Provide the EIN of your business if you have one, and it is not a part of the offer.
Section 2: Tax Periods	In this section, you will list the tax years for each tax type for which you owe back taxes, or wish to have included in the offer.
1040 Income Tax-Year(s)	List all 1040 tax years for which you owe a balance or wish to have included in the offer (example: 2008, 2009, 2010, etc.).
1120 Income Tax-Year(s)	List all 1120 Income tax years for which your business owes a balance or that you wish to have included in the offer (example: 2008, 2009, 2010, etc.).
941 Employer's Quarterly Federal Tax Return – Quarterly period(s)	List all quarters and years for which your business owes 941 payroll taxes (example: 03/2008, 06/2008, 09/2008, 12/2008, etc.).

Line Item on Form	Instructions on How to Complete Line Item
940 Employer's Annual Federal Unemployment (FUTA) Tax Return – Year(s)	List all years for which the business owes 940 unemployment taxes (example: 2008, 2009, 2010, etc.).
Trust Fund Recovery Penalty (TFRP) as a responsible person of	Enter the corporation name for which incurred a TFRP.
For failure to pay withholding and Federal Insurance Contributions Act taxes (Social Security taxes) for period(s) ending	List the tax period and years for which you owe TRFP (example: 03/2008, 06/2008, 09/2008, 12/2008, etc.).
Other Federal Tax(es)	Provide the type(s) and period(s) for which you owe other tax debts.
Note: If you need additional space, you may add an attachment and title it	"Attachment to Form 656 dated (add date)." Make sure to sign and date the attachment.
Section 3: Reason for Offer	In this section, select the option for why you are submitting the offer.
Doubt as to Collectability	Check this option if you have insufficient assets and income to pay the debt in full.
Exceptional Circumstances (Effective Tax Administration)	Check this option if you owe the amount and have sufficient assets to pay the debt in full, but due to exceptional circumstances, requiring you to pay the debt in full would cause an economic hardship or would be unfair and inequitable. Also submit a written narrative explaining your circumstances.
Explanation of Circumstances	In this section, provide an explanation of why you are submitting the offer. You may also submit proof of your circumstances.
Section 4: Low Income Certification (Individuals Only)	Check the box in this section if you meet the low income guidelines based on the chart provided. If you are eligible, you do not need to submit any payments during the consideration of your offer.
Section 5: Payment Terms	In this section, you will select the type of offer you are submitting.
Lump Sum Cash: payable in 5 months or less	Enter the amount of your offer on the line provided and check the box if you will pay your offer in 5 months or less.

Line Item on Form	Instructions on How to Complete Line Item
Total Offer Amount	Enter the total amount of your offer.
20% Initial Payment	Enter 20% of your offer.
Remaining Balance	Enter the amount remaining by subtracting 20% from the total offer amount.
You may pay the remaining balance in one payment after acceptance of the offer or up to five payments.	On the lines provided, enter the following: **I. In the first column,** enter the monthly payment (Monthly payment = Remaining balance/5) **II. In the second column,** enter the day you will make your monthly payments (from 1 – 28). **III. In the third column,** enter the month after acceptance that the payment will be made (enter 1 – 5).
Periodic Payment	Enter the amount of your offer and check the box if you will pay your offer amount in more than 5 monthly installments.
Enclose a check for one month's installment	**I. Your monthly installment** will be determined by dividing your total offer by 24. Remember that no payment is necessary if you meet the low income guidelines in Section 4. **II. Enter the amount of your payment** on line one and two, and then the day in which you will make your payments on line three. **III. You must continue to make** these payments while the IRS is considering your offer. Failure to make your regular monthly payments will cause your offer to be returned.

Line Item on Form	Instructions on How to Complete Line Item
Section 6: Designation of Down Payment and Deposit (Optional)	**I. On the first line,** write the tax form that you would like to have your deposit applied to if your offer is not accepted (example, 1040).
	II. On the second line, write the tax year and quarter you would like your deposit to be applied if your offer is not accepted (example, 2008/12). Note: if you leave this section blank, the IRS will apply the deposit to the oldest tax year.
	III. Check the box if you are making an additional deposit with the offer, and write the amount on the line provided. If you are not making an additional deposit, leave this section blank.
Section 7: Source of Funds and Making Your Payment	**I. On the lines provided,** provide an explanation of where you will obtain the funds to pay for your offer (from wages, borrow from family member, etc.).
	II. Include separate checks for your application fee and deposit and make checks payable to "United States Treasury," and attach to the front of the Form 656. All payments must be made in US dollars.
Section 8: Offer Terms	Provide the terms of the Offer in Compromise.
Section 9: Signatures	By signing this section, you certify: "Under penalties of perjury, I declare that I have examined this offer, including accompanying schedules and statements, and to the best of my knowledge and belief, it is true, correct, and complete.
Signature of Taxpayer/ Corporation Name	**I. The first line** should be signed by you or in the case of married individuals, based on the order of names in Section 1. If signed by a Corporate/Business Officer, write the name of the business.
	II. Provide your Phone Number or Phone Number if being filed on behalf of a Corporation.
	III. Provide the date the Form was signed.

Line Item on Form	Instructions on How to Complete Line Item
Signature of Taxpayer/ Authorized Corporate Officer	**I. This line should be signed** by your spouse or corporate officer if the offer is being filed on behalf of a business. **II. Provide** your spouse's or Corporate officer's phone number. **III. Provide the date** the Form was signed.
Section 10: Paid Prepare Use Only	This section is to be prepared by the individual who prepared the offer on your behalf.
Signature of Preparer	**I. This line should be signed** by the individual who prepared your offer. **II. Phone Number** of the Preparer. **III. Date signed** by the Preparer.
Name of Paid Preparer	Preparer should print their name on this line.
Preparer's CAF number or PTIN	**I. Preparer should provide** their CAF number or PTIN on the line provided. **II. Preparer should also include** a valid, signed Form 2848 or 8821 with this application if one is not on file.
Firm's Name, Address, and Zip Code	Preparer should list the name of their firm and the address on this line.
Section 11: Third Party Designee	**I. Complete this section** if you would like a third party to discuss your offer with the IRS (usually your paid preparer). **II. If no,** check no, then you are ready to mail the forms. **III. If yes,** check yes, then provide the designee's name and telephone number (if you paid a preparer, Attorney, CPA or Enrolled Agent, they will likely be the ones you authorize in this section).
IRS Use Only	This section will be completed by the IRS. Do not complete this section. You are done and ready to submit your Offer in Compromise.
Privacy Act Statement	Read the Privacy Act Statement.

APPENDIX E

How Do I Know If I Am Required to File a Tax Return?

This Chart is to assist you in determining whether you are required to file a Federal Income Tax Return. The information provided is based on the year 2014 and may change in the coming years.

Filing Status	Age at December 31, 2012	Gross Income
Single	Under 65	$10,000
	65 or Older	$11,500
Married Filing Jointly	Under 65 – both spouses	$20,000
	65 or Older – both spouses	$22,400
	Under 65 - one spouse	$22,200
Married Filing Separately	Both Under or Over 65	$3,900
Head of Household	Under 65	$12,850
	65 or Older	$14,350
Qualifying Widow(er)	Under 65	$16,100
	65 or Older	$17,300
Dependent	Any Age	$6,100
Self-Employed	Any Age	$600

Special Cases that Require You to File a Tax Return
Without regard to your gross income, you are generally required to file an income tax return if any of the following applies to your case:

1. You owe ALTERNATIVE MINIMUM TAX.

2. You owe HOUSEHOLD EMPLOYMENT TAXES.

3. You owe additional taxes on a RETIREMENT PLAN or HEALTH SAVINGS ACCOUNT.

4. You must repay the 2008 HOMEBUYER CREDIT (or any other recapture taxes).

5. You owe Social Security and Medicare taxes on unreported TIP INCOME.

6. You had net SELF-EMPLOYMENT INCOME of $400 or more.

7. You earned $108.28 or more from a tax-exempt church or church-controlled organization.

8. You received distributions from an MSA or HEALTH SAVINGS ACCOUNT.

9. Your spouse files a separate return and itemizes deductions and your total income is $5 or more.

APPENDIX G

Points of Contact at the Internal Revenue Service

1st Person to answer your call	Operator	They will try to transfer you to the right department. They know very little about resolving cases.
1st Person if you call the Practitioner Priority Line (PPL)	PPL representative	They can give basic information about case, but often get the information wrong. Cannot do any resolution except maybe a Streamlined Installment Agreement (SIA) under $25,000.
2nd Person you might get transferred to	Streamlined Installment Agreement (SIA) unit	They give better basic information – what years you need to file for, what you owe. Cannot do any resolution except maybe SIA under $25,000.
2nd/3rd Person you might get transferred to	ACS Business	They know what they are doing (most of the time). Can give you good information on businesses and setup most resolutions except OIC, personal cases, and cases over $100,000. Need manager approval for CNC.
3rd/4th Person you might get transferred to	Revenue Officer	If you have a Revenue Officer assigned to your case, you will deal solely with him or her. They usually know a lot but at times need to be reminded what your rights are.
Offer lines	Offer Unit	If you file an Offer in Compromise (OIC) there is an operator that will transfer you to an Offer Examiner handling your case once assigned. See section on OIC cases for more information.

APPENDIX G

How Do I Determine the Amount That the IRS Will Levy From My Income?

This table shows the amount of your income that is exempt from an IRS levy for 2014.

Filing Status: Single							
Pay Period	Number of Exemptions Claimed on Statement						
	1	2	3	4	5	6	More than 6
Daily	39.4	54.23	69.42	84.62	99.81	115.00	23.85 plus 15.19 for each exemption
Weekly	195.19	271.15	347.12	423.08	499.04	575.00	119.23 plus 75.96 for each exemption
Biweekly	390.38	542.31	694.23	846.15	998.08	1,150.00	238.46 plus 151.92 for each exemption
Semi-monthly	422.92	587.50	752.08	916.67	1,081.25	1,245.83	258.33 plus 164.59 for each exemption
Monthly	845.83	1,175.00	1,504.17	1,833.33	2,162.50	2,491.67	516.66 plus 329.17 for each exemption

Filing Status: Head of Household							
Pay Period	Number of Exemptions Claimed on Statement						
	1	2	3	4	5	6	More than 6
Daily	50.19	65.38	80.58	95.77	110.96	126.15	35 plus 15.19 for each exemption
Weekly	250.96	326.92	402.88	478.85	554.81	630.77	175 plus 75.96 for each exemption
Biweekly	501.92	653.85	805.77	957.69	1,109.62	1,261.54	350 plus 151.92 for each exemption
Semi-monthly	543.75	708.33	872.92	1,037.50	1,202.08	1,366.67	379.16 plus 164.59 for each exemption
Monthly	1,087.50	1,416.67	1,745.83	2,075.00	2,404.17	2,733.33	758.33 plus 329.17 for each exemption

Filing Status: Married Filing Joint Return (and Qualifying Widow(er)s)							
Pay Period	Number of Exemptions Claimed on Statement						
	1	2	3	4	5	6	More than 6
Daily	62.88	78.08	93.27	108.46	123.65	138.85	47.69 plus 15.19 for each exemption
Weekly	314.42	390.38	466.35	542.31	618.27	694.23	238.46 plus 75.96 for each exemption
Biweekly	628.85	780.77	932.69	1,084.62	1,236.54	1,388.46	476.93 plus 151.92 for each exemption
Semi-monthly	681.25	845.83	1,010.42	1,175.00	1,339.58	1,504.17	516.66 plus 164.59 for each exemption
Monthly	1,362.50	1,691.67	2,020.83	2,350.00	2,679.17	3,008.33	1,033.33 plus 329.17 for each exemption

Filing Status: Married Filing Separate Return							
Pay Period	Number of Exemptions Claimed on Statement						
	1	2	3	4	5	6	More than 6
Daily	39.04	54.23	69.42	84.62	99.81	115.00	23.85 plus 15.19 for each exemption
Weekly	195.19	271.15	347.12	423.08	499.04	575.00	119.23 plus 75.96 for each exemption
Biweekly	390.38	542.31	694.23	846.15	998.08	1,150.00	238.46 plus 151.92 for each exemption
Semi-monthly	422.92	587.50	752.08	916.67	1,081.25	1,245.83	258.33 plus 164.59 for each exemption
Monthly	845.83	1,175.00	1,504.17	1,833.33	2,162.50	2,491.67	516.16 plus 329.17 for each exemption

Table for Figuring Additional Exempt Amount for Taxpayers at Least 65 Years Old and/or Blind						
Filing Status	*	Additional Exempt Amount				
		Daily	Weekly	Biweekly	Semi-monthly	Monthly
Single or Head of Household	1	5.96	29.81	59.62	64.58	129.17
	2	11.92	59.62	119.23	129.17	258.33
Any Other Filing Status	1	4.62	23.08	46.15	50.00	100.00
	2	9.23	46.15	92.31	100.00	200.00
	3	13.85	69.23	138.46	150.00	300.00
	4	18.46	92.31	184.62	200.00	400.00
*Additional Standard Deduction claimed on Parts 3, 4, and 5 of levy.						

Source: IRS.gov/pub/irs-pdf/p1494.pdf

APPENDIX H
Additional IRS Forms

Note: The Forms listed below are more simplified and user friendly. As a result, no line by line instructions are necessary.

433-A (OIC): The 433-A (OIC) is the simplified version of the 433-A. It was designed by the IRS to be more user friendly. You may use this form as well to submit an Offer in Compromise for an individual.

IRS.gov/pub/irs-pdf/f433aoi.pdf

433-B (OIC): The 433-B (OIC) is the simplified version of the 433-B. It was designed by the IRS to also be more user friendly. You may use this form as well to submit an Offer in Compromise for a business.

IRS.gov/pub/irs-pdf/f433boi.pdf

433-D: Installment Agreement Request. This form may be used to request an Installment Agreement (IA) with the IRS. You may complete this Form and mail it to the IRS to request an IA. If approved or denied, the IRS will send you a letter in the mail. This is a rather time consuming way to obtain an IA, and can take 30-60 days before you receive a response from the IRS. It is always best to contact the IRS over the phone as this is the fastest way to obtain a resolution on your case.

IRS.gov/pub/irs-pdf/f433d.pdf

Glossary

Glossary

Above-The-Line Deductions: deductions that are subtracted from a taxpayer's income prior to calculating their adjusted gross income.

Accountant: individual whose job is to keep or inspect financial records.

Accounts Receivable: money owed to a business by others.

Actual Expense: all expenses being paid by an individual, and also include payments for allowable expenses that exceed the national standards.

Additional Child Tax Credit (ACTC): a refundable credit that may be claimed by taxpayers who were not eligible to claim the maximum amount of the child tax credit because it exceeded their tax obligation.

Adjusted Gross Income (AGI): gross income minus applicable reductions.

Adoption Tax Credit: a nonrefundable tax credit that may be claimed by a taxpayer who incurred qualifying expenses in an adoption.

Alimony: a fixed payment made to an ex-spouse that was ordered by a court of law.

Allocate: to distribute.

Allowable Expense: an expense that meets the Necessary Expense Test (NET) requiring that the expense be necessary for the health and welfare of the individual, or for the production of income.

Alternate Average Income Method (AIM): alternate calculation used by the IRS to determine the monthly gross income by taking the average of three or more consecutive paystubs. (**Formula:** (paystub1 + paystub2 + paystub3) ÷ (total number of paystubs) x (number of weeks paid annually) ÷ (12)).

Alternative Minimum Tax: a tax imposed on individuals, businesses, estates, and trusts that is different from the regular income tax, and is payable if it exceeds the regular income tax.

American Opportunity Tax Credit: provides a tax credit of up to $2,500 for qualifying educational expenses incurred by taxpayers who are students or for educational expenses paid for qualifying dependents.

Annuity: a fixed sum of money paid to an individual annually or for a specified term (i.e. until the death of the individual).

Appeal: applying to a higher authority or neutral party for a review or reversal of a decision.

Appeal's Officer: IRS employee/agent reviewing a matter on appeal.

Appendices: a section found at the end of a book containing additional material.

Assess: to set or determine an amount of tax, penalty, interest, or fine, etc.

Asset: an item of value that you own (house, car, bank account, stocks, bonds, etc.).

Attorney: Person legally appointed to represent an individual or business in a legal proceeding.

Audit: the examination of a taxpayer's tax return to make sure it accurately calculates the taxpayer's tax liability in accordance with the Internal Revenue laws of the United States.

Automated Collection System (ACS): a technological system used by the IRS to collect back taxes owed.

Automated Underreporter Program: a computerized method used by the IRS to select a tax return for audit when the income reported on a tax return is less than that reported to the IRS.

Average Income Method (AIM): method used to calculate income by calculating the average of gross income reported on three or more consecutive paystubs. (**Formula:** Monthly Gross Income = (paystub 1 + paystub 2 + paystub 3) ÷ 3(total number of paystubs) x (Pay Frequency Multiplier).

Bad Debts: loss incurred by independent contractors/self-employed individuals, or business entities resulting from non-payments or uncollected accounts payable owed that were not paid, and were determined to be worthless.

Bankruptcy: a legal proceeding filed by individuals or businesses that are unable to pay off their outstanding debt.

Behavioral Control: providing extensive instruction on how the work is to be performed or carried out by an employee or independent contractor.

Bi-Weekly: pay period in which an individual is paid every other week.

Burden of Proof: duty placed on an individual, business, or entity to prove or disprove a disputed item.

Bureaucracy: a system of government in which state officials make most of the important decisions rather than the elected officials.

Business Debts: unpaid expenses incurred by a business.

Business Expense: the costs incurred in operating a business or performing tasks as an independent contractor, or self-employed individual.

Business Levy Exemption: an amount predetermined by the IRS to be excluded from the value of trade and business tools when an Offer in Compromise is submitted by a self-employed individual.

Business Income: money received by independent contractors/1099, self-employed individuals, or business entities for work performed, services rendered, or goods sold, etc.

Business Owner: individual or entity that owns a business.

Business Tax Account: tax account of a business entity that has an Employer Identification Number.

Capital Gain: income derived from an investment.

Cash Business: a business in which customers ordinarily pay with cash or a financial instrument that can be easily converted to cash (i.e. taxi cab, hair salon, car wash, wait staff, etc.).

Casualty: a loss.

C-Corporation (C Corp): a business entity that is taxed separately from its owners.

Certified Public Accountant (CPA): an accountant who has passed the educational and examination requirements and has been licensed and registered in accordance with applicable state laws.

Chapter 7 Bankruptcy: legal proceeding seeking discharge of all or a portion of your debts.

Chapter 13 Bankruptcy: legal proceeding seeking repayment plan to payoff outstanding debts.

Charitable Contribution: a donation made to a charitable/non-profit organization that is recognized by the IRS.

Charitable Non-cash Contribution: donation of items to charity, rather than money.

Chief Financial Officer (CFO): executive of a business entity charged with overseeing its financial operations on a daily basis.

Child and Dependent Care Credit: a nonrefundable tax credit that allows working taxpayers to claim unreimbursed child and dependent care expenses.

Child Tax Credit (CTC): a non-refundable tax credit of a maximum of $1,000 per qualifying child that reduces the taxable income of a taxpayer subject to the income level of the taxpayer.

Closely held Corporation: a corporation in which more than half of its shares are owned by less than five individuals.

Collections Appeal: a request filed to obtain a review on collection activity taken by the IRS, or to review an adverse decision made by an IRS agent/representative.

Collection Agency: a company or business that operates to collect the debt owed by individuals and businesses.

Collection Due Process Hearing (CDP): a hearing available to taxpayers who experienced collection action by the IRS, or could not agree to a resolution with the IRS and would like to dispute the action taken.

Collections Department: department of the IRS charged with the collection of back taxes and negotiating arrangements to resolve back taxes owed.

Collection Status: status placed on accounts in which the IRS is actively taking collection action.

Collection Statute Expiration Date (CSED): tentative date upon which tax obligations expire.

Colossal: massive, or extremely large.

Compliance: current with your ongoing tax obligations.

Competent: possess the skill, knowledge, or ability to complete a given task successfully.

Computerized Underreporting: the selection of a return for an audit through detection of inaccurate information by the IRS automated system.

Constitutional: consistent with or permissible by the Constitution of the United States.

Correspondence Examinations: audit conducted via mail by the requesting of information by the IRS in order to resolve inconsistent or inaccurate information reported on a tax return.

Credit Bureau: company that records credit ratings of individuals and makes them available to financial institutions and credit card companies.

Criminal Penalty: punishment imposed for wrongdoing which may include a fine, forfeiture of property, or imprisonment.

Currently Not Collectible Status (CNC): (hardship status) resolution that does not require monthly payments to be made by taxpayers experiencing a hardship and are unable to repay their tax debt.

Current Tax Payments: allowable expenses paid for tax obligations such as Federal Income Tax, Social Security, Medicare, and State and Local taxes.

Custodial Parent: the parent with whom the child lives most of the time or as specified by a court document.

Date of Assessment: date upon which tax obligations are assessed which is typically the date the tax return was processed, or tax obligation was determined.

Deadline: specified time in which a response is required by the IRS.

Delay: to make a process slower than usual or late.

Department of Justice (DOJ): a department of the executive branch of the federal government that is responsible for the enforcement of law and administration of justice in the United States.

Dischargeable Debt: debt in which the obligation to repay has been released.

Disclose: to make known or reveal.

Disregarded Entity: an entity that is not treated as separate from its owner for tax purposes (i.e. single member LLC).

Dissipated Asset: an asset that may have been transferred, sold, gifted, or spent such that they are no longer available to pay towards your IRS tax debt.

Distributee: person to whom funds were issued.

Distribution: funds given to a recipient.

Distributor: person or entity that issues funds to a recipient or recipients.

Do-It-Yourself Filer: taxpayer who prepares and files their income tax return on their own.

Domestic: located in the United States.

Domestic Partnership: business entity owned by two or more individuals and operated as a partnership that is located in the United States.

Double Dipping: IRS rule that prevents independent contractors or self-employed individuals from claiming an IRS allowance for a given expense if that expense was already claimed on the profit / loss statement (i.e. cannot claim car payments on the profit/loss statement and on the form 433-A).

Double Taxation: the payment of taxes on the same income (i.e. corporation paying taxes on its profits, and then shareholder pays taxes on the dividends received from the corporation's profits).

Earned Income Credit (EIC): a refundable credit for low and medium income taxpayers with a qualifying child or children.

Educator: a teacher or one in a similar profession or capacity (i.e. professor, instructor, etc.)

Electronic Filing: the process of filing tax returns utilizing the internet through the use of IRS approved tax preparation software.

Employer Identification Number (EIN): a federal tax identification number that is used to identify business entities, estates, and trusts.

Employment Tax (Payroll Tax): taxes that an employer must submit on behalf of employees (i.e. Federal Income Tax, Social Security Tax, Medicare Tax, and Unemployment Tax).

Enrolled Agent (EA): an individual authorized by the US Department of Treasury to represent individuals before the IRS.

Equity in Assets: the amount you can reasonably expect to collect from an asset.

Error: a mistake or inaccurate data.

Estate: all property and debts left by an individual upon death.

Estate Tax: A tax imposed on the net value of a deceased person's estate before it is distributed to their heirs.

Estimated Tax Payments: periodic tax payments made to the IRS in advance for income generated monthly, quarterly, or annually.

Examination: inspection or investigation of an individual or business income tax return, operations, or financial affairs.

Excise Tax: a tax imposed on the sale of a particular good or item.

Exclusive: restricted or limited to a particular matter.

Exemption: a specified amount/item that is not subject to taxation, or reduces a taxpayer's tax obligation.

Expense: money spent to acquire something or to complete a job or task.

Extension: to grant more time.

Face-to-Face Meeting: Audit conducted by physically meeting with the IRS auditor/examiner.

Fair Market Valuation (FMV): price at which an item of value may be sold and purchased by a buyer.

Field Examination: Audit conducted at taxpayer's place of business or location where records are kept.

Financial Control: the ability of an individual or business to control its own ability to make a profit or suffer a loss.

Financial Information: report of individual or business entity's income, assets, expenses, and other information used to determine their ability to repay back taxes owed to the IRS.

Financial Statement: document or form that provides an individual or entity's income, assets, and expenses.

Flow Through Entities: entities that are not subject to double taxation.

Foreign Account Tax Compliance Act (FATCA): law that requires individuals to report their financial accounts held outside of the United States and requires foreign financial institutions to report any financial accounts that are owned by US citizens.

Foreign Bank Account Report (FBAR): annual report that must be filed by a US Citizen to report their bank account and other financial accounts held outside of the United States.

Foreign Financial Account: any bank account, securities, brokerage, or other assets held outside of the United States.

Foreign Trust: trust not governed by the laws of the US.

Form 433-A: form used by the IRS to obtain financial statement/information for individual taxpayers.

Form 433A OIC: IRS form that provides the financial information of wage earners and self employed individuals when submitting an Offer in Compromise (can be used instead of the 433-A).

Form 433-B: form used by the IRS to obtain financial statement/information for business entities.

Form 433-B OIC: IRS form that provides financial information for a business (I.e. Partnership, Corporation, Limited Liability Company, etc.) and is used when submitting an Offer in Compromise for the business (can be used instead of the 433-B).

Form 433-F: form used by the IRS to obtain financial statement/information for individual taxpayers.

Form 656: form used when filing an Offer in Compromise (OIC) that provides the amount of the offer, basis for the offer, and type of offer being filed.

Form 1040: tax form used to prepare and file annual individual income tax return.

Form 1099: form used to report income paid to independent contractor/ self-employed individual or business that is reported to the IRS annually and provided to the independent contractor/self-employed individual or business.

Form 13711: form used to request an appeal of an Offer In Compromise determination.

Fraudulent: inaccurate or false.

Fraudulent expense: inaccurate amount reported for an expense, or claiming an expense that was not actually incurred.

Full-Pay Agreement: method of resolving back taxes by offering to pay off the tax debt in full.

Full Release: when the IRS agrees to release the full amount of a bank levy or fully stop a wage garnishment.

Future Income: a calculation done by the IRS when an Offer In Compromise is filed that is determined by multiplying any net income remaining after deducting allowable expenses by a specified number of months based on the type of offer filed.

General Partnership: a business entity owned by two or more persons or entities called partners who carry on an activity for the purpose of making a profit.

Gift Tax: a tax imposed on the transfer of value or items of value from one individual to another while the giver was alive.

Gross Income: a taxpayer's total income received from all sources prior to any deductions.

Hardship: having allowable expenses that exceed your income, or documentation showing that you are behind on paying allowable expenses.

Head of Household: a taxpayer that is unmarried, paid more than half the cost of maintaining a home for themselves and a dependent, and has a qualifying dependent.

Health Coverage Tax Credit: a refundable tax credit available to individuals qualifying under the HCTC program.

Health Insurance Premium: amount paid periodically to an insurance company for coverage of medical expenses.

Heightened Hardship Standard: requirement imposed by the IRS when a bank levy release is requested that requires taxpayers to demonstrate that the levy caused them insufficient income to pay necessary bills, which must be demonstrated by either a financial showing that their expense exceed their income, or that they have past due notices or shut off notices for necessary expenses.

Hold: a temporary delay on collection activity by the IRS for a specified time period.

Hold Status: a notation placed on the taxpayer's tax account showing a temporary suspension of collection activity for a specified length of time.

Hope Credit: nonrefundable credit that may be claimed by taxpayers for qualified educational expenses for the first two years or dependents first two years of post secondary education.

Household: the size of a family determined by the number of exemptions claimed on an individual's tax return.

Household Furnishings: item used to furnish your home or needed for personal use (i.e. furniture, electronics, appliances, etc.).

Income: money derived on a regular basis from employment, self-employment, or investments (i.e. wages, salary, dividends, interest, royalties, in some cases monetary gifts, etc.).

Income Source: method by which you obtain income.

Income Tax: Annual tax imposed by the US Government on income generated by individuals and businesses.

Income Tax Refund: the returning of excess income taxes paid by a taxpayer or business for a given tax year.

Income Tax Return: tax form filed by individuals or entities that is used to report their income and tax obligation.

Independent Contractor: a person, business, or corporation that provides goods or services under a contractual agreement (i.e. person receiving a 1099 rather than a W-2).

Independent Reviewer (IR): an employee of the IRS that is required to make an impartial decision solely on the information provided.

Individual Tax Account: tax account for an actual person who holds a Social Security Number (SSN) or Individual Tax Identification Number (ITIN).

Individual Tax Identification Number (ITIN): a nine-digit tax processing number issued by the IRS to individuals who are not eligible for a Social Security Number (SSN).

Installment Agreement (IA): resolution that allows individuals or businesses to make monthly payments toward their back taxes owed established by providing their financial information.

Interest: an amount charged at a particular rate for delaying the repayment of taxes owed.

Interest Rate: a percentage charged to a sum of money borrowed, or debt owed.

Internal Revenue Code (IRC): federal tax laws drafted by congress for regulation and collection of taxes in the United States.

Internal Revenue Manual (IRM): manual containing taxation guidelines used by IRS employees in performing work related tasks.

Internal Revenue Service (IRS): agency of the Department of Treasury that is responsible for the collection, enforcement, and interpretation of the Internal Revenue Code.

Investment Income: earnings received by investors from their investments such as dividends, interests, capital gains, etc.

Itemized Deductions: eligible expenses that a taxpayer may deduct in order to decrease their taxable income.

Internal Revenue Service: an agency of the Federal Government that is responsible for the collection of tax revenue for the United States, processing your income tax returns, and interpreting and enforcing tax laws written by Congress.

International: Operating between two or more nations or countries.

Investment: purchase of an asset that is used to generate income (i.e. stocks, bonds, IRA, 401K, mutual funds, etc.).

Judgment Payments: payments ordered by a court of law that are payable on a continuous or periodic basis.

Large Business: a business earning taxable income of $1 million or more annually for any three years prior to the current tax year, or if less than three years, for the amount of years that it has been in existence.

Large Business and International Division: Department of the IRS that handles tax matters related to large businesses (business earning taxable income of $1 million or more annually) and International businesses, as well as individuals owning assets or working in foreign locations.

Levy: a method used by the IRS to collect unpaid taxes by confiscating a given asset (i.e. funds in a Bank account).

Levy Exemption: a predetermined amount that the IRS excludes from the valuation of an asset or from collection during a wage garnishment.

Levy Exemption Table: table established by the IRS that must be used by employers in determining the proper amount to be withheld from the salary or wages of an employee.

Liability: an obligation for which one is held responsible.

Liable: individual or entity responsible for the debt.

Licensed Tax Preparer (LTP): (*also called* Registered Tax Return Preparer (RTRP) is an individual that prepares income tax returns and has passed the IRS preparer competency test and registration requirements.

Lifetime Learning Credit: a tax credit of up to $2,000 that a taxpayer may claim for qualified higher education expenses incurred by the taxpayer or their dependents.

Limited Liability: prevents creditors of the business entity from demanding payment from the individual owner personally, but can demand payment only from the assets of the entity.

Limited Liability Company (LLC): a business entity defined under state law which generally provides limited liability to all of its owners.

Limited Partnership (LP): business entity organized under a specific provision of state law, which has at least one general partner and one or more limited partners.

Limited Liability Partnership (LLP): business entity in which each limited partner is personally liable for the debts of the partnership caused by his or her own wrongful acts.

Liquidate: to cash out.

Lock-In-Letter: a letter sent by the IRS to an employer requiring that they change an employee's exemptions to zero "0" so that the maximum amount of taxes can be withheld.

Loss: a deficit in revenue resulting after deducting all expenses from gross income.

Lump Sum Cash Offer in Compromise: Offer in Compromise in which the proposed offer will be paid in five months or less.

Manager Call Back: a request made in which the individual demands a call from the manager of an IRS agent/representative.

Mandatory Payments: payments that are not voluntary, but must be paid by the taxpayer.

Marital Status: whether you are married, single, divorced, or widowed at the end of a given tax year.

Married Filing Jointly: a filing status used by taxpayers who are legally married at the end of a given tax year (December 31), and file an income tax return together.

Married Filing Separately: a filing status used by a taxpayer who is legally married at the end of a given tax year (December 31), but files a separate income tax return that does not include their spouse.

Mirroring the Account: a method used by the IRS when two parties are liable for a tax debt but only one proposes a resolution, in which case, the party establishing the resolution will be protected from further collection action, but the IRS will continue to pursue collection action against the other party.

Misclassification: to place in the wrong category.

Monthly: pay period in which an individual is paid once per month, usually on a specified date (first of every month, end of every month, first Friday of every month, etc.).

National Standards: predetermined amounts that the IRS will allow for certain allowables, such as food, clothing and miscellaneous items.

Necessary: required in order to complete a given task or achieve a certain goal, or to maintain a taxpayer's wellbeing.

Necessary Expense Test (NET): test used by the IRS in order to determine whether an expense is necessary for the health and well-being of a taxpayer and/or the production of income.

Negotiation: the act of conferring with another in order to resolve a dispute.

Net Income: amount of income of a 1099/self-employed individual that is obtained by subtracting business expenses from the gross receipts (**Formula:** Net Income = Average Monthly Gross Income – Total Monthly Business Expenses).

Ninety-Day Letter (90-Day Letter): notice provided by the IRS after the close of an audit providing 90 days to request a redetermination of the audit in Tax Court.

Non Liable Party (NLP): individual who does not owe back taxes to the IRS but resides in a home that includes an individual owing back taxes to the IRS.

Non Liable Spouse (NLS): married individual who does not owe back taxes to the IRS but is married to an individual who does.

Nonresident Alien: an individual who is neither a resident alien nor US citizen.

Normal Status: a status given to tax accounts that have no back taxes owed or noncompliance.

Notice of Assessment: notice provided by the IRS to a taxpayer notifying them of taxes owed, or providing the results of an audit/examination.

Notice of Levy: a letter sent by the IRS to a bank or employer requesting that funds be withheld from the taxpayer's bank account or wages and submitted to the IRS.

Offer in Compromise (OIC): resolution that allows taxpayers to settle their tax debt for less than the amount owed either through a lump sum payment or periodic payments.

Offer Examiner: IRS employee/agent that reviews an Offer in Compromise.

Office Examination: an audit conducted by a face-to-face meeting at the IRS Examiner's office.

Offshore Accounts: financial accounts held outside of the United States.

Open Audit: an audit that has not been concluded/closed by the IRS and is still undergoing investigation.

Partial-Pay Installment Agreement: a payment arrangement to repay back taxes that will not pay off the debt in full within the Collection Statute Expiration Date (CSED).

Partial Release: when the IRS agrees to reduce the amount being levied or garnished.

Partnership: business entity in which the business is owned by two or more individuals.

Passive Activity: activity or venture in which one did not materially participate (i.e. investing in a business rather than running the business).

Passive Activity Rule: Section 469 of the tax code that defers the use of net losses (until disposition) for activities in which the taxpayer did not materially participate.

Passive Foreign Investment Companies (PFIC): includes foreign partnerships, mutual funds, and other pooled investments that have at least one US shareholder, at least 75 percent of its income is passive, and at least 50 percent of its income is derived from dividends, interests, and/or capital gains.

Pay Frequency: period by which an individual is paid by an employer (i.e. weekly, bi-weekly, semi-monthly, monthly, etc.).

Pay Frequency Multiplier: predetermined amount established by the IRS for each pay frequency that is used to calculate the monthly gross income.

Payroll Liability: taxes owed due to failure of an employer to pay required payroll taxes.

Payroll Taxes: tax collected from the wages of employees (W-2 wage earners) by employers that is payable to the IRS.

Penalty: a monetary punishment imposed for failure to comply with IRS tax laws and regulations.

Periodic Payments: payment received on a specified date or dates (i.e. Social Security Income, Annuity, Pension, etc).

Personal Exemptions: pre-set amounts established by the IRS that a taxpayer may deduct for themselves and any dependents claimed on their income tax return.

Personal Expense: costs incurred that are not related to operating a business or performing a job.

Personal Property: items of value that are moveable (car, jewelry, art, etc.)

Point: percentage of your mortgage loan.

Primary Residence: place where individual lives, or stays for most of the year.

Profit: having a surplus in revenue after deducting all expenses from the gross income.

Profit/Loss Statement: a financial statement used by independent contractor, self-employed individuals, or businesses that lists their income and expenses in order to determine whether they have received a surplus or a deficit in revenue.

Pro-rate: method used by the IRS to divide shared expenses based on portion of income contributed to a household.

Protest Letter: letter written by taxpayer to an IRS Appeals Officer providing an explanation for the protest and why the examination report should be reviewed.

Qualifying Child: a relative either by birth or adoption; under the age of 19 or a full time student under the age of 24, or permanently disabled regardless of age; a child that the taxpayer has provided more than half of the individual's support; resided with taxpayer for more than half of the year; cannot file a joint return if he or she is married; and claimed by only one person who is entitled to claim them, either by law or mutual agreement.

Qualifying Dividends: distributions from a corporation's profits.

Qualifying Relative: under the age of 19 or a full time student under the age of 24, or permanently disabled regardless of age; a child that the taxpayer has provided more than half of the individual's support; resided with taxpayer for more than half of the year; cannot file a joint return if he or she is married; and claimed by only one person who is entitled to claim them, either by law or mutual agreement.

Qualifying Widow(er) with Dependent Child: a filing status used by a taxpayer within two years of their spouse's death and has a qualifying dependent.

Quarterly Tax Payments: Tax payments made to the IRS for payroll taxes or estimated tax payments for income or wages earned every three months (there are four quarters in a year).

Quick Sale Value (QSV): selling price of item if sold immediately (i.e. IRS reduces all assets to 80 percent of its Fair Market Valuation (FMV)).

Random Selection: a process used by the IRS to select a tax return for an audit without the existence of known errors or bias.

Real Property: land and buildings (i.e. house, farm, timeshare, etc.)

Reasonable: fair or sensible, and not too expensive or unrealistic.

Recession: a period of economic decline.

Refinance: to borrow again typically at a lower interest rate.

Regime: a government or system.

Registered Tax Return Preparer (RTRP): (*also called* Licensed Tax Preparer) is an individual that prepares income tax returns and has passed the IRS preparer competency test and registration requirements.

Rejected Offer in Compromise: an appealable decision made on an Offer in Compromise by an Offer Examiner in which it was determined that an offer was not accepted.

Relative: person connected to you by blood, marriage, or adoption.

Research Audit: Audit conducted on a taxpayer's income tax return in search of errors.

Resident Alien: an individual who was not born in the US, but was lawfully present in the US for at least 31 days during the current tax year, or 183 days during a three year period.

Retired Debt: occurs when an allowable expense is expected to expire prior to the months allotted for the Offer In Compromise or Collection Statute Expiration Date (CSED), and will affect the taxpayer's ability to pay back the tax debt.

Returned Offer in Compromise: a final decision made on an Offer in Compromise in which an event/issue prevented the IRS from making a determination on the offer.

Revenue Officer (RO): an employee of the IRS assigned to a tax account for the purpose of collecting the taxes due or to enforce compliance with tax requirements and obligations.

Schedule C: tax form used to calculate and report 1099 income/self-employment income that is filed with the Form 1040.

S-Corporation (S Corp): a business entity in which an election was made with the IRS to be taxed as an S-Corporation which passes the tax obligation to its owners.

Secured Debts: debts secured by collateral (i.e. student loans, loans state installment agreements, and non-reimbursed work related expenses/payments, etc.).

Seizure: forcible taking of property or asset by the IRS in order to collect back taxes owed.

Self-assessment: taxation system in which each taxpayer is responsible to provide the IRS with the information necessary to determine the taxpayer's tax liability.

Self-Employed: an individual that works for themselves rather than for an employer (i.e. business owner or 1099 independent contractor).

Semi-Monthly: pay period in which an individual is paid twice per month, usually on two specified dates (i.e. 5th and 20th of every month, or 15th and 30th of every month, etc.).

Settlement: an agreement made in order to resolve a dispute.

Short-Term Period Payment Offer in Compromise: an Offer in Compromise in which the proposed offer will be paid in 24 months or less.

Significant Investment: the purchase of goods by an independent contractor in order to perform a service.

Single Filing Status: a taxpayer that is single, unmarried, or divorced at the end of a given tax year (December 31).

Small Business: a business earning taxable income of less than $1 million annually.

Small Business/Self-Employed Division: Department of the IRS that handles tax matters related to small businesses or 1099/self-employed individuals.

Social Security Number (SSN): a nine-digit number issued by the Social Security Administration to US Citizens, permanent residents, or resident aliens, that is used to identify individuals and is used by the IRS to track their tax payment history and tax obligations.

Sole Proprietorship (SP): business entity owned by one individual in which the owner is personally liable for the debts of the business.

Source: place, person, or thing from which income or information is derived.

Specified Foreign Financial Asset: any financial account, securities, stocks, financial instrument, or interest in a foreign entity that is not maintained by a financial Institution in the US.

Standard Deduction: a predetermined amount based on a taxpayer's filing status that a taxpayer may deduct from their adjusted gross income.

Start-Up Costs: expenses incurred in opening up a business for the first time.

Statute of Limitation (SOL): a law specifying the length of time available for a legal proceeding to be brought, or to enforce a right.

Streamlined Installment Agreement (SIA): resolution of tax obligation that allows taxpayers to make monthly payments in order to repay their back taxes owed within a specified number of months for balances under $25,000 or 50,000, and in most cases without having to provide financial information.

Substantial Understatement of Income: failure to report more than 25 percent of income earned in a given tax period.

Substitute for Return (SFR): an income tax return prepared by the IRS on behalf of an individual having a requirement to file a tax return for a given tax year, that failed to file the income tax return.

Summons: a notice processed by a court of law ordering compliance with a given act or to make an appearance in a legal proceeding.

Social Security Income/Benefits (SSI/SSB): Income received from the Social Security Administration for retirement or disability.

Statement of Annual Estimated Personal and Family Expenses: Form 4822 requested in an Office Examination that requests that a taxpayer provides estimated living expenses as well as personal assets.

Tax Avoidance: to utilize existing tax laws in order to pay the least amount of taxes possible.

Tax Code: laws that govern the execution of collecting taxes in the United States.

Taxable Income: the portion of a taxpayer's income used to calculate their tax obligation which is calculated by subtracting personal exemptions, standard deductions, and/or itemized deductions from their adjusted gross income.

Tax Court: a court of law authorized by congress to resolve disputes concerning taxes, penalties, interest, and other tax related matters.

Tax Credit: an amount of money that the IRS permits for certain qualified expenses or status that reduces the amount of taxes owed.

Tax Deduction: an expense that the IRS permits that reduces the amount of income that can be taxed by the IRS.

Tax Deposit: sum submitted to a specific tax account to be paid on tax obligations of an individual or business.

Tax Evasion: the avoidance of paying your tax obligation by concealing information, or through a misrepresentation of your financial affairs.

Tax Exempt and Government Entities Division: Department of the IRS that handles tax matters related to tax exempt organizations and government entities.

Tax Lien: notice of a legal claim to the assets of an individual or business owing back taxes to the IRS that notifies creditors or potential buyers that a debt is owed to the IRS by the individual or business.

Tax Obligation: the amount of taxes a taxpayer is expected to pay based on their taxable income.

Taxpayer Advocate Service (TAS): an independent organization within the IRS that assists taxpayers and businesses in resolving their disputes with the IRS.

Tax Preparer: individual that prepares income tax returns.

Tax Professional: tax consultant or advisor specially trained in tax law (i.e. Tax Attorney, CPA, LTP, RLTP, TPA, Enrolled Agent, etc.).

Term Life Insurance: life insurance for a specified period of time that is payable upon death of the insured.

Third Party: an individual or entity or group other than the two that are primarily involved in the situation or dispute.

Thirty-Day Letter (30-Day Letter): notice sent by the IRS in an audit providing a 30 day deadline to request a review of the audit by an Appeals Officer.

Tolled: to delay or place on hold a statute of limitation or deadline.

Trade or Business Tools: items that are used as a regular part of your trade or business to produce income.

Trust: a fiduciary relationship in which an individual (Trustor), gives the right to hold title to property or assets to another party (trustee) for the benefit of a third party (beneficiary).

Trust Fund Recovery Penalty (TFRP): penalty imposed by the IRS upon employers failing to pay required payroll taxes.

Unconstitutional: contrary to or not permissible by the Constitution of the United States.

Underreporting: the inaccurate reporting of income by providing a lower amount than what was reported to the IRS from other sources.

Undischargeable Debt: obligation in which the requirement to repay cannot be released.

Unreported Income: income not reported on an individual or business tax return, or not disclosed to the IRS.

Unsecured Debts/Loans: debts or loans not secured by collateral (i.e. credit card, personal loan, etc.).

US Citizen: individuals born or naturalized in any of the United States or US Territories (i.e. Puerto Rico, Guam, Northern Mariana Islands, Virgin Islands, American Samoa, or Swain's Island).

US Person: includes U.S. citizens and resident alien individuals as well as all entities created or organized in the United States or under the laws of the United States.

Voluntary Disclosure: reporting of one's income or assets without force, or prior to the income being reported by a third party to the IRS, or prior to being audited or investigated by the IRS.

Voluntary Disclosure Program: program extended to individual and entities in which the IRS will not impose penalties in exchange for voluntary disclosure of offshore accounts and compliance with filing and payment of tax obligations.

W-2: Tax Form used by employers to report income and deductions of an employee for a given tax year that is filed with the IRS and provided to the employee annually.

W-2 Wage Earner: individuals who typically work for an employer as an hourly or salaried employee.

Wage: payments made to an employee by an employer on a consistent periodic basis (i.e. Weekly, bi-weekly, semi-monthly, annually).

Wage Garnishment: a method used by the IRS to collect back taxes due by deducting a portion of income from the wages of an employee.

Wage and Investment Division: Department of the IRS that handles tax matters related to wage earners and investors.

Weekly: pay period in which an individual is paid every week.

Whistleblower: person who exposes another person or entity for illegal activity or failure to comply with IRS tax laws.

Whole Life Insurance: life insurance that is payable upon death of the insured that earns cash value over time.

Withholding: portion of an employee's wages that are deducted for income taxes.

Year-to-Date Method (YTD): method used to calculate monthly income by dividing the year-to-date gross income provided on your paycheck by the number of months worked. (**Formula:** Monthly Income = YTD income ÷ number of months worked).

Year-to-Date Method (YTD) Alternate Method: used by the IRS to calculate monthly income by dividing the year-to-date gross income by the number of pay periods worked up to the date reported on your paycheck stub multiplied by your pay frequency. (**Formula:** Monthly Income = YTD income ÷ number of pay periods x pay frequency).

Index

Index

How to Work
with Steven Melnik
Attorney - Media Expert - Speaker

Y ou can work with Steven Melnik, and his associates, in a variety of ways:

Professional Legal Services

- IRS and State Tax Debt Resolution and Audit Representation;
- Estate Planning (will, trusts) and Estate Administration (includes probate);
- Sophisticated Asset Protection,
- Medicaid/Elder Law,
- Medicaid Fraud Representation
- Tax Planning
- Personal Injury and Medical Malpractice
- Formation and Support of Non-profit and other Organizations.
- Retirement, Financial, and Pension Planning

Referrals to Professionals

Steven Melnik can also refer you to professionals that cover your local area.

Speaking and Media Appearances

As an expert in legal, financial and tax strategies, having Steven Melnik talk to your group will bring insight from a warrior for the average individual and family. He is available for speaking engagements, webinars, Google Hangouts, seminars, media appearances and interviews. To get updates on speaking, seminars, and media appearances, his personal website carries an up-todate calendar and direct contact. Sign up for his high content newsletter at:

ProtectYourAssetsCentral.com

Ways to Contact Steven Melnik:

Phone: (800) 975.8929

Email: Contact@ProtectYourAssetsCentral.com

Website: ProtectYourAssetsCentral.com

Steven V. Melnik
Professor, LLM (Tax), J.D., CPA

Steven Melnik is one of the nation's leading educators and authorities in the area of tax law and specifically, IRS representation. He and his associates specialize in Integral Comprehensive Personal Strategic Planning encompassing the interconnected areas of Asset Protection, Elder Law/Medicaid, Retirement, Financial/Health Emergency as well as related Estate and Tax Planning, Tax Debt, Tax Relief, and Tax Resolution.

In addition to being a licensed attorney, a Certified Public Accountant (CPA), and possessing a prestigious post-doctorate degree in law from the New York University School of Law-LLM in Taxation, he is a tenured and distinguished professor of tax law, Director of Graduate and Undergraduate Tax Programs, and a Chairman of Continuing Education Programs for Tax Professionals at the City University of New York. Under his guidance, he has educated tens of thousands of professionals. For over a decade, he has assisted individuals and businesses with their various tax and asset protection related needs—from tax return preparation and sophisticated tax planning to Internal Revenue Service (IRS) and State tax audit and tax resolution representations.

As a sought-after guest expert on major national news networks, he made appearances on *NBC, CBS, CNBC,* and *Bloomberg News,* and was quoted in *Forbes Magazine.* In addition, Steven hosts regular radio and national educational television programs. His articles and recommendations for tax and financial strategies are regularly published widely, including professional and academic publications.

Each year, he hosts and moderates the annual IRS continuing education seminars for tax professionals in New York City where he lectures with senior representatives of the IRS on topics of IRS Audit Representation, as well as IRS tax debt resolution and settlement. With his extensive knowledge and skill in presenting complex topics with a common sense vocabulary and approach, he presents lectures with the Federal Government's Office of Social Security Administration on topics of Retirement and Medicaid planning.

Dedicated to the community he lives and works within, he is a founder and a member of the board of directors of many non-profit community and professional organizations and has been recognized by them for his numerous contributions as well as by political organizations and leaders, leaders that include federal and state senators, assemblymen, and presidents of various municipalities. He is active both on local and national levels including serving as president of one of the national Bar Associations and a board member of one of the Political Action Committees.

Made in the USA
Middletown, DE
29 June 2016